WBI DEVELOPMENT STUDIES

Korea as a Knowledge Economy

Evolutionary Process and Lessons Learned

Edited by
Joonghae Suh
Derek H. C. Chen

Korea Development Institute
and
The World Bank Institute

The World Bank
Washington, DC

© 2007 The International Bank for Reconstruction and Development /
The World Bank
1818 H Street NW, Washington, DC 20433
Telephone: 202-473-1000
Internet: www.worldbank.org
E-mail: feedback@worldbank.org

Library of Congress Cataloging in Publication Data
Korea as a knowledge economy : evolutionary process and lessons learned / edited by Joonghae Suh, Derek H. C. Chen.
    p. cm. — (WBI development studies)
Includes bibliographical references and index.
  ISBN 978-0-8213-7201-2 — ISBN 978-0-8213-7202-9 (electronic)
1. High technology industries—Korea (South). 2. Knowledge management—Korea (South). 3. Korea (South)—Economic policy—1960– I. Suh, Joonghae. II. Chen, Derek Hung Chiat.

HC470.H53K67 2005
330.95195—dc22   2007022259

ISBN13: 978-0-8213-7201-2
e-ISBN13: 978-0-8213-7202-9

Contents

Foreword

The Republic of Korea has been experiencing rapid, and more importantly, sustained economic growth since the 1960s. This has resulted in its real GDP per capita increasing rapidly enabling the once low-income country to join the ranks of high-income industrialized nations within a short time span of four and a half decades. Moreover, the majority of this growth can be attributed to knowledge accumulation, rather than to the accumulation of traditional factors of production of capital and labor. Korea had achieved this knowledge-based growth by investing heavily in education and training, boosting innovation through intensive research and development, and developing a modern and accessible information infrastructure, all coupled with a stable economic and conducive institutional regime that enabled the knowledge-related investments to flourish. Due to this, Korea has ably made its transition to a knowledge economy, that is, an economy that uses knowledge as the key engine of growth. Its successful knowledge-based development experience offers many valuable lessons for developing economies.

Korea as a Knowledge Economy: Evolutionary Process and Lesson Learned has been jointly produced by the Korea Development Institute and the Knowledge for Development (K4D) Program of the World Bank Institute. It is a follow-up to the joint World Bank Institute-OECD report on *Korea and the Knowledge-Based Economy: Making the Transition* (2000) that was produced at the request of the Government of Korea. This first report, which targeted Korean policy makers in the main, looked at the Korean economy just after the 1997 financial crisis. It focused on providing knowledge-economy related policy recommendations to overcome the crisis and to prevent the reoccurrence of a similar economic downturn.

In contrast, this new report on Korea is geared towards policy makers from developing countries that are in the midst of, or are intending to, embark on the transition towards the knowledge economy. It provides pragmatic policy lessons drawn from Korea's forty-five years of knowledge-based growth. This report not only looks at the current policies and challenges of today's high-income Korea, but also reviews its historical economic development since the 1960s when Korea was still a low income country. It follows Korea through the decades as it undertook an array of knowledge strategies that propelled it through the various income levels. The report therefore provides compelling policy lessons that are relevant for developing countries at different stages of economic development.

Jung Taik Hyun   Frannie Léautier
President   Vice President and Head
Korea Development Institute   World Bank Institute

Acknowledgments

This report was jointly developed by the Korea Development Institute (KDI) and the Knowledge Development (K4D) Program of the World Bank Institute (WBI). It was funded mainly by the World Bank Trust Fund for the Korea Knowledge Partnership Program on Sharing Knowledge for Development, sponsored by the Korean Ministry of Planning and Budget. The team of Korean authors was headed by Dr. Joonghae Suh (KDI) and consists of Dr. Cheonsik Woo, Dr. Siwook Lee, Dr. Wonhyuk Lim, and Dr. Moon Joong Tcha of KDI; Dr. Dong-pyo Hong and Dr. Sangwon Ko of the Korea Information Strategy Development Institute (KISDI); Professor Anna Kim of Ewha Womans University; Dr. Byung-Shik Rhee of the Korea Educational Development Institute (KEDI); and Dr. Sungchul Chung of the Science and Technology Policy Institute (STEPI). The K4D team for the report was headed by Dr. Derek H. C. Chen and includes Dr. Jean-Eric Aubert, Mr. Alexey Volynets, and Mr. Do-Geol Ahn.

Dr. Carl Dahlman, former K4D Program Manager at WBI and currently professor at Georgetown University, initiated the project and Dr. Hong-taek Chun, former Vice President of KDI, supported the initiative by arranging for additional resources. Mr. Il Whan An, who had served as a Senior Public Policy Specialist at WBI as a secondee from the Korean Ministry of Planning and Budget, made substantial contributions including valuable comments and suggestions, in addition to undertaking extensive coordination between K4D and KDI.

In addition to the authors, many other Korean scholars contributed to this report. Among them, we would like to thank Professor Inho Lee at Seoul National University for his brief note on Korea's venture business policy and Professor Joon-Mo Yang at Yonsei University on Korea's industrial policy. Dr. Yong-Kook Joo and Dr. Young-Sun Ra at Korea Research Institute for Vocational Education and Training provided data and materials on Korea's lifelong education. Dr. Young-Sub Kwon at Korea Research Institute for Human Settlements kindly provided figure 7.8 of the report.

Earlier drafts of the report were reviewed by several outside readers. Valuable comments were received from two external reviewers, Professor Michael Hobday and Dr. Dieter Ernst, and from participants in knowledge economy workshops held in Korea (Seoul), Russia (Mosow), and Chile (Santiago).

We are grateful to Ms. Suyeon Jeon at KDI for her able research assistance, to Ms. Eun-Hee Jeong and Mr. Jin Park at KDI School for their administrative assistance for several knowledge economy workshops in Seoul, and to Ms. Minjung Lee at IGN Design Co for creating the cover design. We thank to Ms. Faythe Calandra of K4D for her tireless administrative contributions to the development of this report and the entire portfolio of Korean activities at the K4D Program. This report and the accompanying Overview was edited and typeset by Grammarians, Inc. Lastly, we would like to acknowledge our appreciation to Mr. John Didier of WBI for shepherding this report through the publication process.

Abbreviations

ADSL	asymmetric digital subscriber line
ADTV	advanced-definition television
ATM	automated teller machines
BERD	business expenditures on research and development
BK21	Brain Korea 21
CATV	cable television
CDMA	Code Division Multiple Access
Dacom	Korea Data Communication Corporation
DRAM	Dynamic Random Access Memory
EPB	Economic Planning Board
ETRI	Electronics and Telecommunications Research Institute
FDI	foreign direct investment
FSPs	full service providers
FTAs	free trade areas
FTTC	fiber to the curb
FTTH	fiber to home
G4C	Government for Citizens (system)
G-7	Group of Seven
gbps	gigabits per second
GDP	gross domestic product
GERD	gross expenditure on research and development
GNDI	gross national disposable income
GNI	gross national income
GNP	gross national product
GRIs	government research institutes
HAN Project	Highly Advanced National Project
HCIs	heavy and chemical industries
ICTs	information and communications technologies
IMF	International Monetary Fund
IPF	Informatization Promotion Fund
ISO	International Standardization Organization
IT	information technology
K4D	Knowledge for Development Program
KAIS	Korea Advanced Institute of Science

KAIST	Korea Advanced Institute of Science and Technology
KAM	Knowledge Assessment Methodology
KBE	knowledge-based economy
KCC	Korea Communication Commission
KDI	Korea Development Institute
KDIC	Korea Deposit Insurance Corporation
KE	knowledge economy
KEI	Knowledge Economy Index
KICC	Korea Industrial Complex Corporation
KII	Korea Information Infrastructure Plan of 1994
KII-G	Korea Information Infrastructure–Government Plan
KII-P	Korea Information Infrastructure–Public Plan
KIS	Korea's innovation system
KISDI	Korea Information Strategy Development Institute
KIST	Korea Institute of Science and Technology
KMA	Korea Management Association
KMT	Korea Mobile Telecom
KOSDAQ	Korea Securities Dealers Automated Quotation
KPC	Korea Productivity Center
KRIHS	Korea Research Institute for Human Settlements
KSA	Korea Standards Association
KSE	Korean Stock Exchange
KT	Korea Telecom
KTA	Korea Telecommunication Authority
LAN	local area network
LCD	liquid crystal display
mbps	megabits per second
MIC	Ministry of Information and Communication
MOE & HRD	Ministry of Education and Human Resources Development
MOFE	Ministry of Finance and Economy
MOST	Ministry of Science and Technology
NASDAQ	National Association of Securities Dealers Automated Quotations
NPLs	nonperforming loans
NRDPs	national research and development programs
NSTC	National Science and Technology Council
NTFCs	new technology financing companies
NURI	New University for Regional Innovation
OECD	Organisation for Economic Co-operation and Development
OEM	original equipment manufacturing
PISA	Programme for International Student Assessment
PPP	purchasing power parity
R&D	research and development
SCI	Science Citation Index
SICs	start-up investment companies
SMBA	Small and Medium Business Administration
SMEs	small and medium enterprises
S&T	science and technology

TBOP	technology balance of payments
TFP	total factor productivity
TIMSS	Trends in International Mathematics and Science Study
UN	United Nations
USPTO	United States Patent and Trademark Office
W	won (Korean currency)
WIPO	World Intellectual Property Organization
WMEC	Wŏnju Medical Equipment Cluster
WTO	World Trade Organization

1

Introduction

Derek H. C. Chen and Joonghae Suh

The Knowledge Economy Framework

The Knowledge Revolution and Global Competition

Over the past quarter-century, the global rate of knowledge creation and dissemination has increased significantly. One reason is that the rapid advances in information and communications technologies (ICTs) have considerably decreased the costs of computing power and electronic networking. With the increased affordability, the use of computing power and electronic networking has surged, along with the efficient dissemination of existing knowledge. Modern ICTs also enable researchers in different locations to work together, which consequently enhances researchers' productivity, resulting in rapid advances in research and development and the generation of new knowledge and technologies. One indicator of the creation of new knowledge and technologies is the number of patents granted by the United States Patent and Trademark Office (USPTO) each year. Figure 1.1 shows that the total number of patents granted by the USPTO increased from 71,114 in 1981 to 157,747 in 2005. The share of patents granted to inventors outside the United States also grew, from 39 percent in 1981 to 48 percent in 2005. The increased rate of creation of new knowledge and technologies thus reflects a recent global trend.

The increased speed in the creation and dissemination of knowledge has led to the rapid spread of modern and efficient production techniques, plus the increased probability of leapfrogging, which has consequently resulted in the world economy becoming much more competitive. The share of world trade (exports and imports) in world gross domestic product (GDP), which is an indicator of globalization and competition in the global economy, increased from 24 percent in 1960 to 47 percent in 2003 (figure 1.2). International trade increases the number of consumers and producers participating in the market and hence increases the level of competition. Thus, the knowledge revolution, together with increased globalization, presents significant opportunities for promoting economic and social development. How-

Figure 1.1 *USPTO Patent Count, 1981–2005*

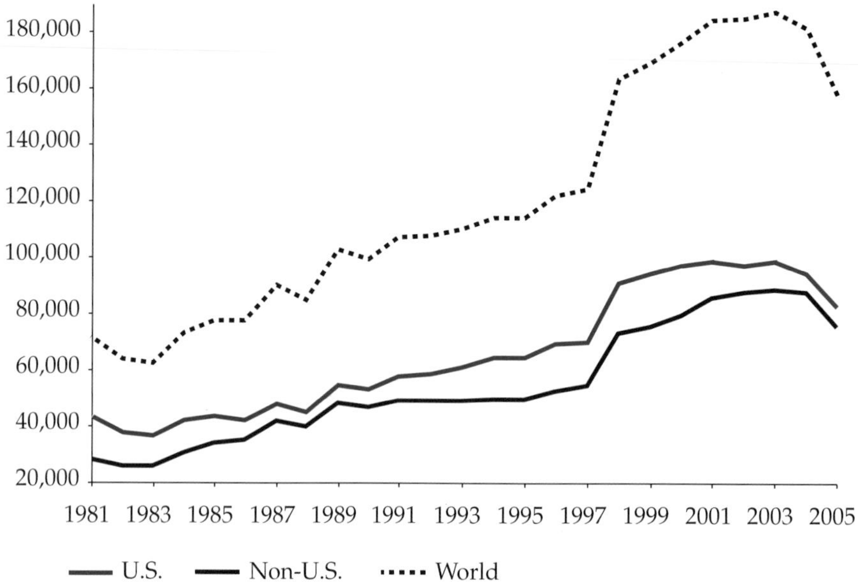

Source: Authors' construction based on data from the USPTO Web site.

ever, countries also face the very real risk of falling behind if they are not able to keep up with the rapid pace of change.

> The knowledge revolution, together with increased globalization, presents significant opportunities for promoting economic and social development as well as increased risk of falling behind if countries are not able to keep up with the pace of rapid change.

In addition to the increased level of competition, the nature of competition also has been changing. Competition was once based on just cost; now it has evolved so that speed and innovation are also essential. Commodity production is usually allocated to the lowest-cost producers, but intense competition resulting from globalization tends to drive profits on commodity production to nearly zero. As such, it has become crucial to derive additional value added by using various means to differentiate products, including innovative design, effective marketing, efficient distribution, and reputable brand names. Thus, for industry to prosper, it must be able to contribute productively to global value chains and generate new value chains, of which the key part is not necessarily production but innovation and high-value services.

In light of this, sustained economic growth in the era of this new world economy depends on developing successful strategies that involve the sustained use and creation of knowledge at the core of the development process. At lower levels of development, which typically imply lower levels of science and technological capability, knowledge strategies typically involve tapping existing global knowledge and

Figure 1.2 World Trade, 1960–2005

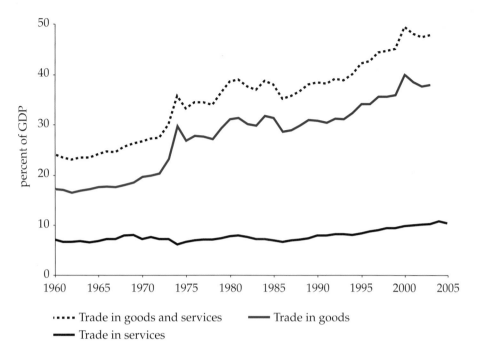

··· Trade in goods and services   — Trade in goods
— Trade in services

Source: Authors' construction based on data from the World Bank SIMA database 2007.

adapting foreign technologies to local conditions to enhance domestic productivity. At higher levels of development, which typically imply higher levels of science and technological capability, knowledge strategies also hinge on domestic innovation and underlie the move to produce products and services that are higher value added to be consistent with the high wages that are characteristic of these economies.

> Sustained economic growth in the new world economy depends on developing successful strategies that involve the sustained use and creation of knowledge at the core of the development process.

The Knowledge Economy

A knowledge economy is one that uses knowledge as the key engine of economic growth. It is an economy in which knowledge is acquired, created, disseminated, and used effectively to enhance economic development. Contrary to some beliefs, the concept of the knowledge economy does not necessarily revolve around high technology or information technology (IT). For example, the application of new techniques to subsistence farming can increase yields significantly, or the use of modern logistical services can enable traditional craft sectors to serve broader markets than before. The successful transition to a knowledge economy typically involves elements such as making long-term investments in education, developing innovation capability, modernizing the information infrastructure, and having an economic environment conducive to market transactions. The World Bank has termed these elements the pillars of the knowledge economy (KE), and together they constitute the knowledge economy framework.

Specifically, the four pillars of the KE framework are

- an economic incentive and institutional regime that provides good economic policies and institutions, which promote efficient allocation of resources and stimulate creativity and incentives for the efficient creation, dissemination, and use of existing knowledge;
- an educated and skilled labor force that continuously upgrades and adapts skills to efficiently create and use knowledge;
- an effective innovation system of firms, research centers, universities, consultants, and other organizations that keeps up with the knowledge revolution, taps into the growing stock of global knowledge, and assimilates and adapts new knowledge to local needs; and
- a modern and adequate information infrastructure that facilitates the effective communication, dissemination, and processing of information and knowledge.

The KE framework thus asserts that investments and interactions among these four pillars are necessary for the sustained creation, adoption, adaptation, and use of knowledge in domestic economic production. The result will be goods and services with higher value added, which increases the probability of economic success in the current highly competitive and globalized world economy.[1]

The Korean Context

Rapid Economic Growth and Structural Transformation

Korea has experienced rapid and sustained economic growth over the past four decades. In the aftermath of World War II, Korea's GDP per capita was comparable to levels in the poorer countries in Africa (figure 1.3). Then the Korean War, from 1950 to 1953, made conditions even worse; the Republic of Korea was considered by many to be a hopeless case after four years of mass destruction. However, 45 years after the full-scale, government-led industrialization drive that started in the early 1960s, Korea's GDP per capita has increased more than 12-fold, to more than US$13,000, which is on par with the medium economies of the European Union (figure 1.4).

---

1. Chen and Dahlman (2004) provide a brief literature review on the contribution of each of the four KE pillars to economic growth. In addition, using various indicators as proxies for the four pillars, they also found econometric evidence showing that the four pillars exert significant positive effects on long-term economic growth.

Despite dire initial conditions, South Korea has experienced rapid and sustained economic growth since the 1960s, resulting in GDP per capita increasing more than 12-fold. This is almost a unique occurrence on the world stage in the 20th century.

Figure 1.3 GDP Per Capita (Constant 2000 US$)

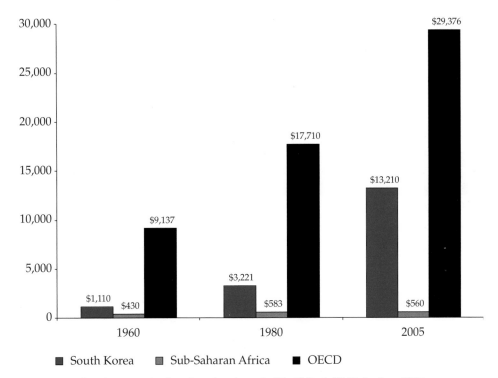

Source: Authors' construction based on data from the World Bank SIMA database 2007.

Figure 1.5 presents the decomposition of the Republic of Korea's economic growth over the past four decades and clearly highlights the contribution of knowledge, represented here by total factor productivity (TFP), to Korea's economic miracle. It shows that about 75 percent of the increase in real GDP per capita from 1960 to 2005 is attributed to TFP growth. By comparison, Mexico's GDP per capita in 1960 was about 2.5 times larger than that of Korea; however, by 2005, Korea's GDP per capita was more than twice Mexico's. Without the contribution of knowledge, Korea's real GDP per capita in 2005 would still be below that of Mexico. It is this rapid and sustained knowledge-based economic growth that makes the Korean case particularly interesting to analyze. In addition, its journey toward the knowledge economy offers valuable policy lessons for other developing economies that are seeking to make that transition.

The accumulation of knowledge was the main contributor to Korea's long-term economic growth.

Figure 1.4 *The Growth Path of the Korean Economy*

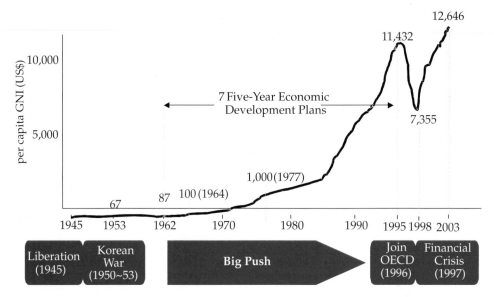

Source: Authors' construction.
Note: GNI = gross national income.

Figure 1.5 *Effect of Knowledge on Korea's Long-Term Economic Growth (1960–2005)*

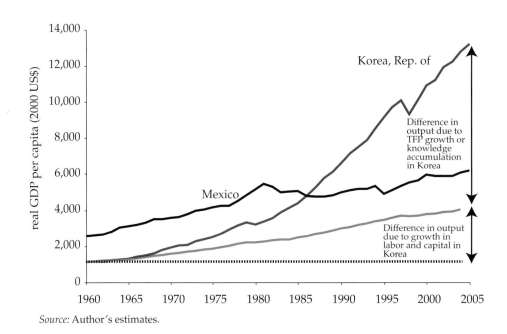

Source: Author's estimates.

The Korean Development Strategy

The Catch-Up Period: 1950–97

The Republic of Korea's rapid and sustained economic growth from the time when it was starting out as a low-income country was an outcome of the knowledge economy approach, even though an explicit knowledge economy development strategy was not laid out. During this time, from 1950 to 1997, Korea's economic development hinged on the critical interactions among the four pillars of the knowledge economy, which have evolved with the various stages of economic development. In particular, the pragmatic development strategies focused on achieving sustained productivity growth by consistently increasing the value added of output. These strategies involved intensive learning processes consisting of active technological capability building and complementary human resources development. At the same time, the Korean government assumed the very necessary proactive leadership role of supporting the market and providing an environment that would foster and sustain the transformation.

> The economic development of Korea hinged on critical interactions among the four pillars of the knowledge economy.

In the 1960s, Korea embarked on the promotion of both export- and import-substitution industries, starting with subsistence agriculture (rice) and labor-intensive light manufacturing sectors (textiles and bicycles). Considerable capital accumulation and investment in primary education during this period allowed a gradual shift up the value added chain toward more sophisticated commodities. Key to this shift was also the use of technologies obtained through foreign licensing and adapted for domestic production.

In the mid-1970s, the government's use of a well-targeted industrial policy resulted in a major shift to the development of heavy industries (for example, chemicals, shipbuilding). Along with industrial targeting, policies were enacted to further improve technological capabilities, together with improving access to and quality of technical and vocational training.

In the 1980s, Korea undertook efforts to ensure a market-conducive environment by deregulating various sectors and liberalizing trade. Concurrently, it expanded higher education while investing in indigenous research and development through the establishment of the National Research and Development Program.

Korea continued to pursue high-value-added manufacturing in the 1990s by promoting indigenous high-technology innovation. Domestic wage hikes and the appreciation of the Korean won had resulted in chronic current account deficits, which sparked a series of reforms, including the reform of the financial market. Together with the setting up of a modern and accessible information infrastructure, there was continued expansion of research and development capabilities in Korean industries, which drew on the skilled labor force that had resulted from the government's aggressive expansion of the higher education system.

> The central theme of this report depicts the evolution of Korea's economic history through crucial interactions among the knowledge pillars, demonstrating the relevance of the knowledge economy approach to developed as well as developing and low-income countries.

The 1997 Economic Crisis and Economy-Wide Reforms

The Korean model of development had been very successful in propelling economic growth for nearly four decades, but it did have some limitations. The mechanism of resource allocation by which the government wielded discretionary power over the market had been effective when the economy was burgeoning. However, it approached its limits as the economy developed and became larger and more complex. The financial crisis of 1997 manifested the limitations of discretionary resource allocation and underscored the urgent need for widespread economic reform. The old policy framework and institutions that had led Korea in the early high-growth era turned out to be bottlenecks for sustained economic growth in the new economic environment (see figure 1.6).

In the aftermath of the financial crisis, policy efforts were made to transform the Korean economy into a knowledge-based one in which innovation can thrive, enhancing overall productivity and thereby sustaining economic growth. The implementation of Korea's new growth strategy, transforming it into an advanced knowledge economy, was based on the KE four pillars: a conducive macroeconomic framework, a modern information infrastructure, human resource development, and an effective innovation system. Korea's efforts to make the transition to an advanced knowledge economy have been assessed to be very successful.

Figure 1.6 Delayed Economic Reform and the 1997 Financial Crisis

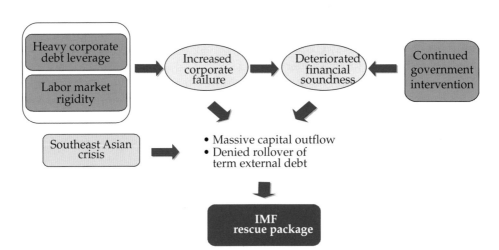

Source: Authors' construction.
Note: IMF = International Monetary Fund.

Many factors have enabled Korea's rapid change. The development strategy for the knowledge economy that the government initiated during the reform period of the economic crisis received proactive responses from both the people and private enterprise. The nationwide concerted effort achieved successful results. Structural restructuring caused the unemployment rate to increase sharply for the short period, but afterward the economy returned to its normal growth path and employment became stabilized when the reform efforts had brought substantive results. Despite the boom and bust of the venture business, the venture industry policy, one of the strategic policy areas in Korea's KE strategy, has contributed to the growth of technology-based firms and boosted the crisis-ridden economy. Today's Korea is facing challenges, many of which are different from those in crisis years: for example, a rapidly aging society raises different socioeconomic problems and people are more concerned about welfare than growth. But the fundamental principles and strategies have not changed, and the KE framework offers very valuable guidance. In this respect, Korea's KE strategy is not complete, but still moves forward. There is much room for further improvement if Korea aims to be a highly advanced knowledge economy.

Korea as a Knowledge Economy

Figure 1.7 illustrates Korea's performance in terms of the knowledge economy according to the basic scorecard of the Knowledge Assessment Methodology (KAM). The KAM[2] is a tool developed by the World Bank that assists comparisons across countries in terms of their advancement toward the knowledge economy. Comparisons within the KAM are performed on the basis of the 81 variables for the 132 countries included in the database. The basic scorecard of the KAM includes 2 performance indicators (GDP growth and the Human Development Index) and 12 preselected, widely used knowledge indicators, with 3 indicators representing each pillar of the knowledge economy. Because the indicators take on different ranges of possible values, all variables within the KAM are normalized onto an ordinal scale of 0 to 10, with 0 being the weakest and 10 being the strongest.

It can be seen in figure 1.7 that Korea's performance in terms of the basic scorecard knowledge indicators is strong and relatively well rounded, with all but one of the indicators ranking above the 50th percentile and a number of them in the 80th percentile or higher. This was true in 1995 as well as the most recent year, typically 2005. A well-rounded basic scorecard is important because it denotes balanced development across the four KE pillars, which in turn tends to indicate that the pillars are in a position to complement and reinforce one another to spur technological progress and economic growth. Although Korea has improved on most of the variables since 1995, it has lost ground in terms of the economic and institutional regime variables, namely, tariff and nontariff barriers and the rule of law, and the education variable, secondary enrollment ratio.

Figure 1.8 compares Korea with the average of the G-7 countries and the average of countries in the high-income category in terms of the KAM basic scorecard.

---

2. Further details of the KAM are presented in appendix 1.1.

Figure 1.7 *The KAM Basic Scorecard, Rep. of Korea, 1995 and Most Recent Year*[a]

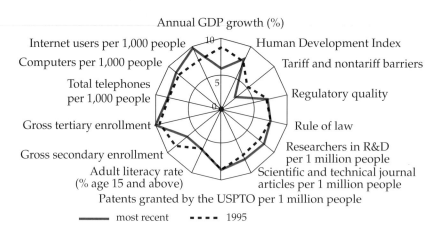

Variable	Korea, Rep. of (most recent)		Korea, Rep. of (1995)	
	Actual	Normalized	Actual	Normalized
Annual GDP growth (%)	4.5	5.9	7.1	8.9
Human development index	0.9	8.0	0.9	7.6
Tariff and nontariff barriers	3.5	2.6	3.5	5.0
Regulatory quality	0.8	7.1	0.6	6.9
Rule of law	0.7	7.5	0.8	7.7
Researchers in R&D/million people	3,187.0	8.1	2,189.9	7.1
Scientific and technical journal articles/ million people	287.6	7.9	84.4	7.2
Patents granted by USPTO/million people	88.4	8.9	29.2	8.5
Adult literacy rate (% age 15 and above)	97.9	6.6	97.0	6.5
Gross secondary enrollment	90.9	6.2	100.9	8.5
Gross tertiary enrollment	88.5	9.8	52.0	9.4
Total telephones per 1,000 people	1,302.8	8.1	448.9	8.0
Computers per 1,000 people	544.9	8.7	107.7	8.1
Internet users per 1,000 people	656.8	9.6	8.1	7.9

Source: KAM, December 2006 (www.worldbank.org/wbi/kam).
a. The most recent year ranges from 2004 to 2006.

Korea is at par or almost at par with the terms of the innovation and information infrastructure pillars. However, Korea is relatively weaker in terms of the economic and institutional regime and the education pillars, indicating that Korea still has room for improvement in these areas. However, it is noteworthy that in terms of gross tertiary enrollment, Korea outperforms the average G-7 and high-income country. Later in the report, it will be elaborated on that having highly skilled human resources is particularly important for facilitating domestic innovation or research and development.

Figure 1.9 shows Korea's performance in the KAM Knowledge Economy Index (KEI) relative to other countries. The KEI is an aggregate index that represents the overall level of development of a country or region in the knowledge economy. It

Figure 1.8 *The KAM Basic Scorecard, Rep. of Korea, G-7, High-Income Countries, Most Recent Year*[a]

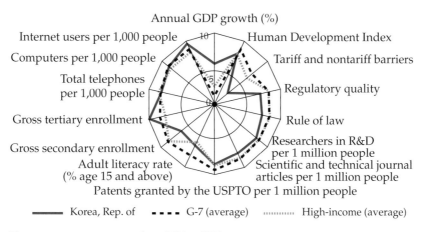

a. The most recent year ranges from 2004 to 2006.

summarizes performance over the four KE pillars and is constructed as the simple average of the normalized values of 12 key knowledge indicators in the basic scorecard. The horizontal axis in figure 1.8 plots countries' and regions' performance in the KEI in 1995; the vertical axis plots countries' and regions' performance in the KEI for the most recent year, currently 2004–05. The diagonal line represents the locus of points where the KEI values in 1995 and in the most recent year are equal.

Figure 1.9 *The Knowledge Economy Index for Selected Countries, 1995 and Most Recent Year*[a]

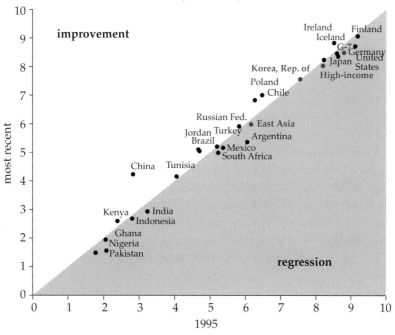

(Figure continues on the following page.)

Figure 1.9 (continued)

Country	Most recent	1995	Change
Finland	9.12	9.21	−0.09
Iceland	8.83	8.54	0.29
United States	8.74	9.13	−0.39
G-7 (average)	8.50	8.81	−0.31
Germany	8.48	8.63	−0.15
Japan	8.42	8.63	−0.21
Ireland	8.27	8.23	0.04
High-income countries (average)	8.06	8.24	−0.18
Korea, Rep. of	7.60	7.56	0.04
Poland	7.04	6.48	0.56
Chile	6.86	6.27	0.59
East Asia (average)	6.03	6.18	−0.15
Russian Federation	5.98	5.85	0.13
Argentina	5.41	6.07	−0.66
Turkey	5.22	5.20	0.02
South Africa	5.19	5.38	−0.19
Jordan	5.12	4.64	0.48
Brazil	5.10	4.73	0.37
Mexico	5.04	5.22	−0.18
China	4.26	2.83	1.43
Tunisia	4.20	4.06	0.14
Indonesia	2.96	3.25	−0.29
India	2.71	2.80	−0.09
Kenya	2.62	2.39	0.23
Ghana	1.97	2.05	−0.08
Nigeria	1.57	2.07	−0.50
Pakistan	1.51	1.76	−0.25

Source: KAM, December 2006 (www.worldbank.org/wbi/kam).
a. The most recent year ranges from 2004 to 2005.

Countries and regions that appear above the diagonal line have made an improvement in the KEI since 1995, and countries that appear below the diagonal line have experienced deterioration in the KEI.

Korea's KEI for the most recent year is 7.6, implying that it ranks in the 76th percentile of the 132 countries included in the KAM database. Although the KEIs for the average G-7 (8.5) and high-income country (8.06) are higher than that of Korea, they have fallen since 1995, and that of Korea has improved since 1995 (7.56). This shows that Korea is on its way to catching up with the G-7 and high-income countries. Also, note that Korea is a relatively strong performer in the East Asia region, with the KEI for the average country in the region being 6.03.

Overview of the Study

This report characterizes the Korean model and Korea's march toward a knowledge economy from a poverty-ridden economy before the launch of full-scale industrialization in the early 1960s. The time span of the study covers those four decades, but the report focuses considerably on the recent years. It contrasts the catch-up model that Korea implemented during the high-growth era before the financial crisis of 1997 and the renewed KE model that Korea has incessantly pursued to overcome the crisis and sustain economic growth afterward. The report emphasizes Korea's achievements, as well as the remaining tasks within the four KE pillars, with a common theme throughout—how Korea has narrowed the gaps in its knowledge and institutions in global competition with world leaders.[3]

Designing a New Macroeconomic Framework

Economies need a stable and favorable macroeconomic environment to develop into knowledge-based economies. For Korea, in particular, the economic crisis in 1997 that has beset the economy since 1997 demonstrated the need to reexamine the macroeconomic environment and institutional regime. Chapter 4 reviews both what has been accomplished since 1997 and what has yet to be achieved with the economy to provide better conditions for economic players. Government-led interventionists faced a dramatic challenge in the radical changes that accompanied the 1997 crisis, and efforts were made to modernize the economic structure and environment and the institutional regime. All of the government's efforts since the crisis—redefining the role of government, creating and leveling the playing field for economic actors, improving the soundness and efficiency of the financial system, and increasing the flexibility of the labor market—are crucial for the economy to build a strong institutional infrastructure and fortify the rule of law. In this regard, the progress is inevitably related to the Korea's success in making the transition to a knowledge-based economy.

Building an Information Infrastructure

Korea's successful movement toward an information society is the result of concerted efforts by the government and industry. This report investigates this process of change from two perspectives—the government's role and leadership in building an information society and industry's response and efforts to make best use of information infrastructure and technologies. The government has tried to lay down the information infrastructure, whereas industry, benefiting from the government's initiative, has consistently tried to capitalize on the information infrastructure and existing technologies. Since the mid-1990s, Korea has pushed for a strong national and social information infrastructure. As a result, it now has one of the world's top broadband Internet infrastructures. At the end of 2000, 144 major cities and regions were connected by high-speed broadband networks through fiber-optic cables. As of June 2004, 66 percent of the population had access to the Internet.

---

3. As mentioned in the Foreword, the first World Bank knowledge economy report on Korea, *Korea and the Knowledge-Based Economy: Making the Transition* (World Bank and OECD 2000), which focuses on the new development strategies Korea needed to overcome the financial crisis and sustain economic growth in the longer term. That report is a companion volume to this report.

However, despite the widespread use of IT, Korea has yet to translate the rapid spread of its information infrastructure into qualitative results, such as increased industrial competitiveness and entrepreneurial innovation. Korea now needs to improve transparency and efficiency in all sectors of society, including politics and the economy, where the information infrastructure will play an important role. All of these efforts will be made with the ultimate goal of stimulating economic growth through the development and best use of ICTs. Chapter 5 reviews this process, with particular focus on the government's role in Korea's march toward an information society, and it also assesses the strength and weakness of Korea's ICT-related industries.

Meeting Skill and Human Resource Requirements

Korea's education system has achieved very rapid growth over the past four decades. One factor specific to Korea, "education fever," has acted as a key driver for the rapid expansion of the country's education system, but it has also created a chronic problem, the lack of quality in education. The problem now is being exacerbated by Korea's move toward an advanced knowledge economy. Transformation to a advanced knowledge economy can only be achieved with an adequate supply of capable human resources. In fact, the potential of Korea's human resources is among the highest in the world; however, up to now, that potential has not been adequately realized because of the rigid and closed education and training system.

The minimal effectiveness of public education creates problems in human resource supply and leads to social tension. Along with universities' efforts to develop high-caliber scientists and engineers, industries' absorptive capacity for those graduates needs to be elevated. Catching up with fast-moving technologies and thereby meeting the skill requirements for incumbent labor will require establishing a new system of job training in industry. For example, the links between tertiary institutions, and other forms of education and training, such as adult education, job training, and employer-based training, will be more important. The Korean government has been concerned about the adequacy of current and future supplies of skilled labor for the projected growth in demand from existing industries and expanding industries. The transition to an advanced knowledge economy will require a new policy framework, with education reform being a major component. These necessary changes and other pertinent aspects of the Korean education system are taken up in chapter 6.

Harnessing the Potential of Science and Technology

Although Korea, as a late-industrializing country, has depended heavily on foreign technologies, it has also made an effort to accumulate technological capabilities. At the initial launch of its economy-wide development plan, Korea was poorly endowed with factors necessary for industrialization, except for a plentiful labor force. Furthermore, the technological competence of Korean firms was far below world standards. Consequently, it was inevitable or natural that it would look toward foreign sources for technologies. After the industrialization process was launched in 1962, there was remarkable growth in imports of foreign technologies.

The process of technological capability building in Korea is characterized as a dynamic process involving the interplay between imported technologies and indigenous R&D efforts. The configuration of Korea's innovation system has largely been shaped by overall economic development strategies. This catch-up model has brought both limitations and advantages to the Korean innovation system. Chapter 7 briefly reviews the process of building technological capability within the broader framework of economic development. The development strategies that have influenced the shape of the Korean innovation system can be summarized as (a) government-led mobilization of strategic resources for achieving development goals; (b) export promotion along with rapid market expansion; (c) selective industrial promotion, notably in the heavy and chemical industries; (d) governmental support for the growth of big business; (e) use of foreign technologies; and (f) construction of science and technology infrastructure, institutions, and R&D programs for industrial demands.

New Challenges and Tasks Ahead

Today's Korea faces new challenges. The slowdown in growth momentum raises concerns about "jobless growth." The rapid rise of low-wage economies forces Korea to move quickly up the quality assurance ladder. However, despite the rapid changes, Korea still suffers from the knowledge and institutional gap in comparison with other Organisation for Economic Co-operation and Development (OECD) member countries. In short, Korea's 20th century transition to the knowledge economy is not complete. For the Korean economy to sustain economic growth, it is essential to refurbish the economic system in which creativity and entrepreneurship thrive. Korea's economic development experiences, success stories, and mistakes over the past four and a half decades offer valuable lessons for other developing economies.

Appendix 1.1

The Knowledge Assessment Methodology (KAM)

The transition to a knowledge economy requires long-term strategies that focus on developing the four KE pillars. Initially, this means that countries need to understand their strengths and weaknesses, then act upon them to develop appropriate policies and investments to give direction to their ambitions and mechanisms to enable the policy makers and leaders to monitor progress against the set of goals.

To facilitate this transition process, the World Bank Institute's Knowledge for Development (K4D) Program has developed the KAM (www.worldbank .org/wbi/kam), which is an Internet-based tool that provides a basic assessment of countries' and regions' readiness for the knowledge economy. The KAM is a user-friendly, interactive diagnostic and benchmarking tool that is designed to help client countries understand their strengths and weaknesses by comparing themselves with neighbors, competitors, or other countries that they may wish to emulate based on the four KE pillars. The KAM is therefore useful for identifying problems and opportunities that a country may face, and where it may need to focus policy attention or future investments, with respect to making the transition to the knowledge economy. The unique strength of the KAM lies in its cross-sectoral approach that allows a holistic view of the wide spectrum of factors relevant to the knowledge economy.

Comparisons in the KAM are made on the basis of 81 structural and qualitative variables that serve as proxies for the four KE pillars. Currently, 132 countries and 9 regional groupings are available in the KAM. The comparisons are presented in a variety of charts and figures that visibly highlight similarities and differences across countries. The data on which the KAM is based are all published by reputable institutions, and the data sources are clearly cited. The data are continuously updated, and the country coverage is expanded whenever possible.

Because the 81 variables contained in the KAM span different ranges of values, all variables are normalized from 0 (weakest) to 10 (strongest), and the 132 countries and 9 regions are ranked on an ordinal scale. Details of the KAM normalization procedure can be found on the KAM Web site.

Given its ease of use, transparency, and accessibility over the Internet, the KAM has been widely used by government officials, policy makers, researchers, representatives of civil society, and the private sector. The KAM has also been used by multilateral and bilateral aid agencies, research institutions, consultants, and others to undertake preliminary single or multicountry KE assessments.

Because countries are ranked on an ordinal scale, the KAM illustrates the relative performance of a country compared to other countries in the KAM database. As such, when a country's performance in a specific variable is indicated to have declined, it could have occurred for two reasons. The country's performance in that variable declined, resulting in lower values in absolute terms. Alternatively, the country's performance could have improved and resulted in large absolute values, but other countries experienced even larger improvements, leading to the country's ordinal ranking falling and resulting in a lower value in relative terms.

2

Overview of Korea's Development Process until 1997

Joonghae Suh

> Korea's rapid and sustained economic growth since the 1960s was an outcome of the KE approach, even though an explicit KE development strategy was not laid out.

Industrialization in general is the process of changing a country's industrial structure such that productive resources are reallocated to sectors with more value added. For latecomers to industrialization, the process also involves learning to create a competitive advantage against world leaders. The Republic of Korea's modern economic history clearly shows these two aspects of industrialization. More specifically, Korea's industrial transformation to the knowledge economy has been achieved through intensive learning processes in which building technological capability and developing human resources have played decisive roles. Therefore, the rapid and sustained economic growth that Korea experienced from the time when it was starting out as a low-income country was an outcome of the KE approach, even though an explicit KE development strategy was not laid out. During this time, Korea's economic development hinged on the critical interactions among the four pillars of the knowledge economy, which have evolved together through the decades in sync with the various stages of economic development.

> Korea's transformation to the knowledge economy have been achieved through intensive learning processes in which building technological capability and developing human resources were critical.

Another distinctive aspect of Korea's industrialization process is the active leadership role that the government assumed to support the market and provide an environment that fostered and sustained the transformation. In retrospect, there seem to be different paths that the government could have pursued at the start of the big march to modernize the traditional economy, and experts debate the development strategies that Korea adopted. For example, government intervention in the market to mobilize resources to promote heavy and chemical industries (HCI) in the 1970s seemed to many to distort the market mechanism and result in static inefficiency in resource allocation. But these industries have since become the growth engines of the Korean economy, which makes a case for government intervention to create dynamic comparative advantages.

The Korean path to the knowledge economy also represents the numerous successes and failures of risk-taking entrepreneurs, painstaking learning efforts of the workforce, and the government's trial and error experience in creating the right business environment. This chapter reviews Korea's development process over three-and-a-half decades, from 1962 to 1997, from two angles: the development strategies and policies that try to make the best use of existing resources and the industrial structures that reflect the stages of industrialization. Using these two viewpoints as a basis, this chapter discusses the successful elements of Korea's economic development and the problems that caused the financial crisis in 1997.

Development Strategies and Policies—Chronological Review

A noticeable feature of Korea's development process is the strategic policy planning in which the government set up development goals and deployed various policy tools to attain them. The blueprints for industrialization took shape through the series of economic development plans. The chronological review in this section is based primarily on official government publications about seven five-year economic development plans.

> A characteristic feature of Korea's development process is the strategic policy planning in which the government set up development goals and deployed various policy tools to attain them.

Before Industrialization

Poorly endowed with natural resources and devastated by the Korean War (1950–53), Korea had remained an agrarian society until the end of the 1950s. Industrial activities were mostly confined to light industries such as simple assembly and processing of raw materials. Economic conditions before the full-scale industrialization were dismal. The efforts to establish the national identity during the years after the liberation in 1945 had been mostly unsuccessful and filled with social unrest and turmoil. However, during this period, the Korean government implemented two important policies: compulsory education and land reform. The constitution of 1949 declared it the duty of the government to educate and the right of the people to be educated, and the government introduced compulsory education in primary schools. The introduction of compulsory education helped create an abundant pool of knowledgeable people that would be instrumental in industrialization in later years. The land reforms of 1947 and 1949 laid another foundation for later industrialization as more equal distribution of wealth equalized opportunities for the people. But in 1950, the efforts to build institutional bases for the newly born country were stopped abruptly by the three-year war, which almost devastated the emerging industrial bases.

> The introduction of compulsory education in the 1950s created an abundant pool of knowledgeable people that would be instrumental in industrialization in later years.

After the war, efforts to rebuild the country's roads, railroads, buildings, and plants showed only minor achievements because of the limitations of the government's budget and the shortages of necessary resources. The government budget depended heavily on U.S. aid, which contributed more than 40 percent of total government expenditures. Industrial and trade policies during the postwar 1950s were based on import substitution that aimed to restrict imports and try to produce daily necessities. High tariffs were levied, and the quantities of imports were tightly controlled to protect domestic industries. The restoration of a domestic consumer goods industry was aided by overvalued foreign exchange rates, but this had detrimental effects on exports, so the yearly volume of exports decreased until 1960.

Although the Korean government had primarily emphasized political stability rather than systematic economic development during the 1950s, after the military coup in 1961, the new political leadership decided that modernization of the Korean economy and rapid economic growth should be the highest priorities.

Launch of Industrialization: 1960s

At the beginning of the 1960s, Korea was an essentially agrarian society with a very limited endowment of natural resources. The majority of the workforce was employed in the agriculture, forestry, and fishery sectors, mostly producing foodstuffs for domestic use. But the very limited area of available arable land (only one-fourth of the total surface area of the country) did not allow much scope for the expansion of output or the production of substantial quantities of exportable agricultural products. The mining sector had no natural endowment of resources to develop, except for limited quantities of tungsten and some other exportable minerals. In the manufacturing sector, 80 percent of the products were consumer goods, particularly food and textiles. The postwar average annual population increases of 2.8 percent aggravated the problem of unemployment and underemployment in the agricultural and services sectors. Services such as transportation and electricity were in extremely short supply.

The development strategies of the 1960s were aimed at terminating the vicious circle of low savings, low investment, and low growth through policies designed to promote an increase in government savings and a rise in foreign capital inflow, with priority attention given to export-led industrialization (Tae 1973). The government set up some principles for industrialization:

- Fiscal and monetary policies, which had been used as instruments for maintaining stable prices, are a necessary condition for the inducement of domestic savings.

- Investment resources should be allocated by the price system; at the same time, price variables such as foreign exchange rates, interest rate, and wages should reflect the opportunity cost of the resources, thus alleviating direct controls over production, prices, wages, imports, and exports.
- Because investment allocation by the price mechanism cannot prepare for the dynamic development of the economy over the long run, the government can use its own investment resources for the construction of key industries and for the formulation of social overhead capital.

Specific policies were developed from these principles:

- Before the 1960s, the industrialization process depended mostly on import-substitution industries under extensive protection in domestic markets, and export promotion was very much neglected. Consequently, the increase in reinvestment through capital accumulation was negligible, and there was no incentive to cultivate new technology and management skills. For further development, industrialization based on the growth of export industries was essential.
- For increased exports, industrialization needed to start in areas of light consumer products for which capital requirements could be minimized.
- Exports of labor-intensive commodities face keen competition, so the low export margin could be compensated for by government policies on export subsidies, such as raw material tariff exemption, preferential loans, tax exemption, and subsidized public utilities.
- For both export diversification and import substitution, the important decisions were based on the profit motivation of private enterprises, and relaxed import restrictions encouraged greater attention to exports and at the same time produced competitive pressure to improve management.
- Education should be designed for productive activities, with new emphasis on vocational training.

In summary, the development strategy of the 1960s was based on the promotion of both the export- and import-substitution industries, beginning with the labor-intensive light manufacturing sectors. In a country such as Korea, with limited raw materials, a nonintegrated industrial structure, and a skilled labor force that received low real wages, it was inevitable that at that stage, exports should consist mainly of labor-intensive processing of imported raw materials and intermediate goods. The capital accumulation that was attained through this process was then used for both the development of the agricultural sector and for the promotion of the HCI to accelerate the industrialization process. In addition, although the government assumed leadership in development efforts, voluntary activities such as private creativity and

> The development strategies of the 1960s were aimed to increase government savings and a rise in foreign capital inflow to terminate the vicious circle of low savings, low investment, and low growth. There was also the active promotion of both import-substitution and export-led industrialization, beginning with the labor-intensive light manufacturing sectors.

initiative were encouraged. The principle of the market mechanism was accepted as the basic premise of the economic order in the 1960s. Measures such as normalization of interest rates, adoption of flexible exchange rates, and liberalization of trade were used to improve the operation of the price mechanism.

Upgrading of the Industrial Structure: 1970s

In the mid-1970s, the Korean government adopted a new set of development strategies, shifting from the promotion of labor-intensive export industries in the 1960s to the development of HCI. The government acknowledged that the industrial policy of the 1960s overemphasized the quantitative growth of industry, which took place under heavy government protection and support. This led to imbalances in growth and weaknesses in international competitiveness. For the future, therefore, government support aimed to be intensive but more selective. Furthermore, the economy could no longer rely on foreign funds for its increasing investment needs or on imports for its increasing demands for equipment and materials. The development of HCI was seen as a means for the economy to adapt itself to changes in its international and domestic environments and as a move toward a more resilient economy, capable of further growth and maturity. The targeted industries, including machinery, metallurgical, chemical, and shipbuilding, were leading industries that provided a strong driving force for the development of other industries.

Alongside the industrial targeting, the HCI plan explicitly stated the importance of technological and human resources development along with strategies to upgrade the technology and technical workforce. A decisive factor was the technical workforce. In particular, the education system for training technicians had to be remodeled to increase quality and produce a greater diversity of skills (see chapter 6). This policy shift significantly deepened the industrial structure but also accelerated inflation and increased economic inefficiencies. The adverse effects mainly resulted from the overly ambitious investments, which outgrew the technological and financial capacities of the economy. Large enterprises were crucial in the process of heavy and chemical industrialization because of the economies of scale, but the importance of large enterprises led to the concentration of economic power in the hands of a few big Korean businesses (chaebols). Moreover, the development of assembly industries without the concomitant development of component parts and materials industries deepened the economy's dependence on foreign imports.

> In the mid-1970s, the Korean government adopted a new set of development strategies and shifted to the development of HCI. The strategies also included the simultaneous development of technological and human resources to meet and complement the forthcoming industrial needs and structure.

Rationalization of the Industrial Structure: 1980s

The 1980s were a transition period for Korea, from an authoritarian government to a more democratic society. During the 1980s, the Korean economy had continued its high-growth trend with an improved balance of payments. However, the economy

Box 2.1 Debate on the Effectiveness of Korea's HCI Policy

Korea's industrial policy to promote HCI in the 1970s has been a much-debated issue in industrial policy. According to Lee (1991, p. 461), there are two contrasting views regarding the HCI plan for Korea's economic development. The viewpoint that is critical of the plan consists of the following points: First, contrary to the logic underlying the HCI plan, the plan's execution led to misallocation of resources, thereby weakening the Korean economy's growth potential. Second, the process of implementing the HCI plan distorted various market prices. Third, implementation of the overly ambitious plan was responsible for the rapid inflation of the late 1970s and early 1980s. Fourth, the plan led to excessive concentration of economic power and an uneven distribution of wealth and income. Fifth, some of the HCI plan's for projects have put great strains on Korea's resources while producing poor results. Sixth, the success of various HCI sectors in the later years stems from the revival of private initiative and market function that resulted from the painful structural adjustment efforts of the 1980s.

The contrasting positive viewpoints are based on the following arguments: First, considering its changing pattern of comparative advantage, Korea had no alternative but to build up HCI sectors; therefore, the policy goals set by the HCI plan could not be challenged. Second, the huge cost involved in implementing the HCI plan has been more than paid off by the successes of the HCI projects in later years and by external economies generated by the plan. Third, given the nature of HCI sectors and the difficulties involved in building them, a nation can hardly expect to build a sophisticated industrial structure by simply responding to price signals. Price signals usually do not carry information about the future, especially in developing economies. Fourth, some of the criticisms directed at the HCI plan have been misleading or misdirected. For example, the high capital-output ratio suggested as a cost of the HCI plan would be lower if the ratio were calculated after HCI projects are fully operational.

Contending that the critics have overemphasized the costs of the HCI plan while ignoring its dynamic benefits to Korea's economic development, Lee (1991) concludes that the construction of HCI contributed to the success of Korea's economic development. There are several elements of success. First, Korea launched its HCI plan to participate in the international division of labor. Second, Korea had a solid light industrial base, which contributed to earning valuable foreign exchange and providing employment opportunities. Third, while the HCI plan was being vigorously executed, Korea had a well-educated and motivated industrial labor force. Also, the abundance of engineers and skilled workers that resulted from the HCI plan's workforce training measures greatly helped to resurrect the Korean economy in the 1980s. Fourth, Korea's entrepreneurs were vigorous and experienced in competing in the world market. Thus, when they were freed of regulations and forced to survive on their own, they took innovative, bold measures to vitalize the HCI projects. Fifth, the Korean government was pragmatic and bold enough to reform the entire incentive and economic management regime when circumstances dictated it. Sixth, the Korean economy benefited tremendously from a favorable world economic environment characterized by low interest rates, low oil prices, and above all, a realignment of exchange rates in Korea's favor.

paid a high price, such as increased labor disputes in the process of democratization. Continued wage hikes led to mounting inflationary pressures. To cope with the new challenges, during the 1980s, the government promoted economic autonomy as one of its key policy goals. The government simplified various procedures for approval and authorization that had hindered private initiatives and creativity.

In the early 1980s, the major focus of the government's development policies was solving the economic problems that stemmed from the development of HCI in the 1970s. Strong economic stabilization measures were implemented to curb the inflationary trends. Economic deregulation, which reduced government intervention and allowed more individual freedom, was actively pursued. Steps were also taken to internationalize and liberalize the economy. Anticipating the Seoul Olympic Games in 1988, the government began to pursue more active internationalization policies. The accelerated import liberalization policies during the five years of the sixth economic development plan resulted in an almost complete liberalization of manufactured imports. Tariff rates were also substantially lowered. These initiatives were also intended to promote the international competitiveness of domestic industries through greater exposure to foreign competition. Fair trade and competition policies were strengthened to reduce the inefficiencies of domestic industrial structures and to curtail abusive practices of monopoly enterprises. By twice revising the Monopoly Regulation and Fair Trade Act, in 1986 and 1990, the government strengthened the institutional basis to regulate unfair and anticompetitive trade practices.

These stabilization, deregulation, and liberalization policies helped check the inflationary pressures and substantially improved the international competitiveness of the export industries. Still, problems caused by the big gap between the large and small business firms, imbalances between the urban and rural sectors, and unequal income distribution remained. In the 1980s, the government therefore exerted major efforts to improve income distribution and enhance social equity. The democratization movement in the 1980s has had an immense impact on labor relations, among other things. The Declaration of Democratic Reform of June 27, 1987, marked an important turning point in labor-management relations in Korea. Labor-related laws, including the three basic labor laws, were extensively revised to promote workers' rights and guarantee the freedom of labor union activities. Social equity and welfare were also significantly improved during the late 1980s. The government enacted the minimum wage law in 1988 and introduced the national pension system in 1988 and a nationwide medical insurance system in 1989.

Liberalization of the Economy: 1990s

Policy measures introduced during the 1980s seemed to be successful. For instance, the Korean economy regained its high-growth path, and 1986 marked the first current account surplus since the launch of the export-led industrialization. But the trade deficits returned in 1989, and new problems emerged. Manufacturing wages rose rapidly, surpassing productivity growth. Combined with the appreciation of the Korean currency, the competitiveness of the Korean economy deteriorated, with chronic current account deficits. Excessive expansion of domestic demand and rapid wage hikes during the period of trade surplus led to the balance-of-payments deficits.

Confronted with the new challenges, in February 1993 the new government initiated a series of economic reforms known as the Five-Year New Economy Plan. The plan was based on the premise that the various institutions built during the earlier years would no longer work in the new economic environment. Under the authoritarian regimes of the preceding 30 years of economic development, the absence of explicit socioeconomic systems and rules did not seem to hinder economic and social development. However, the new democratic order, which gives more individual freedom, and the movement toward internationalization call for clearly defined economic rules and systems that are more consistent with the international norm.

Financial reform was at the top of the policy priorities. Interest rates had been rationalized since the late 1980s, and the financial reform measures culminated in 1993, when the new government adopted its real-name financial transaction system, which requires all financial transactions to be made on a real-name basis. The reform measures were pursued at the outset with an imperative urgency; however, those measures were not implemented consistently throughout the new government's ruling period. In particular, the appreciation of Japanese currency during the 1990s allowed a boom in Korean exports, which slackened reform efforts.

Table 2.1 tabulates the various KE policies implemented since the 1960s along with the associated stages of economic development, since the 1960s.

Elements of Success for Korea's Economic Growth

The Korean economy has continued to have high economic growth since it began its march toward industrialization, albeit with cyclical fluctuations, as shown in figure 2.1. The average GDP growth rate of the 1960s was 8.5 percent, twice that in the 1950s. The average GDP growth rate of the 1970s was 7.7 percent, but excluding 1980, when the oil shock hit the country with negative economic growth, the 1970s had economic growth rates of 8.8 percent, higher than the previous decade. That high-growth trend continued in the 1980s, with average GDP growth rates of 9.1 percent, but as the economy entered a mature stage of economic development in the 1990s, the economic growth rate declined to 7.2 percent. In 1998, the economy showed negative growth because of the financial crisis at the end of 1997. The growth trend recovered, but on average was far lower than in previous decades. The growth trend after the financial crisis manifests that Korea is now entering into a lowered growth path.

In addition to the rapid increases in per capita income, the economic developmental process has proceeded with "the transformation of techniques, organization, and composition of production in the direction of higher productivity, ordinarily with concomitant growth" (Landes 1998). Table 2.2 summarizes some of the key features of these transformations. While the population grew from 27 million in 1962 to 48 million in 2005, the share of the economically active population also grew, from 56 percent to 62 percent for the same period, while the unemployment rate decreased from 8.2 percent to 3.7 percent. At the beginning of industrialization, 48 percent of the population suffered from absolute poverty, but, as of 2000, that number had declined substantially, to 6.4 percent. The concomitant improvement in people's welfare is revealed in the steady increases in per capita gross national product (GNP) for the years of industrialization: from US$87 in 1962 to US$16,413 in 2005. Hence, the goals of economic development, "to establish a self-reliant economy and to make the people's life worth living" (Government of the Republic of Korea, 1962, p. 4), are effectively achieved.

Table 2.1 *KE Policies and Development Stages of the Korean Economy*

	Development goals	Major policy directions	Macroeconomic policy framework	Human resource development	Science and technology
1960s	• Build production base for export-oriented industrialization	• Expanding export-oriented light industries • Mobilizing domestic and foreign capital	• Preparation of legal and institutional bases to support industrialization	• Decreasing illiteracy • Establishing national infrastructure	• Building scientific institutions: legal and administrative framework
1970s	• Build self-reliant growth base	• Promoting HCI and upgrading industrial structure • Building social overhead capital	• Maximization of growth: expand policy loans • Government intervention in the markets	• Increasing vocational training • Improving teaching quality • Increasing college graduates in engineering	• Setting up scientific infrastructure: specialized science and technology institutions, Daeduck Science Town
1980s	• Expand technology-intensive industries	• Increasing industrial rationalization • Decreasing export subsidy and expanding import liberalization	• Stabilization • Enhancement of private autonomy and competition	• Expanding higher education system • Developing semi-skilled human resources	• R&D and private research center promotion • Launching national R&D programs (NRDPs)
1990s	• Promote high-technology innovation	• Supporting technology development • Building information infrastructure	• Liberalization • Reform and restructuring	• Building high-skilled human resources in strategic fields: IT, biotechnology, and so on • Developing a lifelong learning system	• Taking a leading role in strategic areas with the goal of technological catch-up
2000s	• Make transition to knowledge-based economy	• Using government as a market supporter • Promoting venture businesses and small and medium enterprises	• Globalization • Balanced national development	• Increasing research productivity • Improving quality of university education • Focusing on regional development	• Building national and regional innovation systems

Source: Author's compilation.

Figure 2.1 Average Annual GDP Growth Rates

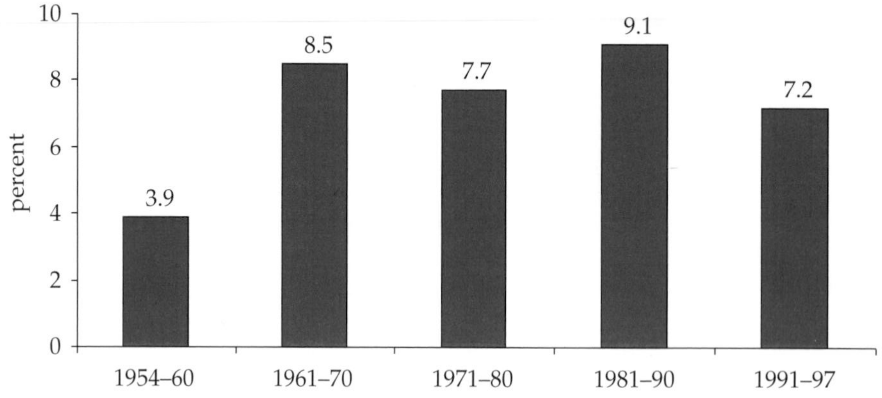

Source: Bank of Korea, *National Accounts*, various issues.

Managing the Economy for Industrialization

Accomplishing the vision of industrialization requires great effort from both the government and industry. The government implemented interventionist policies to achieve its development goals, and industry responded by venturing into the new businesses. Creating institutional frameworks to mobilize resources toward targeted areas was one of the government's primary tasks, whereas the assimilation of technologies is among industry's main tasks. Industrialization is the result of both accumulation and assimilation, which was made possible by the concerted efforts of both the government and industry.

The government's active role has several dimensions, of which the economic development plan is the clear manifestation. The government body responsible for designing and implementing the development plans, the Economic Planning Board (EPB), was created in 1961. The EPB, as a central agency for economic planning and coordination, had a great deal of control over other economic ministries until it was transformed into the Ministry of Finance and Economy (MOFE) in 1994. The Korean government had formulated a series of five-year plans beginning in 1962, and for 35 years, each five-year plan set the development goals for the Korean economy (see box 2.2).

The five-year plans sought national agreement on the direction of medium- and long-term policies by harmonizing various opinions from different social strata. Usually, individual government ministries and agencies designed their own goals and strategies within the realm of their own missions, and the EPB took the role of social planner by coordinating those plans and thereby designing a final comprehensive plan that was coherent at the national level (see box 2.2). In the earlier stages of economic development, the government took the leading role in formulating the plans. The major issues of the plans were sectoral investments and mobilization of domestic and foreign capital to finance such investments.

As the economy grew and the economic structures became more complex, the government-led economic development strategy became less effective. Therefore, since the 1980s, the five-year plan has evolved into an indicative plan that respects

Table 2.2 Economic Structure of Korea, 1962–2005

	1962	1972	1982	1992	2005
Population (millions)	26.5	33.5	39.3	43.7	48.1
Economically active population (%)	56.4	57.7	58.6	60.9	62.0
Unemployment rate (%)	8.2	4.5	4.4	2.5	3.7
Absolute poverty (%)	48.3[a]	23.4[b]	9.8[c]	7.6[d]	6.4[e]
Macroeconomic indicators					
GNP (US$ billions)	2.3	10.7	74.4	329.3	790.1
GNP growth rate (%)	2.2	4.6	7.5	5.9	4.2
GNP per capita (US$)	87	320	1,893	7,527	16,413
Gross investment (% of GNDI)	11.0	21.4	28.9	37.2	30.2
Gross savings (% of GNDI)	9.9	17.0	25.7	36.8	32.9
Industrial structure (% of value added)					
Agriculture, forestry, fishing, and mining	37.0	28.7	15.9	7.7	3.4
Manufacturing	16.4	20.8	27.0	27.2	28.7
Services	46.7	50.5	57.1	65.1	67.8
Employment structure (%of all industries)					
Agriculture, forestry, fishing, and mining	63.4	50.5	32.1	14.0	7.9
Manufacturing	7.5	14.1	21.9	26.5	18.6
Services	29.1	35.4	46.1	59.5	73.5
Trade structure					
Export (US$ millions)	55	1,624	21,853	76,632	284,429
Share of capital goods exports (%)	4.9	9.8	25.2	37.5	43.9
Import (US$ millions)	422	2,522	24,251	81,775	261,238
Share of capital goods imports (%)	16.5	29.9	25.7	37.7	34.7
Human resources					
Illiteracy rate (%)	29.4[a]	12.4[b]	7.2[c]	4.1[d]	2.2[e]
University enrolment ratio of high school graduates (%)	29.2	29.0	37.7	34.3	82.1
Number of university graduates	20,452	29,544	62,688	178,631	268,833
Share of science and engineering graduates (%)	34.6	45.7	46.4	40.9	39.4
Technology indicators					
GERD as share of GDP (%)	0.25[h]	0.29	0.96	2.03	2.99
Private enterprises' share of GERD (%)	22.2[i]	31.9	50.4	82.4	75.0
Number of researchers	1,750[j]	5,599	28,448	88,764	234,702
Patents (per million population)	10.0[f]	6.5	66.3	240.1	1,527.0

Source: Author's compilation from government statistical resources.

Note: All currency is in 2005 U.S. dollars. GERD = gross expenditure on R&D; GNDI = gross national disposable income.

a = 1961 data; b = 1970 data; c = 1980 data; d = 1990 data; e = 2000 data; f = 1968 data; g = 1960 data; h = 1963 data; i = 1967 data; j = 1963 data.

> The five-year plans sought national agreement on the direction of medium- and long-term policies by harmonizing the goals and strategies of the various government ministries into one coordinated strategy coherent at the national level.

Box 2.2 Development Strategies and Government Plans

Korea's development processes since the early 1960s can be divided into several phases. Government's development plans have clear, distinctive characteristics from early phases to later years. Broadly speaking, Korea's four and half decades of rapid economic development experience can be distinguished into three regimes: government-led industrialization years from the early 1960s to 1992; transitional period of two governments of President Kim Young-Sam (1993–1997) and President Kim Dae-Joong (1998-2002); and balanced growth regime of the incumbent government. The three regimes are different in many respects: for an instance, in terms of the nature of the governments, authoritarian ones in industrialization periods versus democratic ones in later years; or, the degree of autonomy in the private enterprises, where as the economy grows steadily, the private sector becomes more important in later years. The Three regimes were also distinctive in the fundamental nature of the government's plans.

The interventionist approaches during the industrialization phase are clearly exposited in five-year economic development plans. At the start of the industrialization drive, the first to fourth development plans were blueprints of the national economy, containing very specific goals and targets for each five-year period. In particular, since the economy was in dire shortage of almost all the resources for substantial economic growth, the utmost goal of the economic plans was the maximum mobilization of national resources and efficient allocation thereof via government plans. In contrast, the fifth and sixth plans were more of the nature of indicative plans, where government set the development goals but the allocation of resources tended to rely more on the market mechanism. There were, among others, two factors that led to the move from national blueprints to indicative plans. First, the aftereffect of government intervention, for example HCI drive in 1970s, that caused inefficiency of resource allocation, forced government to reconsider the ways and approach of the development plans. Second, having benefited from the successful economic growth of the 1960s and 1970s, markets and private enterprises had grown enough to be an autonomous force of economic growth.

The 1990s was a transition period in many ways. In tandem with the nationwide democratization process, the seventh economic development plan was devised under a partnership between the government and the private sector, and the plan specifically contained the social dimensions of economic development. The seventh plan was the last in the series of government's five-year plans, as the outbreak of the financial crisis of 1997 forced the government to tackle the urgent task of crisis management. After the immediate crisis years, government unfolded the Knowledge-based Economy (KBE) Development Plans. The KBE plan was by nature no longer the kind of previous government plans. It contained policy goals and targets for Korea as a KBE, but the role of the government was to create the environment for new-technology based firms.

Currently, the Korean government no longer regulates directly the economy as in the past years, since the basic role of the government is supposed to complement the market mechanism. However, long-term planning from a nationwide perspective and thereby preparing socioeconomic issues far in advance becomes ever more important. A five-year, but yearly rolling, fiscal plan, the National Fiscal Management Plan (NFMP) is instrumental in this regard. NFMP is the most comprehensive review of government's spending programs in Korea. It contains evaluation of program outcomes and sets up goals or targets to be achieved for the five-year time period. The reviewing process is open to the public, which is important in building consensus on priorities over national agenda and deciding expenditure limits in various government spending programs. In this regard, NFMP plays the role of past development plans in a different manner.

The table contrasts government plans in three broadly delineated development regimes, with highlights on key features of plans, focuses of government policies, and examples of fiscal policy targets. As shown in the figure, a clear trend of the priorities of government expenditures appears. Throughout the industrialization period, government

Development Regimes and Government Plans

Development regimes	Government-led industrialization		Transforming to market-led economic growth		Balanced growth
	1962–	1982–	1993–	1997–	2003–
Major plans	Five-year ED Plans (1st to 4th)	Five-year ED Plans (5th and 6th)	New economy ED plan (7th)	KBE Development Plan	National Fiscal Management Plan
Key features of plans	Mobilization and allocation of national resources	Rationalization and restructuring	Private sector's participation in government's planning	Crisis management and institutional reform	Long-term fiscal planning
Focuses of government policies	Export promotion, HCI drive	Strengthening industrial competitiveness	Internationalization and economic liberalization	Four-sector reform and moving towards a KBE	Maintaining social equity and sector/ regional balances
Key targets of fiscal policies	Supporting industrialization, Strengthening defense capabilities	Restoring fiscal prudence, Priorities on education and social welfare	Strengthening industrial competitiveness, Priorities on economic sectors	Assisting reforms, Expanding welfare spending	Harmonizing growth and welfare

Source: Author's compilation based on government documents.
Note: ED = economic development, KBE = knowledge-based economy, HCI = heavy-chemical industries.

put highest priorities on programs of economic development. The high share of defense spending is the result of the Korea's confrontation with North Korea, but the defense spending share has continuously decreased over the years. The sharp increases in economic development spending are noticeable in two periods: the late 1970s, when HCI drive was the main cause; and the late 1990s during which public funds had been funneled to cope with the financial crisis. The share of education expenditures has been around 15 percent. As is explained in chapter 6, relatively smaller increases in government spending in education have been compensated by private expenditures. Welfare spending has steadily increased, taking the largest share in 2005.

Sector Composition of Government Expenditures

Source: Ministry of Planning and Budget.

the initiative and the creativity of the private sector. The plans formulated in the earlier years focused on expanding the productive capacity and mobilizing the required resources, whereas in later years, industrial rationalization and macroeconomic stabilization aimed to make the economy more efficient and productive. Despite the active role of the government in designing and implementing the economic plans, the plans had consistently emphasized the importance of the market as the main mechanism by which the plans were to be implemented.[1]

> Despite the active role of the government in designing and implementing the economic plans, the plans had consistently emphasized the importance of the market as the main mechanism by which the plans were to be implemented.

In tandem with organizational arrangements, the government had made far-reaching interventions in the financial market. Earlier, in 1961, the military government had expropriated the majority of bank shares that were owned by big businesses and limited the voting powers of private owners, which enabled the government to directly control the banking system. The following year, the law of the Bank of Korea was revised in a way that gave the EPB more discretionary power over financial and banking policy. Furthermore, the private banks were required to deposit some of the savings in the government-owned Korea Development Bank so that the deposits could be funneled to the industrial development projects. Policy loans had reached more than one-third of total bank loans at the height of industrialization (see table 2.3). In addition to the policy loans earmarked for spending on targeted areas, the government had maintained two different interest rates. To attract domestic savings, interest rates for one-year savings deposits were doubled, from 15 to 30 percent in 1965, whereas those for export loans remained at 6.5 percent per year, thereby offering a direct incentive for exports (Park 2004). Throughout these actions, Korea's banking system was transformed to support the industrial development goals of the government.

> Requiring private banks to leave a portion of their deposits with the government-owned Korea Development Bank meant that private savings could be tapped for industrial development projects.

Despite these measures, however, Korea suffered chronic shortages of domestic savings, which made it necessary to rely heavily on foreign capital to finance the rapid industrialization. To facilitate the inflow of foreign capital, in 1962, the government had enacted a law on foreign capital. One of the key mandates of the law was the payback assurance of imported foreign capital by the Bank of Korea, backed in turn by the government. Medium- and long-term loans and FDI amounted to a mere US$308 million in the first plan period but increased substantially in the

---

1. This is the fundamental difference between Korea's economic planning and plans adopted by former socialist economies.

Table 2.3 *Size and Share of Policy Loans by Deposit Banks*
(billion won, %)

Year	Total	General loans		Policy loans			
				Nonexport loans		Export loans	
1970	722.4	510.5	(70.7)	211.9	(29.3)	55.9	(7.7)
1975	2,905.5	2,117.9	(72.9)	787.6	(27.1)	339.2	(11.7)
1980	12,204.4	7,904.8	(64.8)	4,299.6	(35.2)	1,720.8	(14.1)
1985	33,810.7	23,382.6	(69.2)	10,428.1	(30.8)	3,129.9	(9.3)

Source: Bank of Korea.
Note: Numbers in parentheses are percentage share of total loans.

subsequent two plan periods, to US$2.3 billion and US$6.0 billion, respectively (see table 2.4). For the four years during the fourth plan period, the amount of foreign capital reached US$10.7 billion. Foreign capital played a very important role in implementing the development strategies.[2]

The rapid increase in foreign capital inflow has not only contributed to economic growth by financing the expansion of production capacity, it also has resulted in the concomitant transfer of advanced technologies that has been the source of the productivity increase. As shown in figure 2.2, there appears to be a close correlation between capital goods imports and royalty payments for licensed foreign technologies, which implies that along with the capital goods imports that were financed partly through the foreign capital, the industry has made great effort to learn to industrialize.

Distinctive Features of Korea's Economic Development

The features of Korea's successful economic development process are varied (see box 2.3). First, in the macroeconomic dimension, the high rates of investment and

Table 2.4 *Inflows of Foreign Capital*
(2005 US$ million)

	First plan (1962–66)	Second plan (1967–71)	Third plan (1972–76)	Fourth plan (1977–80)
Loans	291	2,166	5,432	10,256
Public	116	811	2,389	4,084
Commercial	175	1,355	3,043	6,172
FDI	17	96	557	425
Total	308	2,262	5,989	10,681

Source: Government of the Republic of Korea 1982, p. 5.
Note: Short-term capital and bank loans are excluded.

---

2. Because 30 percent of gross national investments were financed through foreign capital during the 20-year period between 1962 and 1982, Cho and Kim (1997) estimated that, without foreign capital, annual economic growth would be lowered by 3.3 percentage points from the actual rate of 8.2 percent.

Figure 2.2 Royalty Payments and Capital Goods Imports, 1969–92

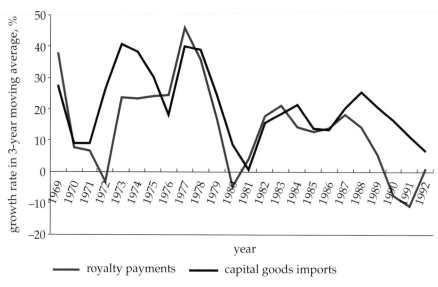

Source: Calculated using data from the National Statistical Office.

savings imply that Korea's economic transformation has been achieved by massive capital investment. Korea's capital accumulation has been made possible through increases in domestic savings; the gap between investment target and domestic savings in the earlier years had been filled using borrowed foreign capital. Second, industrial and labor composition has been changed in the direction of higher productivity as the share of manufacturing has steadily increased. Trade structures have also fundamentally changed, from export of primary goods to export of manufactured products, including capital goods, which were more than 40 percent of total exports in 2002. Third, the changes in the structures of industry, employment, and trade have proceeded with great improvements in human resources and technological capabilities, two of the most important factors for sustaining the economic growth that increases efficiency. Despite the debates on the nature of East

---

Box 2.3 Success Factors of Korea's Economic Growth

Among the factors that account for the success of Korea's economic development, only three issues—the government's role in managing the economy, and technology and human resource development—are discussed in this chapter. Former Prime Minister Nam Duck-Woo was one of the key policy makers during the high-growth era in Korea. He accounts for the factors in successful economic development as follows: Economic factors include (a) an outward-looking strategy, (b) good use of foreign resources, (c) a favorable international environment, (d) education, (e) faith in the free enterprise system, and (f) the activist role of government. Noneconomic factors include (a) ethnic and cultural homogeneity and a strong Confucian tradition that places a high value on education, achievement, and loyalty to the nation; (b) security threats; and (c) political leadership (Nam 1997).

> A major contributing factor in Korea's economic transformation is the large amount of capital accumulation, which was possible because of high Korean savings rates.

Asian growth performance, it is apparent that Korea has poured tremendous effort into upgrading knowledge and human resource bases. Korea's industrialization process was not only a process of capital accumulation; but also involved the learning process, a key concept of the knowledge-based economy.

> Elements of a KE development strategy, such as aggressively improving human resources and domestic technological capability, also played key roles in Korea's economic development in the past four decades.

Saving and Investment Rates

A very noticeable macroeconomic feature is the continued rise in savings and investment rates (see figure 2.3). Savings and investment rates, measured as a percentage of GDP, had remained low during the 1950s, at about 11 percent. The two rates started to increase as the full-scale industrialization unfolded in the 1960s, growing rapidly afterward until they reached a peak in the 1990s, with 35 percent and 37 percent savings and investment rates, respectively. Except in the 1980s, the investment rates surpassed the savings rates, and the deficiency in savings was made up with foreign investment.

The long-run trend of gross investment rates from 1960 to 2006 is shown in figure 2.4, with a trend line that implies a long-run equilibrium path. The figure shows the steep increases in investment rates during the 1960s and 1970s, with rates reaching their peak around the end of the 1980s. The rapid increases in the 1970s were the result of the HCI policies, but those steep increases were slowed in the 1980s by the stabilization and rationalization policies, and the long-run trend began to decline.

Figure 2.3 Savings and Investment Rates

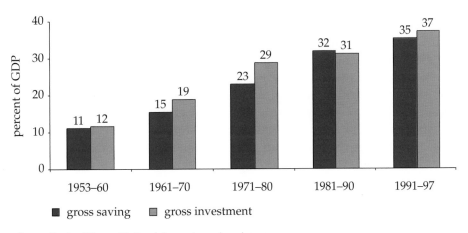

Source: Bank of Korea, *National Accounts,* various issues.

Figure 2.4 *Long-Run Trends of Gross Investment Rates, 1960–2006*

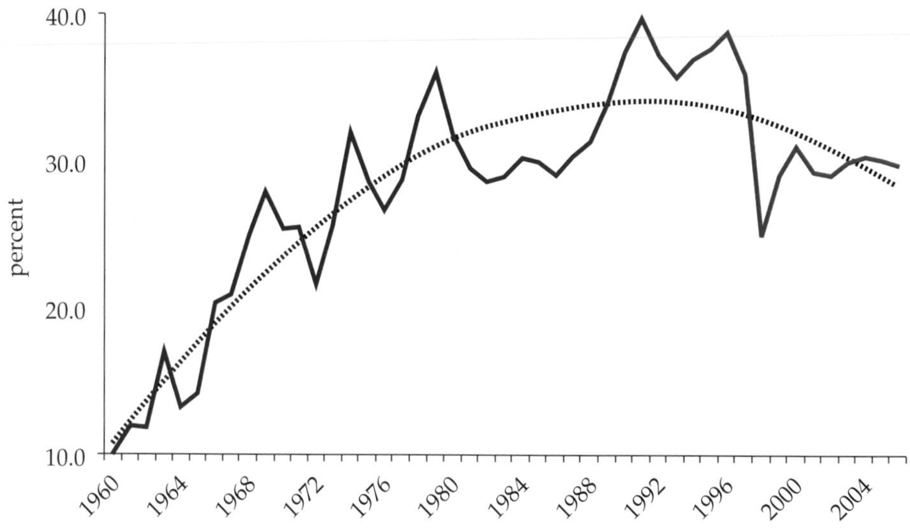

Source: Author's construction.
Note: Gross investment rate is the ratio of gross fixed capital formation to GDP in national accounts. The dotted line is the time trend of investment growth rates regressed with a quadratic equation.

The investment trend described above illustrates how Korea's economic development process can be divided into three distinct phases. Rapid and steady increases in investment rates in the 1960s and 1970s emphatically show that economic development in that period was investment driven. The role of investment in economic development remained high during the 1980s, although with diminishing rates of increase, and reached the peak at the end of the decade. There appears to be a clear turn in the trend after the peak, and since the 1990s, the Korean economy has been less and less dependent on physical investment. After the end of the 1980s, Korea entered into a mature phase of economic development that was different from the past.

It is worth noting that long-term disequilibrium of investment has occurred twice: one time in the 1980s and again in the early 1990s . As mentioned above, the disequilibrium of investment in the 1980s was the result of the industrial policy to rationalize the overinvestment of the 1970s. The rationalization policy was successful, and the Korean economy regained its growth path during the 1980s. However, the overinvestment during the early 1990s, until the financial crisis of 1997, is an opposite case. Entering into the 1990s, the Korean government felt the need to reshuffle its economic structure and tried to implement several reform measures, as discussed before. However, the reform was not consistently implemented; rather, government and industry opted for expanding production capacities.[3]

---

3. Overinvestment in the early 1990s is criticized as being a remote but fundamental cause of the financial crisis. For example, see Chung (2004).

Industrial and Trade Structures

The process of industrialization has been accompanied by radical changes in industrial structure (see table 2.5). The primary sectors, including agriculture, forestry, and mining, took the majority share of 48 percent in 1953; however, as industrialization proceeded after the 1960s, the share of primary sectors significantly decreased to 3.8 percent in 2005. Instead, the shares of manufacturing and services steadily increased, reaching 28 percent and 68 percent, respectively, in 2005. The sectoral composition of manufacturing has also dramatically changed over the years. Until the early 1970s, manufacturing was mainly composed of light industries such as textiles and apparel and food and beverages. Entering the 1980s, the share of HCI exceeded half of manufacturing and continued to increase afterward; as of 2005, about 85 percent of manufacturing was composed of HCI. In addition to the external transformation of the manufacturing sectors' composition, intrinsic contents of production activities in the manufacturing sectors have also changed greatly. For instance, the main production structure of the chemical industry in the 1970s remained mostly the mass production of petrochemicals, but it expanded to specialty chemicals and fine chemicals in later years.

Along with the changes in industrial structure, the leading industries in manufacturing are changing for the different stages of economic development. Table 2.6 shows the changes in manufacturing decomposed into the top 10 leading industries. Each period is marked with leading industries, which changed from labor-intensive light industries including food and beverage and textiles to capital-intensive HCI and to high-technology industries such as the electronics sector. Until the early 1980s, the food and beverage and textile and apparel sectors led in manufacturing share, with about half of manufacturing, but the share of these two sectors shrank over the years. Electrical and electronic products have had the leading role since the 1990s; second were the automobile and the chemical industries in 1990, and in 2000 and 2005, respectively.

The changing composition of manufacturing is the result of changes in factor conditions of the economy, which are also manifested in trade structure. As is

Table 2.5 *Production Structure of the Korean Economy, 1953–2005*
(percent)

	Agriculture, fishery, and mining	*Manu- facturing*	*Light industries (% of mfg)*	*Heavy and chemical industries (% of mfg)*	*Services*
1953	48.4	9.0	78.9	21.1	42.6
1960	38.9	13.8	76.6	23.4	47.3
1970	28.7	21.3	60.8	39.2	50.0
1980	16.7	28.6	45.6	54.4	54.7
1990	9.3	28.9	32.6	67.4	61.8
2000	5.3	29.4	20.7	79.3	65.3
2005	3.8	28.4	15.3	84.7	67.8

Source: Bank of Korea, *National Accounts*, reported years.

Table 2.6 *Top 10 Leading Industries in Korea's Manufacturing Sectors*
(% of total manufacturing value added)

Rank	1970 Industries	Share	1980 Industries	Share	1990 Industries	Share	2000 Industries	Share	2005 Industries	Share
1	Food and beverage	28.6	Textile and apparel	19.2	Electrical and electronic products	14.6	Electrical and electronic products	25.2	Electrical and electronic products	24.7
2	Textile and apparel	20.4	Food and beverage	19.0	Automobile	13.2	Chemicals	13.9	Chemicals	15.2
3	Chemicals	11.5	Chemicals	13.1	Food and beverage	12.9	Automobile	11.3	Automobile	12.2
4	Automobile	9.1	Electrical and electronic products	10.4	Chemicals	12.9	Basic metal	8.0	Basic metal	11.3
5	Paper and printing	5.5	Basic metal	6.7	Textile and apparel	11.5	Food and beverage	6.9	Machinery	7.0
6	Nonmetallic mineral products	5.3	Automobile	6.1	Basic metal	9.0	Machinery	6.9	Food and beverage	6.1
7	Coal and petroleum refinery	4.2	Coal and petroleum refinery	5.5	Nonmetallic mineral products	5.6	Textile and apparel	6.9	Coal and petroleum refinery	5.4
8	Electrical and electronic products	3.7	Nonmetallic mineral products	3.7	Machinery	5.5	Fabricated metal products	4.8	Fabricated metal products	4.5
9	Machinery	2.3	Paper and printing	3.9	Paper and printing	4.6	Paper and printing	4.3	Textile and apparel	3.6
10	Basic metal	1.5	Machinery	3.7	Fabricated metal products	3.8	Coal and petroleum refinery	4.2	Paper and printing	3.5
	All manufacturing (% of GDP)	21.2	All manufacturing (% of GDP)	28.2	All manufacturing (% of GDP)	28.8	All manufacturing (% of GDP)	29.4	All manufacturing (% of GDP)	28.4

Source: Bank of Korea, *National Accounts* and *Statistical Yearbook*, reported years.

shown in figure 2.5, during the earlier years of economic development, the textile and apparel industry was the only sector that showed comparative advantages. Electrical and electronic products began to contribute positively to the trade balance after the early 1970s, followed by transportation equipment, including automobiles and ships. Chemicals as a whole became trade surplus only after the mid-1990s, but the composition of the chemical sectors changed greatly. At earlier stages of development, Korea's chemical industry showed strong competitiveness in industrial chemicals, including petrochemicals, plastic, and rubber, but depended heavily on imported materials and fine chemicals. Only recently has Korea expanded its domestic production of materials and fine chemicals to lower the dependence on imports. Machinery is the least developed sector in terms of international competitiveness, but it is showing gradual improvement.

Building Technological Capabilities

Korea has gone to great lengths to build indigenous technological capabilities. Science and technology have become priority policy areas; for example, when the EPB was designing the first five-year economic development plan, it also produced the first technology promotion five-year plan, which explicitly stated the importance of indigenous technology development efforts for successful industrialization.

In line with the five-year plan, Korea has invested substantially in R&D, and its GERD has grown tremendously in both size and intensity. As shown in figure 2.6, the percentage share of GERD increased from 0.25 percent in 1963 to 2.99 percent in 2005. The number of researchers has increased 120-fold in the four and a half

Figure 2.5 Trade Specialization Index, 1967–2005

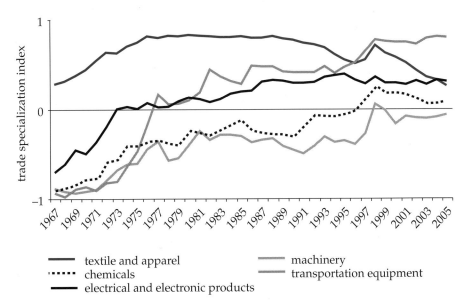

Source: Author's compilation from UN trade data.
Note: The trade specialization index is calculated as (exports – imports)/(exports + imports) for each industry.

Figure 2.6 Long-Term Trend of Korea's R&D Expenditures, 1964–2005

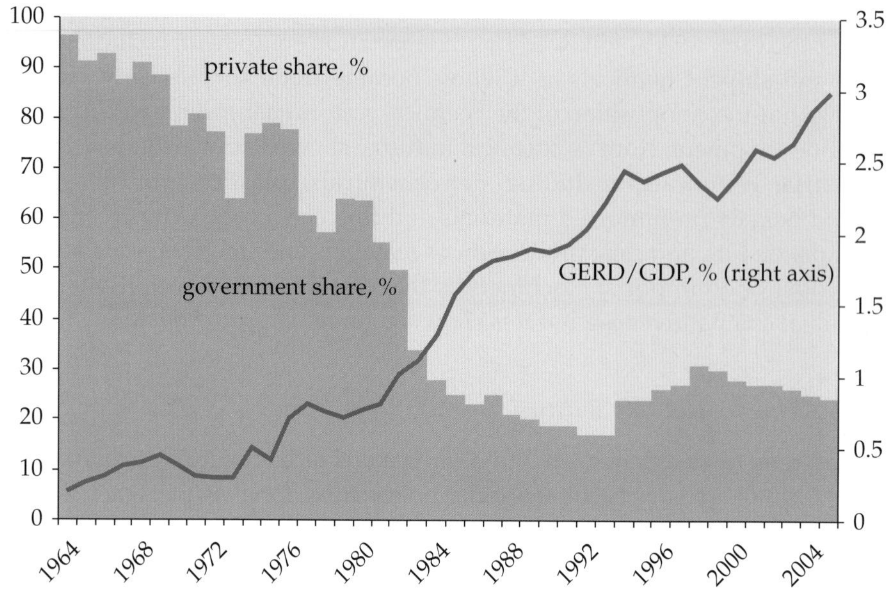

Source: Constructed using data from Ministry of Science and Technology.

decades, from 1,900 to 198,500. See figure 2.7, which plots researchers in R&D per million for selected OECD countries. The rapid increases in R&D have been possible through the active expansion of the private sector's investment. During the earlier years of industrialization, private sector R&D spending was negligible, but as the rapid economic growth has called for commensurate investment in technology development, private enterprises have continuously increased R&D. Consequently, the funding sources have also greatly changed: the government's share of GERD has been continuously declining, and in recent years, only one-fourth of GERD has come from the government (figure 2.6).

The process of technological capability building in Korea can be characterized as the interplay between imported technologies and indigenous R&D efforts. Figure 2.8 plots the trends in the ratio of royalty payments to business expenditures on R&D (BERD) and the ratio of BERD to sales (or R&D intensity) from 1976 to 2005. The ratio of royalty payments to BERD substantially decreased until the early 1980s, which implies that the growth of BERD exceeded that of royalty payments. The R&D intensity, however, had remained at 0.5 percent. After the early 1980s, there was a clear change in the trends; although the ratio of royalty payment to BERD remained at 30 percent, R&D intensity started to increase.

Underlying these changing relationships are the concerted efforts by both the private sector and the government to develop technological capabilities. First, business strategy has undergone a fundamental shift. In earlier years, international competitiveness relied mostly on cost factors such as low wages and scale economies based on mass production. And because imported technologies were of a kind that required simple assimilation and adaptation, there was no need to organize R&D

Figure 2.7 Researchers in R&D, Selected OECD Countries (Average 2002–04)

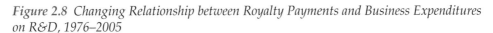

Source: Constructed using data from World Bank SIMA 2007 database.

activities. In later years, in contrast, as the cost advantage of cheap skilled labor was exhausted and the economic structure was transformed into more technology-intensive sectors, the need for institutionalized R&D activities became more pressing. The private sector met this need by establishing in-house R&D laboratories (box 2.4).

Figure 2.8 Changing Relationship between Royalty Payments and Business Expenditures on R&D, 1976–2005

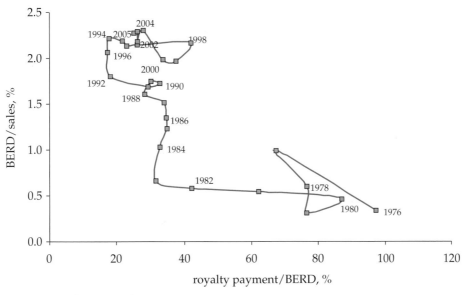

Source: Author's compilation.

In accordance with the stages of economic development, the Korean government has successively changed the orientation of science and technology (S&T) policy. In the earlier years, more emphasis was put on building the infrastructure for techno-logical development, whereas in later years the emphasis shifted toward targeted technological development. In the early years of launching full-scale economic development plans, the Korean government recognized very clearly that S&T would play important roles in the coming years. In the 1960s, two noteworthy policy measures were initiated in this regard: the establishment of two institutions, the Korea Institute of Science and Technology (KIST) in 1966 and the Ministry of Science and Technology (MOST) in 1967. These two institutions, with the Korea Advanced Institute of Science (KAIS), which was established in 1971, have exerted powerful influences over the S&T community in Korea. MOST has been the main designer of Korea's overall S&T policy; KIST has played the role of technological functionary in responding to industrial demands for rapid economic growth; and KAIS (later KAIST—the Korea Advanced Institute of Science and Technology) first implemented the concept of the research-oriented university in Korea's higher education system.

> The orientation of S&T policy has evolved with the stages of economic development, with more emphasis on building the infrastructure for technological development in the earlier years and targeted technological development more recently.

Despite government efforts to build S&T institutions in the 1960s and to set up S&T infrastructures such as specialized government research institutes, in addition to KIST, in the 1970s, S&T policy played a limited role in those years. The technological capability for labor-intensive export industries in the 1960s and for HCI in the 1970s could be easily acquired from foreign sources (OECD 1996, p. 27). Significant changes occurred during the 1980s as many Korean export industries shifted from producing for original equipment manufacturers and began to market internationally under their own brand names. Changes in firms' competitive strategies created new challenges for government policy. In the past, S&T policy had been supply oriented, to provide foundations for adopting foreign technologies. During the 1980s, the direction of S&T policy turned toward encouraging domestic R&D activities. After MOST launched a national R&D program in 1982, other ministries started mission-oriented R&D programs.

Investing in Human Resource Development

Similarly to the innovation pillar of the knowledge economy, Korea's education or human resource development pillar has evolved from one that struggled to provide universal primary education to one that produces highly skilled graduate and post-graduate technical specialists. Government policy for human resource development and the education system as a whole has proceeded with the development stages of the economy. In the earlier years, education policy focused on the expansion of primary and secondary education, which was critical to supply industry with an educated workforce. The most conspicuous feature of educational devel-

---

Box 2.4   What Happened in 1982?

As figure 2.8 indicates, around 1982, the trend in the interaction between imported technologies and indigenous R&D effort changed from a substituting relationship to a complementary one. This turning was not accidental; 1982 marked the launch of the first NRDP, and during that year private enterprises began to establish in-house R&D laboratories. That year is also memorable in that the share of the private sector's R&D spending reached 50 percent of the national total and continued to increase rapidly.

Some of the government's initiatives were instrumental in the change. MOST's newly introduced special R&D program, Korea's first NRDP, aimed to implement a nationwide, full-scale technology development strategy. A year before, the Technology Development Promotion Act was revised to be the legal basis of the special R&D program. The revised act came into effect in 1982, with a new clause stating government's direct financial support for corporate R&D centers. The Military Service Law was also revised in that year to include a special army service exemption for qualified engineers and researchers who opted to work in public and private R&D centers. The government initiatives that supplied financial and human resources, coupled with technology development programs, triggered a burgeoning of R&D activities by private enterprises.

---

opment in the 1960s was its expansion of students' enrollment and the number of schools (figure 2.9). The completion of the six-year compulsory education plan enabled all children of the relevant age group to enroll in schools, and the number of secondary school students tripled compared with the previous decades. Vocational high schools were established in the 1960s to provide training in craft skills for the growing labor-intensive light industries.

Korea's education system was developed in tandem with the various stages of economic development, complementing the other KE pillars.

Strengthening vocational education was one of the priority areas of economic development plans during the 1970s.Vocational junior colleges were set up in the 1970s to supply technicians for the HCI. The framework of vocational training was institutionalized by the 1976 enactment of the Basic Vocational Training Act, which was wholly amended in 1981. In addition to the public vocational training institutions, partial government funding was introduced to support out-of-school training by enterprises. Since 1976, large enterprises have been required to either train their employees or pay a levy to the government for the cost of vocational training in public training institutions.

During the 1970s and 1980s, the rapid expansion of higher education had proceeded by increasing student enrollment and diversifying higher education institutions. As junior colleges took a larger share of tertiary education, their programs were diversified to meet the industrial needs. On July 30, 1980, the government announced an education reform that included such measures as abolishing university entrance examinations, renovating school facilities, and introducing incentives for teachers. To finance the education reform measures, the government introduced the education tax (box 2.5).

Figure 2.9 Republic of Korea: Gross School Enrollment Rates

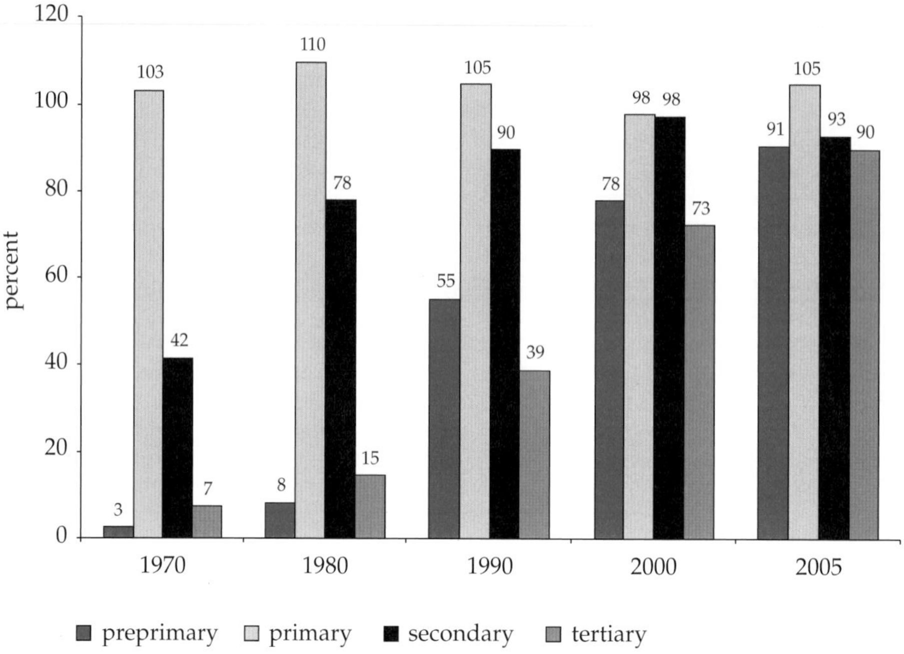

Source: Author's construction using data from the World Bank SIMA database.

The availability of labor became increasingly strained in the 1980s. The portion of the population that was economically active dropped sharply in the 1980s compared with the previous decade, and labor demand continued to increase as the economy grew at a high annual average rate of 10 percent in the second half of the 1980s. The changes in labor demand for a better skilled and higher-caliber workforce in 1980s—the result of rapid economic growth—called for strengthening science and engineering education in universities. Reforming the education and training system to meet the needs of an industrializing society was one of 10 major policy objectives and programs in the Seventh Five-Year Economic and Social Development Plan in 1992.

The Korean education system has undergone a series of reforms like that of July 30, 1980. The focus of the reforms has changed according to the stage of social and economic development, yet the underlying principle of the reforms has been consistent, viewing "education as the prime mover of national development" (Presidential Commission on Education Reform 1997, p. 17). However, the education reforms were not always successful. Quantitative expansion was rather easy to implement; for example, the new industrial needs in the 1970s were met by increasing the university enrollment capacity. But the quality improvement necessitates, among other things, capital investment. The government's investment in education has steadily increased, but not enough to finance the amount of quality enhancement needed. The Presidential Commission on Education Reform's report described the financing problem, stating that although economic growth and social transformation had proceeded "at a breathtaking pace," investment in education

Box 2.5 *Education Tax*

The government's education budget had always run short of the required investment for upgrading the educational system. In particular, the July 30, 1980, education reform necessitated a substantial increase in the government's investment in education, and government introduced an education tax in 1981. An education tax had been in place since 1958, but it was abrogated in 1961 just after the military coup. The new law in 1981 was intended to be effective for only five years; it was revised once in 1986 to extend the tax for another five years and then was changed to a permanent tax in 1991.

When the education tax was enacted in 1981, it was also levied on capital gains income (5 percent), liquor sales (10 percent), tobacco sales (10 percent), and banking and insurance companies' earnings (0.5 percent). The composition of the education tax has since expanded, including, for example, property tax (20 percent) and automobile tax (30 percent). When the government initiated the changes in the education governance system to make it more decentralized in 2000, the education tax played an instrumental role in empowering the provincial authorities. Education taxes that were collected with the local taxes were directly transferred to provincial governments. This approach is expected to give more autonomy in regional education policy to the local government bodies. The education tax has contributed significantly to meeting the increasing needs of the country's educational investment. The education budget has steadily increased over the years, reaching 4.13 percent of GDP in 2004. As shown in the table below, , more than 20 percent of the education budget was appropriated through the education tax until 2000; afterward, the share of the education tax decreased to approximately 10 percent.

Trend of Education Budget and Education Tax, 1996–06

	1996	1998	2000	2002	2004	2006
Total education budget, in trillion won	17.9	19.4	22.9	28.1	33.3	35.0
As share of GDP (%)	4.0	4.0	4.0	4.1	4.3	4.1
Education tax, in trillion won	3.8	4.5	5.8	3.5	3.5	3.4
Share of education budget paid by revenue from education tax (%)	21.2	23.2	25.3	12.5	10.5	9.7

Source: Ministry of Planning and Budget.

had not kept up (1997, p. 18). Since 1995, Korea's gross educational expenditures as a percentage of GDP have been above the average of OECD countries; however, the public investment is far below that of average OECD countries (see table 2.7). The investment gap is mostly supplemented by the private sector (see table 2.8).

In addition to increasing education investment, Korea's education system needs to cultivate creativity. The education reform plan announced in 1997 succinctly stated the challenges faced by Korea: "Korean education, having registered a marked growth in quantitative terms in the era of industrialization, will no longer be appropriate in the era of information technology and globalization. It will not be able to produce persons who possess high levels of creativity and moral sensitivity,

Table 2.7 *Education Expenditures in OECD Countries, 1995*
(% of GDP)

	Korea	Japan	United States	Canada	France	Germany	OECD average
Public education	3.6	3.6	5.0	6.3	5.8	4.5	4.8
Private education	2.6	1.1	1.7	0.7	0.5	1.3	1.2
Gross	6.2	4.7	6.7	7.0	6.3	5.8	6.0

Source: OECD 1998b.

Table 2.8 *Educational Expenditures in Korea*
(% of GDP)

	Expenditure	1993	1995	1997	1999	2001	2003
Korea	Public	3.8	3.6	4.4	4.1	4.8	4.6
	Private	1.9	2.6	2.9	2.7	3.4	3.1
	Total	5.7	6.2	7.4	6.8	8.2	7.7
OECD total	Public	5.0	4.8	4.9	4.6	4.8	5.5
	Private	1.1	1.2	1.2	1.1	1.4	0.8
	Total	6.1	5.9	6.1	5.8	6.2	6.3

Source: OECD 1998b, 2003a, 2005b.

which are required to sharpen the nation's competitive edge in the coming era" (Presidential Commission on Education Reform 1997, p. 17).

The rapid economic growth has had a great impact on human resource development in two ways. On the industrial side, rapid industrialization affected skill formation in workplaces; in particular, for a short time industrial deepening required substantial effort to upgrade workforce skills and knowledge. On the supply side, the education and training system had to change to meet the new requirements of the industry. Hence, Korea's education and training system responded to the growth of the Korean economy by rapidly expanding student enrollment capacity, but this caused an imbalance between the quantitative expansion and qualitative improvement of education and resulted in the skill mismatch between public training and industrial needs. On-the-job training in Korea has always been emphasized by both the government and businesses, but public vocational training has also been criticized for lagging behind the industries' needs. According to some critics, public training was in the form of basic training, whereas industry needed specialized training that would produce workers able to cope with rapid technical and structural change (Koh 1998, p. 64). Korea's education system and human resource development policy has sometimes been successful and sometimes been deficient, exemplifying the incessant process of transformation toward a vision in which education is a prime mover in national development.

Summary

The transformation of the Korean economy over about four decades shows a gradual transition to more sophisticated and advanced industrial structures. The successful transformation has been made possible by the government's use of the appropriate policy framework and industries' active engagement. The government set development goals that clearly indicate where the country should move forward. Those goals and major policy directions have changed according to the stage of development and in response to changes in domestic and international economic conditions.

The government's approaches have been practical throughout the years, and its intervention has been pervasive, as manifested in economic planning. Also, there have been several instances of trial and error, among them, the HCI plan, which caused serious distortions in resource allocation and overinvestment. The Korean government responded to the mistake through rationalization policies that aimed to restore the market mechanism. In this regard, the role of the Korean government is not a substitute for the market; rather, it has been successful because it has complemented the functioning of the market, particularly in the earlier years when the markets and institutions were still at an inceptive stage (Aoki, Kim, and Okuno-Fujiwara 1997).

> The role of the government in the Korean economy is not to substitute for, but to complement, the functioning of the market.

The government's intervention into the market has not been uniform over the years, as shown by the changes in the macroeconomic policy framework, which has moved from direct intervention in the early years to liberalization and autonomy more recently. Managing the economy to support industrialization has brought tremendous benefits but also costs. Without the government's intervention to mobilize the limited resources toward a few targeted industries—under which a small number of large firms enjoyed favorable conditions that fostered rapid growth—Korea might not have built such modernized industries as steel, automobiles, and shipbuilding. However, the cost of these industrial policies was not negligible.

Among other effects, the underdevelopment of the financial sector, which had been subjected to the industrialization goals, not only caused losses in the financial sector itself, it also had economy-wide impacts. The direct cost of the financial repression in the early 1970s turned out to have negatively affected output growth during the period, and its overall effects on the economy were significantly negative (Park, Song, and Wang 2004). In addition, the mismatch between the financial system and the economic system as a whole has made the Korean economy vulnerable to outside financial shocks. Therefore, the Korean government's efforts to refurbish the economic system, including the financial sector in the early 1990s, did not produce satisfactory outcomes as expected.

The government's intervention in general brought about positive effects in two areas: human resource development and S&T. Investment in public goods such as education and innovation has always been advocated as one of the priority areas of the Korean government, and the Korean case shows that practical and stepwise approaches can be performed effectively in line with the overall stages of economic development. A stepwise approach was used in both S&T and human resource development in Korea. The primary policy goal in the earlier years was expanding infrastructure, whereas enhancing the quality of education and innovation was the main focus in later years.

> Investment in public goods such as education and innovation has always been advocated as one of the priority areas of the Korean government, and the Korean case shows that practical and stepwise approaches can be performed effectively in line with the overall development stages.

Investment in strengthening Korea's education and innovation systems is not only important for the sectors' own sake; it is also important for enhancing the productivity of workers, firms, and industry as a whole. In addition, as ICTs became critical in propelling national economic growth, Korea significantly expanded investment in these areas, where the government played a leading role.[4] Korea's goal of building an information society was a rather late movement, arriving after the financial crisis in 1997. However, as chapter 5 shows, information infrastructure was one of the key areas in which government recognized the importance of prioritizing investment for, on one hand, its own development and, on the other hand, its impacts on the rest of the economy.

---

4. As chapter 5 shows, it is more accurate to say that the production and export of electronics hardware propelled Korea's economic growth, not the use of advanced ICTs and the Internet. This issue is recapitulated in chapter 8.

3

The Challenges for Korea's Development Strategies

Cheonsik Woo and Joonghae Suh

Problems that Caused the Financial Crisis of 1997

The financial crisis in 1997 was the critical junction for Korea to rethink and redesign the ways of managing the national economy. During the high-growth years, the Korean government had actively intervened in the market in the form of selective industrial policies, yet there are debates on the effectiveness of these policies (see box 2.1). As explained in chapter 2, in the 1990s, the Korean economy faced the urgent need to reform its economic system, make the financial system more autonomous, and restructure redundancies in the industrial sectors.

Despite the efforts of the new government, however, reform and restructuring were unsuccessful until the outbreak of the financial crisis in 1997. One of the factors in the aborted reform was the short-lived economic recovery that had resulted from the appreciation of the yen in the early 1990s, which fostered complacency and maintained the status quo. However, according to Fukagawa (1997), the fundamental reason for retarded industrial restructuring lies in the "iron triangle of bank-chaebol-government" that hinders the free flow of financial resources that are needed to restructure the overinvested industries. Chang (2003) sees the situation differently, arguing that the cronyism story seems implausible. According to Chang, Korea's selective industrial policies before the 1990s were successful because of the government's ability to discipline the recipients of the state-created rents. The crisis was the result of hasty financial liberalization and the weakening of such disciplinary power (Chang 2003).

However, the self-diagnosis of the Korean government clearly points out the adverse effects of the iron triangle and condemns it as a prime cause of the financial crisis. "The government failed to set either the foundations for a market economy or an environment in which businesses and banks would assume responsibility for their mistakes in free market competition. In various sections of society, moral hazard prevailed where market principles failed to work. Chaebols and financial institutions expected that the government would take fiscal measures to bail them out when the economy declined"(Government of the Republic of Korea 1999, p. 12)

Causes of the Financial Crisis

The causes of the financial crisis might be considered from three aspects—Korea's financial system, international competitiveness, and the failure of the government to build a new economic system. First, from the aspect of the financial system, international capital movements in a global marketplace weaken the autonomy of individual countries to manage their domestic financial markets. The problem gets worse when the financial institutions have weak risk management. Korea's financial sectors had been regulated by the government so that financial market liberalization pursued throughout the mid-1990s exposed the Korean banking system to outside shocks without due preparation, as discussed in *DJnomics:*

> In 1997, many banks and financial institutions became insolvent as they were saddled with the huge unpaid debts of bankrupt chaebols. Nonetheless, such rampant insolvency was not the sole cause for the flight of foreign capital. The Korean foreign exchange crisis was the product of two events. First, the share of short-term debt increased quickly, exceeding that of long-term debt by 1994 [see table 3.1]. Had it not been for this exorbitant accumulation of short-term debt the massive outflow of foreign capital—which in turn triggered the foreign exchange crisis—would not have happened. Second, foreign analysts downgraded the prospects for the Korean economy, further exacerbating the capital flight. The causes for this rapid increase in short-term debt and foreign creditors' negative view of the Korean financial market are varied. The deluge of short-term debt was rooted in the negligence of financial supervision during the process of rapid capital liberalization, combined with instability in the international money market and the government's unsophisticated policy responses to the situation (Government of the Republic of Korea 1999, p. 6)

The key suspected causes of the 1997 financial crisis in Korea are the breakdown in financial system, the erosion of economy's international competitiveness, and weak macroeconomic and institutional environments, which were badly in need of reforms.

Table 3.1 *Trends in Short- and Long-Term Foreign Debt, 1992–97*
(percent)

	1992	1993	1994	1995	1996	1997
Long-term debt share	56.8	56.3	46.6	42.2	41.7	42.4
Growth rate	11.0	1.6	7.3	24.9	32.0	17.2
Short-term debt share	43.2	43.7	53.4	57.8	58.3	57.6
Growth rate	7.6	3.8	58.3	49.0	34.7	14.1

Source: Government of the Republic of Korea 1999.

Second, the continued erosion of the Korean economy in terms of international competitiveness is more fundamental than the financial aspect. The underlying causes of financial insolvency and the bankruptcies of the large firms lie in the deteriorating profitability of businesses in conjunction with rising wages and lowered productivity since the late 1980s. Accustomed to the growth first strategies of the past and under the patronage of the government, those firms had neglected to change their strategies and upgrade nonprice factors of competitiveness. Instead, large enterprises were still preoccupied with expanding their business scale, which was made possible through increased lending by the banks.

The third aspect, which seems to be remote, is the failure of government to build a new economic system. During the 30 years of economic development before the crisis, under the authoritarian regimes, the government had intervened severely in the market. Despite the government's effort to enhance market functions, the pervasive cronyism between political and business circles had a detrimental effect on the economy as a whole. Increased demand for individual freedom after the democratization in the late 1980s called for clearly defined economic rules and systems that are more consistent with the international norm. The government had felt the necessity of reform, and in 1993, the new government tried to introduce several reform measures. But the reform efforts in the 1990s, until the outbreak of the financial crisis in 1997, were aborted because of the short-lived economic recovery that had resulted from the appreciation of the yen, among other things.

New Strategies for Korea's Economic Development

The overarching challenge for Korea after the financial crisis was to secure new, sustainable sources of growth. Korea's potential growth rate during the 1990s had already declined to 6.7 percent from the 8 percent of the preceding decade, mainly because of a sharp fall in labor growth (from 2.6 percent to 1.5 percent). That long-term trend will continue in the future (see table 3.2).

The problem of securing new, sustainable sources of growth for Korea's future thus translates into the problem of enhancing the knowledge base and innovation capabilities of Korean people and firms, because a critical factor here is the produc-

Table 3.2 *Potential Growth Rates and Sources of Growth in Korea*
(percent)

	1980–90	1990–2000	2000–10 High	2000–10 Low	2010–20 High	2010–20 Low
Actual growth rate	9.1	5.7				
Irregular factors	1.1	1.0				
Potential growth rate	8.0	6.7	5.1	4.5	4.1	3.2
Growth in factor inputs	4.5	3.4	2.5	2.4	1.9	1.7
Labor	2.6	1.5	0.6	0.4	0.2	0.2
Capital	2.0	1.9	2.1	1.8	1.7	1.5
Productivity growth	3.5	3.4	2.7	2.1	2.2	1.5
Technological advances	1.1	1.2	1.2	0.9	1.1	0.7

Source: Korea Development Institute (KDI) 2002.

tivity growth resulting from technological progress or advances. Actually, along with economic restructuring, these needs constituted another major thrust of Korea's policy initiatives after the financial crisis, and notable progress has been made in this regard. Indeed, the latest financial crisis can be assessed as an epochal event that precipitated Korea's crossover from the old development paradigm of input-based growth to a new development paradigm of innovation-driven, knowledge-based growth. Korea's strategy to seek and anchor such a new development paradigm is well represented by the knowledge-based economy (KBE) master plan of 1999 and the ensuing three-year KBE action plan (see Woo [2004] for a detailed explanation).

Korea's Master Plan for a KBE in 1999

In general, the transition to a KBE means making the entire society more suitable for the creation, dissemination, and exploitation of knowledge. However, practical and policy implications of the transition to a KBE vary across countries, depending on the stage of economic development, industrial characteristics, and institutional or cultural environments. The gist of the challenge for Korea is to make the most of the existing pool of technologies, intellectual assets, industrial base, and other productive assets, whether they exist within Korea or outside.

> The transition to a KBE means making the entire society more suitable for the creation, dissemination, and exploitation of knowledge. The practical and policy implications of the transition vary across countries, depending on the level of economic development, industrial characteristics, and institutional and cultural environments.

In the 1999 design of the KBE strategy, Korea's assets and disadvantages for the transition to a KBE were summarized as follows:

- Strengths include (a) the high motivation and high absorptive capability of the people, who are equipped with good educational background, and (b) the world-class, modern production facilities, balanced industrial base, and reliable supply chain supported by Korea's indigenous firms, which will guarantee Korea some minimal level of industrial performance for a while.
- Weaknesses are the resources gap and the institutional gap. The resources gap is Korea's disadvantage in core factors of production such as knowledge, technology, and capital compared with the leading industrialized countries. The institutional gap is Korea's lack of a range of system assets, such as a market economy and organizational assets, that are needed to use existing resources efficiently.
- Opportunities are seen in the following. (a) Multinational enterprises are strengthening their northeast Asian strategy, looking for a regional platform for a range of mid- to high-level knowledge-intensive activities. (b) The latest crisis brought about a fortuitous chance for Korea to undertake drastic restructuring and reform measures to make itself more market- and knowledge-friendly.

- Threats include (a) the competitive pressure from low-wage economies, which is escalating, and (b) waning momentum of reform in Korea because of the unexpectedly fast recovery from the financial crisis.

The strategic thrust of Korea's KBE plan includes (a) harnessing the market fundamentals through successful completion of the major structural reforms that are under way; (b) transforming Korea into a fully open, globally connected society by further liberalization measures and proactive policies that promote FDI; and (c) enhancing the indigenous innovation capacity by establishing an advanced system to further national innovation.

> Korea's plan for transition to the KBE included (a) harnessing market fundamentals for the major structural reforms that were in progress; (b) increasing openness by further liberalizing measures and policies to promote FDI; and (c) enhancing the indigenous innovation capacity by establishing an advanced system to further national innovation.

Three-Year Action Plan

Korea's knowledge strategy as envisaged in the KBE master plan was implemented under the auspices of the three-year KBE action plan (see table 3.3). The action plan deliberately focused on the microeconomic side issues of the KBE, such as ICTs, innovation and S&T, education and human resource management, and the digital divide. The plan did not address the macroeconomic side issues of harnessing market fundamentals and fully opening up, because their core policy agendas such as financial, corporate, labor, and public sector reforms were already being fully implemented in the context of Korea's all-out crisis management or system-rebuilding efforts.

Put into effect in April 2000, the action plan set forth three goals: (a) leapfrog to the top 10 knowledge-information leaders in the globe, (b) upgrade educational environments to OECD standards, and (c) spearhead S&T such as bioengineering by upgrading to G-7 standards. Aiming to meet these goals, the plan set out 18 policy tasks and 83 actionable subtasks in the five main areas of information infrastructure, human resource development, knowledge-based industry development, S&T, and methods of coping with the digital divide. To implement the action plan, the government formed five working groups that involve 19 ministries and 17 research institutes, with MOFE assigned to coordinate the overall implementation.

Progress and Attainment

The three-year KBE action plan was implemented in 2000 with adequate budget support. Korea managed to substantially increase its budget spending in the planned action areas, even though the overall budget situation was quite tight as a result of the huge burden of financing the corporate and financial restructuring programs that were under way. In the 2000 budget, the total budget growth rate was 4.7 percent, but growth rates in the information and R&D sectors were 12.9 percent and 13.4 percent, respectively. In 2001, the growth rates in the informatization,

Table 3.3 *Korea's Three-Year Action Plan for the KBE, 2000–03*

Sector	Target tasks (18 total)
Informatization	• Complete a basic information infrastructure, such as an optical cable network • Foster an education information network • Manage a national knowledge and information system • Build a cyber government • Change mindsets with respect to IT • Build a sound and secure knowledge society
S&T and innovation	• Reinforce a strategic approach in R&D investment • Facilitate cooperation among industry, universities, and research centers • Build an efficient support system for research • Enhance an understanding of S&T and scientists
Knowledge-based industries	• Build an industrial infrastructure for a KBE • Nurture a new knowledge-intensive industry • Upgrade traditional industries through IT
Education and human resource development and management	• Reform the education system for creativity and competitiveness • Revamp the vocational training system • Develop a fair and efficient labor market
Digital divide	• Expand access to information and IT training • Empower the vulnerable and enhance their life quality

Source: MOFE 2000.

R&D, and education sectors were 15.7 percent, 16.3 percent, and 19.1 percent, respectively, far exceeding the overall budget growth rate of 5.7 percent.

Greatly helped by such budget support, the action plan has stayed on track. By June 2002, of the 83 programs, 7 had been completed (6 in the informatization sector), and 76 are under way as originally planned. The three goals have not yet been attained, but results are more or less satisfactory. In five main policy areas, the government has achieved great success in the area of information infrastructure and made good progress in the areas of knowledge-intensive industries and innovation and S&T, but progress has been relatively limited in the area of education.[1]

---

1. Chapters 4, 5, 6, and 7 deal with the four areas of the KBE in detail.

4

Designing a New Economic Framework

Siwook Lee, Wonhyuk Lim, Joonghae Suh, and Moon Joong Tcha

As of 2003, Korea had risen to become the 11th largest economy in the world, in terms of total GDP, from one of the most devastated and poorest economies when the Korean War ended in 1953. At least part of this achievement was arguably due to the government-led growth strategy that was based on the fast accumulation of labor and capital, among other factors, in particular since the early 1960s. However, this quantitative growth model has run its course as the economy has continued to become more structurally complex. Recognizing this, the Korean government redefined its role and pursued continuous reforms to convert the economic system into a more market-oriented and autonomous one. The 1997 financial crisis is considered to be an important turning point as the government-led interventionists faced a dramatic challenge because of radical changes that accompanied the crisis. The government tried to establish market discipline in economic activities and consequently minimize the government's intervention in the market. Structural reforms in Korea, starting in the wake of the crisis, have been extensive, covering most of the areas in public and private domains. The scheme of the reforms is summarized in figure 4.1.

The economic reforms since the 1997 crisis had three main objectives:

1. to transform Korea into a market-oriented economy by deregulating across the sectors, thereby promoting competition and entrepreneurship (at the same time, a modern regulatory framework would be set up to support the efficient and equitable functioning of the markets);
2. to improve the institutional regime by improving the rule of law and by having greater transparency, disclosure of information, and accountability on the part of the government as well as the private sector; and
3. to continue the transition to the KBE by developing a relevant and modern legal and institutional infrastructure in such areas as intellectual property rights, valuation of intangible assets, and laws to cover privacy and security in digital transactions.

To encourage a market-oriented economy, the government's objectives were to promote competition and entrepreneurship and deregulate the market to encourage the creativity of the private sector. At the same time, the reform provided a

The three main objectives of Korea's post-1997 economic reforms were encouraging a market-oriented economy, improving the institutional regime, and making the transition to an advanced KBE.

modern regulatory framework to support the efficient and equitable functioning of the markets.

To improve the institutional regime, the Korean government aimed to secure the rule of law and provided greater transparency, disclosure of information, and accountability for market players, as well as for the government.

The government initiated the transition to an advanced KBE, for which it planned to establish modern legal and institutional infrastructures that were relevant for the knowledge economy in such areas as intellectual property rights, valuation of intangible assets, and laws covering privacy and security in the cyber domain and digital transactions. The government acted as a catalyst for a high-speed Internet backbone, promoting new technologies and facilitating networks (among universities, researchers, and firms), while it was careful to foster market-led mechanisms.

As well as the structural reforms, the Korean government had also focused on developing venture business firms. The Korean government has fully recognized the significance of venture business that commercializes the new technologies and ideas characterized by high-risk, high-return opportunities. The Korean govern-

Figure 4.1 Scheme of Economic Reform after the Financial Crisis

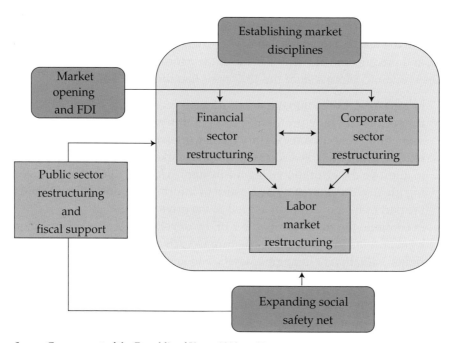

Source: Government of the Republic of Korea 1999, p. 46.

ment has felt the need to systematically support small, technologically agile firms to advance the industry structure and create high-quality jobs.

This chapter discusses structural reforms and other institutional efforts that have strong implications for the Korean economy's transformation into a KBE. All of Korea's efforts since the 1997 crisis are crucial if the economy is to build strong institutional infrastructures and fortify the rule of law. In this regard, the progress is closely related to Korea's success in establishing a KBE.

Financial Sector Reforms

Restoring confidence in Korea's financial system was a top priority for the government in the wake of the 1997 crisis. The crisis stemmed largely from the failures of a banking system that had doled out soft loans to conglomerates, which did not worry about profits. Financial sector reforms are the keystone of far-reaching reforms throughout the economy. The government has embraced the following principles in bringing the financial sector up to world standards in terms of capital structure and prudential supervision: (a) restoration of financial intermediary functions through the elimination of uncertainties that prevailed in the overall financial system; (b) the swift exit of nonviable financial institutions from the market and early normalization of viable institutions through settlement of nonperforming loans and injection of public funds; and (c) prevention of moral hazard through the strict application of loss-sharing principles to the beneficiaries of public funds.

Financial sector reforms have been undertaken in several ways. First, to rehabilitate the financial system, the government liquidated troubled institutions, removed nonperforming loans, and recapitalized promising financial institutions by injecting public funds (see figure 4.2). Following the government's lead, financial institutions also adopted stricter standards, which have greatly contributed to increasing the financial health and profitability of the financial industry. Various institutional reforms also were implemented to avoid a repeat of this kind of disaster. Most notably, the precrisis distortions in financial resource allocation and corporate governance drew great attention.

Figure 4.2 *Method of Financial Sector Restructuring*

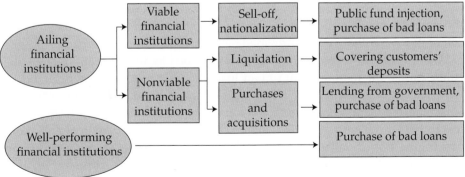

Source: Kim, K. 2003, p. 238.

Cleaning Up Nonperforming Loans

In the wake of the crisis, one of the main challenges that Korea faced was "legacy costs"—problems resulting from mistaken or unlawful decisions of the past. Foremost among these problems were massive nonperforming loans (NPLs) that had resulted from unprofitable investment. The magnitude of NPLs reached a level that it was impossible for banks to clean up themselves. Consequently, after closing the worst of the distressed financial institutions, the government had to step in with public funds and urge financial institutions to take proactive measures against insolvent firms. Although the injection of public funds was likely to generate political controversy, the government decided to withstand criticism and stabilize the financial system.

Once the government decided to inject public funds to rehabilitate the financial sector, the question became what exactly constituted an NPL. Before the crisis, only loans in arrears for six months or more had been classified as NPLs. In July 1998, banks tightened the asset classification standards by redefining NPLs as those loans in arrears for three months or more. Nonbank financial institutions followed suit in March 1999. In December 1999, financial institutions adopted a forward-looking approach in asset classification, taking into account the future performance of borrowers in addition to their track record in debt service. The forward-looking criteria pushed creditors to make a more realistic assessment of loan risks based on borrowers' managerial competence, financial conditions, and future cash flow. Creditors classified loans as substandard when borrowers' ability to meet debt service obligations was deemed to be considerably weakened. NPLs were to include substandard loans on which interest payments were not made. In March 2000, the asset classification standards were further strengthened with the introduction of the enhanced forward-looking criteria, which classify loans as nonperforming when future risks are significant, even if interest payments have been made without a problem up to that point. With the use of the enhanced criteria, NPLs would have increased from 66.7 trillion won (W) to W 88.0 trillion at the end of 1999.

To clean up NPLs and rehabilitate the financial sector, the government injected a total of W 155.3 trillion (approximately US$129 billion), equivalent to 28 percent of Korea's GDP in 2001, as of end-2001. Table 4.1 shows the sources and uses of public funds. Two-thirds of public funds were raised through bonds issued by Korea Asset Management Corporation and Korea Deposit Insurance Corporation (KDIC). More than W 40 trillion was used to settle deposit insurance obligations and provide liquidity to distressed financial institutions. Funds used for recapitalization and purchase of NPLs and other assets made up the rest of the government's injection of W 155.3 trillion, which provided better prospects for recovery.

Along with the restructuring, which was helped by the injection of large-scale public funds, the total amount of bad loans (loans classified as substandard or below) fell to W 31.8 trillion in 2002 from the highest W 66.7 trillion in 1999. At the same time, the share of bad loans out of total loans sharply decreased, from 11.3 percent in 1999 to 1.9 percent in 2004, at and below par relative to many OECD countries (figure 4.3). - Similarly, figure 4.4 shows that Korea's level of nonperforming loans is currently significantly less than before the crisis. The restructuring of the financial sector had been implemented as planned. In that regard, the financial crisis was a blessing in disguise in that it acted as a catalyst for change (Kang 2004).

Table 4.1 *Sources and Uses of Public Funds, 1997–2004*
(trillion won)

	Purchase of NPLs	Settlement of insured deposits	Contribution	Recapi- talization	Purchase of assets	Total
Bond issues	20.5	20.0	15.2	42.2	4.2	102.1
Fiscal funds	n.a.	n.a.	n.a.	14.0	6.3	20.3
Recycled funds	17.4	7.4	2.2	6.0	5.1	38.1
Other funds	1.1	2.9	0.2	0.0	0.1	4.3
Total	39.0	30.3	17.6	62.2	15.7	164.8

Source: Public Fund Oversight Committee 2004.
n.a. not available.

In sum, the liquidation of troubled institutions, removal of NPLs, and recapitalization of promising institutions through injection of public funds have contributed to increasing the financial health and profitability of the financial industry. The Bank for International Settlement ratio of equity, a measure of the financial health of banks, increased from 7.0 percent in 1997 to 10.5 percent in 2002. Banks have increased in size through active mergers and acquisitions in the banking industry. According to the criterion of total assets, only one of Korea's domestic banks was among the world's 200 largest banks in 1997. In 2002, six domestic banks were listed.

Figure 4.3 *Bank Nonperforming Loans (Share of Total Gross Loans), Selected OECD Countries, 2004*

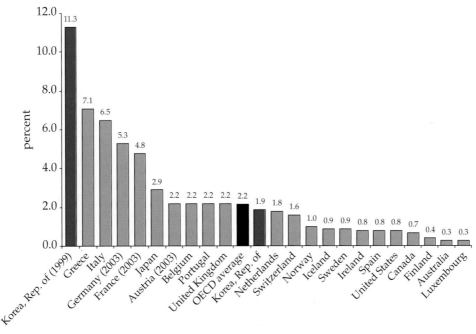

Source: World Bank SIMA database 2007 database.

Figure 4.4 Korea—Nonperforming Loans 1981–2005

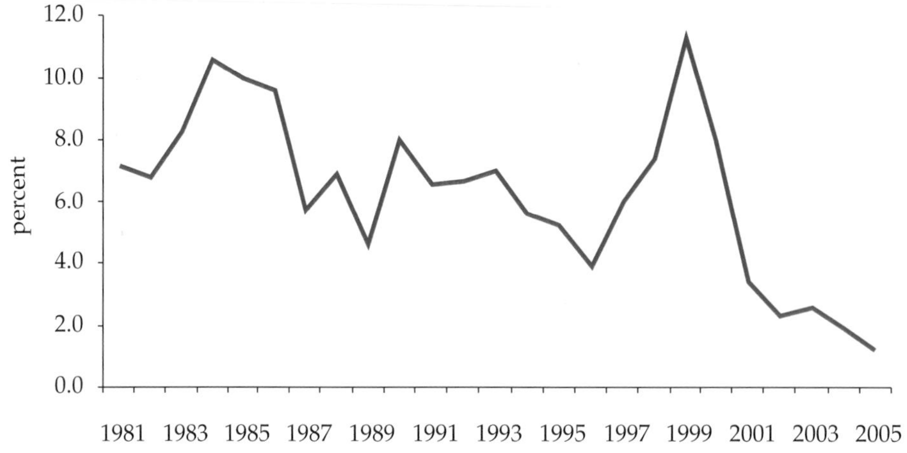

Source: Bank of Korea, internal information.

Enhancing the Financial Sector Infrastructure

The government understood the seriousness of the underdeveloped financial sector, which was one of the major causes of the financial crisis, and knew it would retard the growth process if not improved. The government continued to reform the financial industry by improving the financial market infrastructure and strengthening the stability of the financial system. The major areas in the efforts to enhance the infrastructure of the financial sector included development of capital markets, separation of banking and nonbanking commerce, consolidation of financial regulations, and market-oriented financial supervision. Reform efforts to restructure financially distressed firms have continued. In particular, to complete the restructuring of the financial sector, the restructuring of the nonbank sector was accelerated, and the government-owned financial institutions were privatized. Moreover, to improve the market infrastructure in the financial sector, the government has pursued measures such as the advancing the capital market, overcoming the ill effects resulting from integration of financial regulations, and using market-friendly financial supervision.

However, despite these positive results, the restructuring process in the nonbanking areas, including convertible securities, is not complete. In particular, because of diminishing corporate demand for funding after the financial crisis, once-prevalent corporate loans are now being replaced by household and personal debt, which has emerged as a new restructuring task. The domestic financial industry has not adequately gained the confidence of domestic and overseas investors, in spite of the restructuring that has taken place during the years since the 1997 crisis. As revealed in the accounting scandals in major conglomerates, the problem of transparency in the financial markets continues, and protection of investors against unfair trade practices in the securities market needs to be addressed further.

Corporate Sector Reforms

The financial crisis was triggered when it became publicly known that many large firms, notably chaebols, had large amounts of debts that they could not repay. Previously, the chaebols had rushed into the same new industries to maintain their status, which was the standard expansion strategy regardless of profitability and competence. The expansion strategy of large firms turned out to be no longer sustainable as the bankruptcy of large firms exacerbated the financial market credit system. The relationship between large firms' bankruptcy and the financial market crunch was a kind of vicious circle, as depicted in figure 4.5. Therefore, the first objective of the corporate reform was to eliminate overcapacity. The second broad objective was to encourage firms to reinvent themselves on the strength of their core competencies, by becoming more competitive in the global market.

Enhancing the Corporate Governance System

The Korean government recognized that one of the most important reasons for the economic crisis was the structural weakness of firms. The underdeveloped corporate governance system eroded sound management and made firms vulnerable to shocks. Starting in 1998, the Korean government introduced a number of measures to improve financial disclosure and accounting standards, including the requirement of combined financial statements that cover all companies under the effective control of the same business group, regardless of the level of shareholdings. Another reform would improve the prudence of corporate governance by guaranteeing the voting right of the shareholders.

Major reforms that have continued since the economic crisis are summarized in table 4.2. These institutional reforms, combined with increased scrutiny by investors in the postcrisis period, have led to substantive improvement in the corporate governance of Korean firms. Gone are the days when directors on corporate boards left their official stamps with the company so that decisions made by con-

Figure 4.5 The Vicious Circle of Insolvency

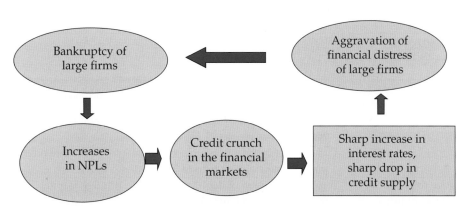

Source: Nam 2004, p. 344.

trolling shareholders could be formally approved without much ado. Although some loopholes in regulations on the transaction of shares remain, attempts to expropriate minority shareholders are no longer likely to go unnoticed. The threats of litigation and damage to reputation are also forcing accountants, auditors, and creditors to become more cautious in their dealings with their corporate customers.

Table 4.2 Major Reform Measures Related to Corporate Governance in Korea in the Post-crisis Period

Policy challenges	Specific measures adopted
Improve transparency	Mandated combined financial statements for the top 30 business groups (January 1998, starting with business year 1999) Adopted international accounting and auditing standards (GAAP and GAAS, December 1998) Mandated board resolution and disclosure for large-scale inter-subsidiary transactions (December 1998) Strengthened law enforcement against "window dressing" and poor auditing Mandated establishment of a committee for appointing independent auditors (January 2000)
Enhance the accountability and independence of the board of directors	Made it possible to hold de facto directors (chongsu) accountable for their decisions and introduced fiduciary duty and cumulative voting (December 1998) Mandated appointment of outside directors: at least one person (1998), no less than one-fourth of the board (1999), no less than one-half of the board (2000, for financial institutions and large listed companies) Mandated establishment of an auditing committee (December 1999)
Protect the property rights of minority shareholders	Lowered filing requirements for motion to dismiss directors and auditors (February 1998) Lowered filing requirements for derivative action suits (May 1998) Lowered filing requirements for inspection of accounting books (February 2001) Lowered requirements for recommending outside directors (February 2001)
Liberalize mergers and acquisitions	Abolished mandatory tender offer (February 1998) Abolished ceiling on equity investment by foreigners (May 1998)
Strengthen the role of creditors in corporate governance	Allowed banks to exercise voting rights on stocks in their trust accounts (September 1998) Mandated periodic assessment of corporate credit risks (March 2001) Gave the KIC the right to investigate unlawful activities on the part of financially distressed firms (March 2001)
Improve the financial soundness of firms	Induced reduction of debt-to-equity ratio through Capital Structure Improvement Plans (1998–99) Prohibited intersubsidiary loan guarantees (February 1998)

Improving Bankruptcy Procedures

For more efficient functioning of failing firms' market exits, reorganization procedures should be implemented quickly. Since the surge in the number of bankruptcies during the financial crisis, laws related to bankruptcy, including the Corporate Reorganization Act, and the Composition Act have been revised. In February 2003, the government submitted a proposal for a recovery and bankruptcy law that integrated corporate reorganization, composition, and bankruptcy. The integrated bankruptcy act removes previously misused negotiation procedures and simplifies the bankruptcy process by focusing on corporate reorganization. Also, mergers and acquisitions among bankrupt firms will be promoted to expedite recovery and retirement of inefficient firms, all to support market competition.

Removing Anticompetitive Regulations

The main role of a government in securing a competitive market system is to ensure fair and equal opportunities to every firm. Market monopolies can be created and maintained by the government's artificial barriers to entry, as well as by technical reasons such as economies of scale. Firms with a monopolistic status produced by artificial barriers to entry usually use their advantages in socially less productive ways, such as lobbying, to maintain their monopolies. Consequently, the government needs to remove artificial barriers to entry and induce price competition among firms. The Korean government has attempted to remove various institutions that inhibit competition; for example, in February 1999, the government dissolved 20 cartels engaged in price collusion, limitation of sales volumes, and partitioning of sales areas. In 2004, the Second Cartel Reformation Act was legislated to abolish anticompetitive laws and systems. The series of institutional reforms that have been implemented is expected to pave the way for fair competition in the market.

Promoting Openness: Korea as a Northeast Asian Economic Hub

For Korea, a country highly dependent on international trade, the continuous opening of its market is a catalyst for strengthening the country's economic constitution by maximizing competition. The Korean government recognized the importance of opening up the nation, and it continued to accelerate its globalization trend by participating in multilateral and bilateral free trade negotiations. The promotion of free trade areas (FTAs), aligning with strategically vital trading partners, helps secure the strategic position of domestic companies by securing a stable export market and overcoming high trade barriers within the region (see box 4.1). FTAs also contribute to the attraction of FDI. FTAs with major countries should further encourage investors to set up production bases in Korea, which may open the door for nontariff exports with those countries. Korea formed an FTA with Chile in 2004 and is currently working on other possibilities with countries that show potential interest.

Labor Market Reforms

Korea's well-trained and hard-working labor force was a key contributing factor for successful industrialization beginning in the early 1960s, and high economic

---

Box 4.1 Korea as a Northeast Asian Hub

Using Korea's geographical potential and creating a systematic framework for economic cooperation among Korea, China, and Japan are essential to making Korea an economic hub of northeast Asia. Forging economic partnerships among the three countries is a mid- to long-term goal of the government, which plans to develop Korea as an economic hub of northeast Asia.

One of the critical aims of the Korean government regarding globalization is to expand growth engines by strategically attracting foreign capital and advancing the economic system. In particular, Korea not only has developed a top-notch manufacturing industry, it also has enhanced service industries such as transports and logistics, banking, and so forth. Besides developing infrastructure such as airports, harbors, and housing complexes, the government is moving forward with core tasks: (a) adjusting the allocation of investment in transportation facilities, (b) encouraging logistics-specialized companies with international competitiveness, (c) clarifying and planning optimal logistics transactions, (d) developing human resources specialized in logistics, (e) improving the international logistics support system and attracting foreign logistics companies, (f) building a logistics information system, and (g) bolstering the level of logistics infrastructure, such as constructing a northeast Asian railroad network.

Source: Government of the Republic of Korea 2004.

---

growth gave new employment opportunities. During this period, until late 1987, wages often increased more than the productivity growth rates (figure 4.6), but this was mostly the result of the labor shortages caused by rapid economic growth. The situation has gradually changed as the economy has matured, and the labor market conditions in terms of labor supply and demand have become tighter than before. The Democratization Declaration on June 29, 1987, marked not only a political turning point for Korea, but also a shift in the nation's labor sector. The wage increase in the post June–29 Declaration period was determined by the institutionalized labor union, not by the market (Yoo 2004). Wage increases that were higher than the productivity growth undermined the competitiveness of the economy. The tension between labor and management, together with increasing wages, emerged as a major obstacle to attracting foreign investment. The financial crisis and restructuring efforts thereafter struck a serious blow to Korea's labor force. Large-scale layoffs, which had been rare during the development era, became common, and this elicited strong national interest in how to maintain the right balance between labor flexibility and social security.[1]

After 1987, real wage increases, determined by labor unions, were higher than productivity growth, thereby undermining the competitiveness of the Korean economy.

---

1. Labor issues are an area where many conflicts of interest and differences in views and philosophies exist. Most of the expositions in the next sections are excerpted from the government's official positions (Government of the Republic of Korea 2004).

Figure 4.6 Growth of Real Wages, Labor Productivity, and Employment

Source: Yoo 2004 and National Statistical Office.

Enhancing Labor Market Flexibility

The term *labor market flexibility* refers not only to adjustments in employment, but also to job-training programs and the infrastructure that enables job seekers to find work. Korea's labor market changed to become more flexible, in part because of the enactment of managerial dismissal rights (the right to dismiss labor for managerial reasons) in the Basic Labor Conditions Act of March 1998, before which managerial dismissals were recognized only in special cases. Labor market flexibility in Korea has been primarily a concern of management, a way of weathering the financial crisis rather than an issue demanding legislation. Because of that, the newly introduced managerial dismissal program has been largely replaced with honorary retirement programs, and managerial dismissal has been permitted only in very limited circumstances. This situation has resulted in a heavy reliance on nonpermanent workers who are irregularly and temporarily employed.

The reform of the labor market also needed to include strengthening the protection of vulnerable workers, expanding employment benefits, and addressing the youth unemployment problem. This challenge was addressed by the establishment of employment centers, an increase in the number of job counselors, and the implementation of the Work-Net facility for job seekers. These measures have contributed substantially to increasing labor market flexibility.

The coexistence of unemployment among the young and shortages in the workforce in small- and medium-size firms suggests that there may be a mismatch between demand and supply in the labor market, as well as reduced numbers of jobs as a result of business depression alone. One reason for the mismatch in the labor market lies in the education system. Although the structure of the labor market changed substantially, school education nonetheless fell short of the needs introduced by changes in the labor market. In 1990, the rate of high school graduates entering college was 33.2 percent, while in 2003, it stood at 79.7 percent. During the period 1995–2003, the number of college graduates grew by 180,000; however, these graduates have not proved capable of commanding the skills necessary to work in the industrial field. This was why education-sector reform had to accompany the nationwide economic reforms.

> Reform of the Korean tertiary education system necessarily accompanied labor market reforms because Korean university graduates, although increasing in number, were not appropriately trained to match the current industrial needs of the Korean knowledge economy.

Korea is rapidly becoming an aging society. Shifts in the paradigm caused by this rapid transformation to an aging society require countermeasures based on sound employment policies. To alleviate the increased social burden stemming from an increasingly dependent senior population, the overall labor force participation rate should be raised. To that end, women, especially highly educated women, should be actively encouraged to join the workforce. The government planned to provide a better environment for women to participate in the labor market, including provision of child care and eradication of gender discrimination. Because countermeasures to an aging society usually bring about few immediately visible results, long-range measures should be pursued.

> To offset the economic effects of an increasing elderly dependency ratio due to the rapid aging of the Korean population, various policy measures were implemented to encourage women to join the labor force.

Improving Labor-Management Relations

The current government has proposed the construction of socially integrated labor relations as a policy target. Having socially integrated labor relations means that transparent management and constructive labor have equal importance, recognizing each other as partners, cooperating, and considering each other's position for the sake of the national economy. The government established the Committee for the Advancement of Labor Relations in May 2003 and initiated the process for improving labor relations. The committee devised a plan to advance labor-related acts through internal discussion and subsequent reports to the concerned governmental body. In September 2003, the government announced its own version of the plan to renew labor relations, which contains basic directives and conceptual approaches.

The aims of reform in labor relations were to minimize the social costs stemming from labor disputes, create a more flexible and stable labor market, and reduce inequities among the various working classes. The government's directive contains major policies and approaches to meet those goals. To minimize social costs, for example, the government proposed the implementation of systems, institutions, and traditions that comply with global standards. These approaches reflect the government's objective of dealing with its own labor unions as entities with rights and responsibilities in solving problems, provided they are within the boundaries of the law.

> The aims of improving labor–management relations were to minimize the social costs of labor disputes, create a more flexible and stable labor market, and reduce inequities among the various working classes.

Public Sector Reforms

Redefining the role of the government has at least two important implications. First, because the government sector constitutes a significant portion of the economy, the redefinition of its role will have a substantial influence on the entire economy. Second, one of the most important roles of the government is to provide an environment within which economic agents act and operate. The redefinition of the government's role will change this environment and affect the activities of the economic agents. The government should respect what the private sector and the competitive market is able to do by providing level playing fields for private sector firms, creating sound macroeconomic environments through institutional reforms, and providing public goods, including information. Korea did well in this regard after the crisis. An efficient and service-oriented government has been achieved, including improved public sector management, such as in the tax system and administration, more transparency in budget processes and human resource management, and greater outsourcing to the private sector.

> Since the 1997 crisis, the Korean government has been allowing the market mechanism to work and the private sector to take the lead in spurring economic activity.

Restructuring the Institutional Regime

Being a reliable government means achieving administrative efficiency by having a more flexible and open system, enhancing transparency, and improving the quality of the administration serving economic agents. Although the effort to reform the government was initiated by Kim Dae-Joong's government, more active reform has been carried out since the current Roh government came to power. To achieve these administrative goals, the Roh government established the Presidential Committee on Government Innovation and Decentralization in April 2003. The committee consisted of both private and government agencies. The government also set up several task forces and established a reform team in each governmental department. These bodies were expected to carry out administrative reforms autonomously and systematically through flexible coordination with the presidential committee.

By continuing systematic and continuous administrative reform, the government hopes to improve the delivery of public services, increase government openness, advance democratic participation, and increase government transparency. The most important institutional variable that the government is planning to control is corruption. In particular, using the crisis as momentum, Korea has attempted to eradicate the connection between business sectors and government or politicians. One of the most important efforts of the government in fighting corruption has been the establishment of an independent body, the Korea Independent Commission against Corruption, in 2002, based on Korea's Anticorruption Act. The government recognized that eradicating corruption is one of the most urgent tasks, and it must be accomplished if the nation wishes to become a fair society and a globally competitive economy. The functions of the commission include formulating and assessing policy, making institutional improvements, responding to whistle blowers, and educating business about and promoting its activities.

Maintaining Fiscal Soundness and Privatization in Fiscal Reforms

One of the factors that enabled Korea to recover from the financial crisis in a short period is the soundness of its budget and fiscal system. As of 2002, the total debt of the central government reached about 21 percent of GDP, which was about twice the level of debt before the crisis. Nevertheless, it was much lower than the OECD average, which was as high as 74 percent of GDP. However, the liability backed by the government increased rapidly because of the restructuring of the financial sector after the crisis. Although the government managed the fiscal system successfully, the burden on the government was not lessening. Since 2000, after the recovery, the central government has managed its budget with a surplus. One of advantages of maintaining a sound budget is having the flexibility to use fiscal policy if need be. The priority of the government's expenditures was the expansion of the social safety net and investment in education, S&T, and R&D. This continued trend of maintaining the soundness of the central government's budget has provided government flexibility and helped the government deal with the expenditure priority, which contributed to the economy's getting back to the growth track.

> By sustaining a budget surplus, the Korean government had the flexibility to implement fiscal policies when necessary, and this contributed to the rapid recovery from the 1997 financial crisis.

Privatization of public corporations helped to increase government revenues and increased the competitiveness of firms by introducing more competition and market principles. In 1998, the government began the plan to privatize 11 public corporations to reduce government intervention in the market, improve the quality of service, increase government revenue, and stabilize the foreign exchange markets. As shown in table 4.3, eight corporations had undertaken the procedure for privatization as of the end of 2002.[2]

---

2. The revenue from the sales of public corporations is not categorized as government revenue in the reformed government fiscal statistics.

Table 4.3 *Privatization Plan for Public Corporations*

Timetable	Enterprise	Number of employees	Sales (billion won)	Number of subsidiaries	Government share (%)	Profit (billion won)	Results
Immediate (by end-1999)	Pohang Steel and Iron Corporation	19,294	9,718	16	26.7	729	Privatized in October 2002
	Korea Heavy Industries and Construction Corporation	7,851	3,008	3	84.3	45	Privatized in December 2000
	Korea General Chemical	263	15	1	98.8	−57	Liquidated in November 2000
	Korea Technology and Banking	163	438	1	10.2	2	Privatized in January 1999
	National Textbook Corporation	739	52	0	40.0	4	Privatized in November 1998
Step-by-step	Korea Telecom Corporation	58,556	7,784	13	71.2	80	Privatized in May 2002
	Korea Tobacco and Ginseng Corporation	7,573	4,243	1	35.3	226	Privatized in October 2002
	Korea Electric Power Corporation	33,036	13,116	7	58.2	561	Government share reduced to 54 percent
	Korea Gas Corporation	2,891	2926	5	85.7	−336	Government share reduced to 51 percent
	Daehan Oil Pipeline Company	385	34	2	48.8	−44	Privatized in November 2000
	Korea District Heating Company	1,044	203	3	72.2	1	Government share remains at 72 percent

Source: Ministry of Planning and Budget (various years).
Notes: Data are from 1997 and include holdings of government-capitalized public enterprises.

Improving the Social Welfare System

Since the financial crisis, the government has gained heightened awareness of the need for welfare participation, and has sought social stability for all people within the framework of growth and distribution. Korea's welfare expenditure was 9.8 percent of the GDP in 1999 and, assuming that the current trend is maintained, expenditures will increase to 14.5 percent in 2020 and 20.6 percent in 2030. If the welfare expenditure increases rapidly as the aging of society progresses, not only will the fiscal deficit and national debt increase, but the burden of tax and social insurance expenses will also increase. This will distort the economy and reduce economic growth.

Korea's four major social insurance programs—pension, health insurance, employment insurance, and workers' accident compensation insurance—began to legally cover the majority of the Korean people in the late 1990s. With regard to public assistance, the minimum living standard, which was introduced in October 2000, guarantees minimum living conditions for all citizens. The standard replaced the Living Protection System, in which living expenses were paid in a limited amount according to the demographic characteristic. Although the government obligation expanded and household obligation was reduced, with the introduction of the minimum living standard for all citizens, the obligation of households remains large. The role of the government has been limited because various requirements were placed on the beneficiaries in addition to the criteria of income and assets.

Venture Business Policy

Korean economic restructuring since the financial crisis has proceeded in a way that was favorable to venture businesses. The Korean government has acknowledged the importance of small and medium-size firms based on the firms' use of new, innovative technology. By systematically supporting such firms, the government would nurture cutting-edge technology, advance the industry structure, and increase employment. This section briefly reviews the venture policy that the Korean government implemented.

> Small and medium-venture business firms that commercialize new technologies and ideas are necessary to sustain innovation and the use of frontier-level technologies in the Korean industrial sector.

After the financial crisis, many large firms went bankrupt, and surviving large firms have restructured their businesses. Taking advantage of this opportunity for a niche business and the rapid IT growth, venture businesses, which were flexible and specialized, could grow rapidly. Labor market restructuring after the financial crisis also had a favorable effect on the venture business industry. In particular, the retirement of workers with accumulated know-how provided promising venture businesses with a competent labor force through the reallocation of human capital.

After the crisis, the Korean government restructured the economic system to make it flexible and gave higher priority to policies that would nurture technology-based small and medium-size firms. The government's support for new venture businesses also served as an alternative plan to solve the unemployment problem caused by the crisis and modify the resource allocation structure that had focused on large firms.

Growth of Korea's Venture Industry and Venture Capital Market

Beginning and developing venture businesses requires a stable supply of risk capital. Therefore, it is necessary to have the capital market and a supporting system that can undertake risk and efficiently allocate the resources. In the early 1980s, markets that could allocate resources to the venture business industry did not exist in Korea. Accordingly, the Korean government actively promoted the formation of venture capital markets that could allocate the resources to the venture business industry as part of the government initiative. Nevertheless, the government-driven venture capital firms did not play a primary role until the mid-1990s because all the necessary conditions had not been satisfied; no sufficiently promising investment opportunities existed, and there was no proper capital market to recoup the return on the investment.

However, after the mid-1990s, the rapid diffusion of the Internet and outstanding development in the IT sector triggered the burst of growth in the venture industry. In particular, as venture businesses secured many kinds of new technologies in the IT industry, the venture capital industry had the opportunity to expand the existing market and pioneer new markets. Because the global IT industry was at the start-up stage, Korean IT venture businesses were not technologically inferior to firms in developed countries, and entry barriers were low. Thanks to the remarkable worldwide development of the IT industry, the commencement and growth of venture businesses based on new IT technology became active and the investment in the IT sector by venture capital firms increased dramatically (see table 4.4).

Table 4.4 Number of Registered Venture Firms by Industry, 1999–2005

	1999	2000	2001	2002	2003	2004	2005
Manufacturing	3,48 (70.49)	5,363 (60.96)	6,889 (60.47)	5,679 (64.70)	5,234 (67.96)	5,487 (68.90)	6,754 (69.40)
Data processing, software	1,248 (25.29)	2,925 (33.25)	3,715 (32.61)	2,390 (27.23)	1,832 (23.79)	1,783 (22.40)	2,054 (21.10)
R&D, services	69 (1.40)	213 (2.42)	333 (2.92)	286 (3.26)	278 (3.61)	323 (4.10)	410 (4.20)
Construction, transportation	65 (1.32)	144 (1.64)	206 (1.81)	172 (1.96)	117 (1.52)	133 (1.70)	194 (2.00)
Retail	26 (0.53)	74 (0.84)	116 (1.02)	119 (1.36)	144 (1.87)	146 (1.80)	184 (1.90)
Others	48 (0.98)	79 (0.90)	133 (1.17)	132 (1.50)	97 (1.25)	95 (1.20)	136 (1.40)
Total	4,934 (100.00)	8,798 (100.00)	11,392 (100.00)	8,778 (100.00)	7,702 (100.00)	7,967 (100.00)	9,732 (100.00)

Source: Small and Medium Business Administration (http://www.smba.go.kr).
Note: Percentage of total businesses is shown in parentheses.

Recognizing the venture businesses as a new economic power group, the Korean government opened the KOSDAQ (Korea Securities Dealers Automated Quotation) market so that venture businesses could easily finance their required funds and venture capital firms could recover their investment. The direct financial market, especially a stock market, was essential for the development of venture businesses and the venture capital industry because the commercial bank–oriented indirect financial market had critical limitations on the financial support for firms in new technology. Thus, to develop the KOSDAQ market as a venture-centered stock market and differentiate it from the Korean Stock Exchange, the government set more relaxed requirements in the KOSDAQ than in the KSE.

> Firms in new technology faced difficulties in obtaining loans from commercial banks, thus the government formed the KOSDAQ market so that venture businesses and venture capital firms could more efficiently finance venture investments.

More specifically, with the explosive growth of the U.S. National Association of Securities Dealers Automated Quotations (NASDAQ) system, the venture capital market was stimulated by the 1999 policy promoting the KOSDAQ market, and that growth brought about the venture industry boom in Korea. The growth of the KOSDAQ market inspired the establishment of venture businesses and accelerated the flow of venture capital into the market. This helped cause the healthy circulation of venture capital, which led to the establishment and growth of venture businesses and the KOSDAQ market boom. The rapid growth of venture-related markets contributed to the advancement of Korea's venture capital market, which was initially formed by the past Korean government. Additionally, it helped the KOSDAQ market serve as the capital supplier and function as a new resource distributor. In this regard, the rapid growth of the venture capital market was significant for the Korean economy. As shown in figure 4.7, Korea ranks among the leading OECD countries in venture capital investment as a share of GDP.

In addition, by establishing the Act on Special Measures for the Promotion of the Venture Business, the Korean government prepared a legal basis to back up various supports for new technology or knowledge-intensive firms. Through this law, the government relaxed many regulations associated with these firms, thus helping to create venture businesses. The law also allowed venture businesses to be officially certified as technology-intensive small and medium-size firms, which was useful in various aspects of business, including financial aid, technological support, tax aid, labor changes and location. This policy was based on the government's judgment that the developing IT technology paradigm was more suitable to small, flexible firms; therefore the government encouraged the allocation of economic resources to the newest industries, such as new technology–based or knowledge-intensive industries.

The venture business industry has grown rapidly because of the provision of business opportunities by developments in the IT industry, the start of the KOSDAQ market, and the Korean government's policies, which nurtured venture businesses during the years of restructuring after the financial crisis.

Figure 4.7 Venture Capital Investment by Stages, 1999–2002
(percent of GDP)

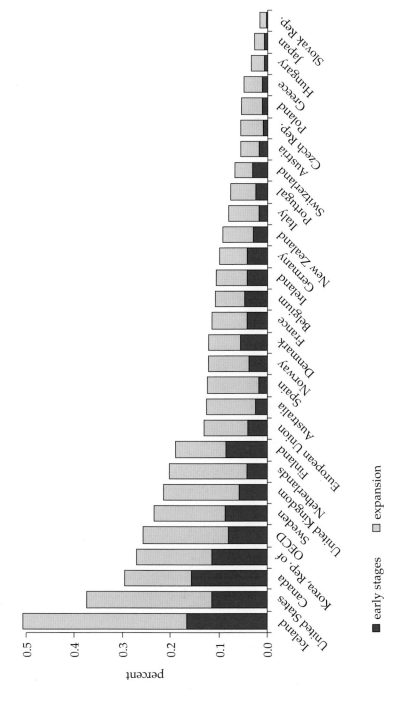

Source: OECD 2005c.
Note: Data for Ireland are for the period 2000–02. Data for Korea, Australia, New Zealand, and Japan are from 1998–2001.

The financial crisis was a painful disaster, but the crisis became a turning point for the venture business industry. In fact, venture businesses, as well as large firms, had a lot of difficulties as a result of the overall economic restructuring and depression following the financial crisis. However, in late 1998, as soon as interest rates and exchange rates went down and were more stable and the real sector started to recover, many funds in the market flowed into the stock markets with the expectation of rapid economic recovery. Attracted by new technology–based industries, many investors traded on the KOSDAQ market rather than the KSE, which was oriented to the traditional industries in which the restructuring process has continued.

Adjustment of the Venture Boom

A dark outlook for venture businesses loomed in 2000. With the crash in NAS-DAQ, the stock prices of venture businesses in KOSDAQ also began to fall steadily. To make matters worse, the illegal activities of some venture businesses' chief executives and venture capitalists, along with unfair trading practices in KOSDAQ, led to the KOSDAQ index falling drastically. The market for initial public offerings was depressed, and many venture businesses had difficulty getting financing through the stock market. Furthermore, this depressed venture capital market constrained the additional financing of venture businesses in need.

This drastic depression was fundamentally due to the excessive valuation and myopic overinvestment in venture businesses. The excessive inflow of funds and high expectations held by investors (without systematic consideration of the businesses' profitability) pushed the stock market into a bubble. The Korean government's excessive intervention also made it more serious. Although the new market and technological opportunities had emerged from the rapid IT development, the competence of the venture businesses and venture capital firms did not improve significantly within that short time. Thus, investments in the stock market expanded too quickly for the promising new technology–based venture businesses to grow. However, even though many had warned about the risks involved in the venture investment fund, the government's excessive intervention in the markets helped expand the bubble. After the bubble burst in 2000, Korea's venture industry underwent an adjustment period, as shown in table 4.5. Since 2001, the number of firms decreased or stabilized, operating income stagnated, and total liabilities decreased and then slightly increased. However, since 2003, the mood of the markets related to venture businesses has become more optimistic. The required investigation of listings in KOSDAQ was enforced, and investments were made only in businesses based on concrete profit models.

Generally, fluctuation in the stock market can be viewed as a natural phenomenon. The adjustment process is therefore a stage during which the market restores its original function. In the long run, this adjustment will get rid of obstacles to the development of venture-related markets (venture business market, venture capital market, and KOSDAQ market). It also will provide a good opportunity to develop healthier markets and restore the markets' primary function of efficient resource allocation.

Table 4.5 Performance Trend of Venture Firms Listed in KOSDAQ, 1998–2003
(millions of won)

	1998	1999	2000	2001	2002	2003
Number of firms	171	234	244	379	340	373
Total assets (A)	6,296,057	12,484,547	19,318,401	28,718,219	24,245,793	26,678,148
Operating income (B)	516,997	972,341	1,211,966	1,048,571	1,052,473	1,302,817
B/A*100	8.21	7.79	6.27	3.65	4.34	4.88
Total liabilities (C)	4,273,547	5,806,513	7,091,118	11,184,646	9,550,174	9,933,722
Cash end of year) (D)	361,081	681,707	1,217,975	1,561,178	1,188,488	1,351,337
Risk (C/D)	11.84	8.52	5.82	7.16	8.04	7.35

Source: KOSDAQ (http://km.krx.co.kr).

Venture Policy—Evaluation and Policy Implications

The rapid development of venture capital and venture-related businesses was important for the Korean economy. Among other things, it provided a foundation on which human and material resources would be distributed to small and medium-size technology-oriented business rather than to conglomerates, with their demand for the factors of production, including labor and capital. In the process of restructuring after the financial crisis, the conglomerate-oriented industrial structure was losing its significance, and the areas dominated by large-scale companies in the past were transferred to venture business. However, a development policy based on the government's direct support is not recommended; an efficient market system can develop only when the government acts as a fair supervisor and improves the financial market's efficiency. The foundations of the venture industry and the development of the venture capital market are, above all, knowledge, technology, and entrepreneurship. Therefore, the Korean government should attempt to lead in expanding knowledge capacity through education, basic science, and original technology support. In addition to expanding financial support for universities and research institutes, the government needs to foster organizations' innovative and management capabilities to increase efficiency in the investment.

Summary and Assessments

The 1997 crisis served as an important turning point for the Korean economy. The government exerted its utmost efforts to establish the market's discipline in economic activities and consequently minimize government intervention in the market. The economic reforms since 1997 have three main objectives: encouraging a market-oriented economy, improving the institutional regime, including the government sector reform; and making the transition to an advanced KBE. The structural reforms have been extensive, covering most areas of the economy, including the financial, corporate, labor, and public sectors. The reforms to shape a new economic framework are summarized below.

First, in the wake of the crisis, the Korean government gave top priority to restoring confidence in its financial sector. Through the liquidation of troubled institutions, removal of nonperforming loans, and recapitalization of promising institutions through the injection of public funds, the financial health and profitability of the financial industry have been greatly improved. The number of financial institutions at the end of 1997 was 2,101, but the number decreased to 1,507 as of January 2003. Along with the restructuring, helped by the large-scale injection of public funds, the total amount of bad loans fell to W 31.8 trillion in 2002, from the highest point, W 66.7 trillion in 1999. At the same time, the share of bad loans out of total loans sharply decreased from 11.3 percent in 1999 to 1.9 percent in 2004. The restructuring of the financial sector had been implemented as planned. In that regard, the financial crisis was a blessing in disguise in that it acted as a catalyst for change (Kang 2004).

> Korea turned the 1997 financial crisis into an opportunity for major, widespread economic reforms.

However, more tasks remain. What had been done was mostly about "hardware" reform, which forced the cleaning up of bad loans and ailing financial institutions. Despite the relatively successful financial restructuring, Korea should put more emphasis on developing a sound and transparent financial system based on international best standards and promoting the financial industry as a KBE. As revealed in the accounting scandals in major conglomerates, the problem of transparency in the financial markets continues, and protecting investors from unfair trade practices in the securities market needs to be further addressed. Consequently, the domestic financial industry has not gained adequate confidence from domestic and overseas investors, in spite of the restructuring that has taken place during the 10 years since the financial crisis.

Second, reforms in the corporate sector have focused on eliminating inefficiencies and encouraging firms to reinvent themselves on the strength of their core competencies. Special efforts have been made to improve the corporate governance system, revise bankruptcy procedures, and remove anticompetitive regulations. Specifically, the Korean government introduced a number of measures to improve financial disclosure and accounting standards and enhance the prudence of corporate governance by guaranteeing the voting rights of the shareholders. These institutional reforms, combined with increased scrutiny by investors in the postcrisis period, have led to substantive improvement in the corporate governance of Korean firms. The Korean government also removed various institutions that inhibit competition to provide a more market-friendly environment for entrepreneurial activities. In addition, recognizing that globalization is a catalyst of structural reforms, the Korean government is actively pursuing free trade agreements with many trading partners. By doing so, the government ultimately aims at developing Korea as an economic hub of northeast Asia.

Third, the basic purpose of labor sector reforms was to make the market principles work properly, including competition and the establishment of and respect for private ownership and property. It is believed that market principles tend to flourish where the flexibility of the labor market is maximized. As a result, labor market reforms focused on labor market flexibility that can support economy-wide restructuring. The Labor Standards Act was revised to legalize layoffs in February 1998. Through the Tripartite Commission—composed of representatives of employers, employees, and the government—labor unions dropped their blanket objection to unemployment, which gave support to the government's efforts to make the labor sector more responsive to market forces.

The current government has proposed the construction of socially integrated labor relations as a policy target. The government established the Committee for the Advancement of Labor Relations in May 2003 and initiated the process for improving labor relations. The aim of reform in labor relations is to minimize the social costs stemming from labor disputes, create a more flexible and stable labor market, and reduce inequities among the various working classes. Mutual trust and reliability can take root in labor and management relations by establishing partnerships based on transparent management and participatory labor.

Along with labor sector reforms, Korea's social safety net was quickly reorganized and enhanced by means of expanded coverage of unemployment insurance and other measures. The social policies that were introduced to remedy the side effects of restructuring have continued. The government is developing a comprehensive and productive social welfare system that will not be a drain on the economy but will provide security in a way that ultimately benefits the economy. In addition, to alleviate the increased social burden stemming from an increasingly dependent senior population, the government should raise the overall labor force participation rate. To that end, women, especially highly educated women, should be actively encouraged to join the workforce.

Fourth, the public sector managed by the government was a central actor in the country's economic and social development. The earlier positive and active role played by the government after the 1997 crisis had been subject to criticism because of the excessive growth of bureaucracy and the procrastination in making the transition to an open economic system. The most important change regarding the role of the government since the 1997 crisis was the reestablishment of the government philosophy that the government would respect what the private sector and the market can do. The government has concentrated on providing a level playing field for the private sector and sound macroeconomic environments through institutional reforms and the provision of public goods, including information.

Like the importance of adopting the market-based approach, opening up is essential to narrowing Korea's knowledge and institutional gaps compared with advanced countries (Government of the Republic of Korea 2004). Korea has made great strides in this regard in the wake of the economic crisis. Various measures have been taken to eliminate remaining barriers against imports and foreign companies' investing in Korea. Especially as regards inbound FDI, the old policy stance of controlled, prudent accommodation was replaced by active promotion, resulting in a surge of foreign investment. However, the vestige of the old Korean system as a semiopen–semiclosed society is still strong.

It is essential for Korea to maintain the newly gained momentum of opening up and pursue it further, including greater acceptance of foreign cultures, mindsets, and social practices. To that end, complementary measures should be devised to open up the trade and finance sector, along with all-dimensional efforts to create a social environment hospitable to foreigners. More specifically, regulations and institutions that are not in line with global standards should be abolished or improved swiftly. Human capital and culture should also be opened to the outside to expand international exchanges and cooperation. To encourage inbound foreign investment, more proactive measures should be taken. Barriers to foreigners' entry into R&D, education, and government procurement should be scrapped. Because the exchange of human resources is the most effective way of encouraging an open mindset, obsolete and exclusive clauses of the immigration law should be revised to aid the inflow of a foreign workforce. Active introduction of foreign culture and exchanges of different cultures are needed to globalize Korean culture as well.

Reforms to address the soundness of the budget and fiscal system have also contributed to helping the economy get back to the growth track. The government has strived to radically change the system into one that is more decentralized and participatory. To create more social cohesion and meet rapidly changing fiscal demands, especially for social welfare, the fiscal system will also undergo an extensive review from the ground up.

Finally, in the process of overcoming the 1997 crisis, the Korean government made a special effort to find, nurture, and develop venture businesses to reduce unemployment and encourage the development of the next generation of industries. Economic restructuring has been favorable to venture business firms. After the financial crisis, many large firms went bankrupt, and surviving large firms restructured their businesses. Taking advantage of this niche business opportunity, combined with the rapid IT growth, venture businesses that had a flexible structure and specialized in a specific business could grow rapidly. The labor market restructuring also contributed to the surge in growth of the venture industry by diverting workers with the accumulated know-how to promising venture businesses.

However, the excessive valuation in the stock market and the myopic overinvestment in venture businesses led to a drastic depression in the venture industry. Because of the government's intentional market making from the start, and its regulatory policies that allocated financial resources to technology-based small venture businesses, the venture capital market in Korea achieved some quantitative growth, but it is unsatisfactory from a qualitative point of view. Future government policy should focus on transferring responsibility from the government to the market. Taxation, financial support, and control should be entrusted to the market to improve the self-sustaining capability of venture businesses. The government's role should be confined to establishing regulations to ensure fair play and to monitoring and supervision to make sure the regulations are followed.

With all of the above mentioned reforms implemented or being implemented, the economic and institutional regime in Korea has improved significantly. Figure 4.8 illustrates the performance in the Knowledge Assessment Methodology (KAM) indicators for the economic regime of the Republic of Korea, the G-7, and the high-income country average, for the most recent year, predominantly 2006. Korea is at par and even exceeds performance compared to the average high-income country for some variables, such as gross capital formation, low interest rate spread, and low cost to enforce a contract. However, for a number of indicators, Korea still has a lot of catching up to do relative to the G-7 and high-income countries, such as soundness of banks, which was still weak because of transparency issues. Similarly,

Figure 4.8 KAM Custom Scorecard—Economic and Institutional Regime
(most recent year)

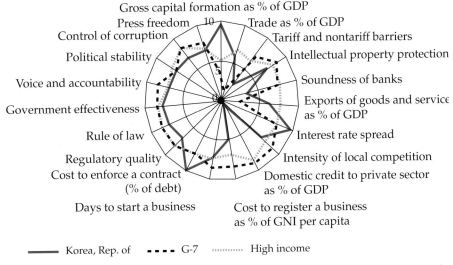

Source: KAM, December 2006 (www.worldbank.org/wbi/kam).

Korea has a lot of ground to catch up in terms of exports of goods and services and domestic credit to the private sector.

In summary, although it is widely recognized that these large-scale reforms contributed to the Korean economy's recovery from the 1997 crisis, Korea still faces a number of challenges, which call for additional structural reforms, in maintaining its high growth potential. Most important, the stagnation of domestic demand since the end of 2002 and slowing inputs of capital and labor have raised concerns about Korea's growth prospects. Sustaining high growth rates in Korea increasingly depends on productivity improvement, especially through technological innovation. Therefore, upgrading the innovation system and transforming the economy into a knowledge-based one is essential to promote faster productivity gains and enhance its high growth momentum. In addition, the government should further promote competition and entrepreneurship and deregulate the market to encourage the creativity of the private sector.

5

Information and Communication Technologies for a Knowledge-Based Economy

Dongpyo Hong, Sangwon Ko, and Alexey Volynets

This chapter examines the ICT pillar of the knowledge economy—or more specifically, the information infrastructure of the Republic of Korea and its evolution over the past four decades. It details the policies that the government implemented to develop the modern information infrastructure currently in place. The second part of the chapter looks at the ICT production industry in Korea. Although the ICT production industry is not part of the information infrastructure, it does provide a unique example of how the various elements of the knowledge economy interacted to produce a dynamic industry that substantively contributed to Korea's economic growth.

Overview

To a very substantial degree, the shift toward a KBE has been driven by ICTs. Governments around the world are formulating policy frameworks for developing this strategically important sector and using ICTs to promote economic growth.

Korea's ICT-related polices have spanned three areas: building information infrastructure; promoting industrial activities, including capacity building of the ICT industry; and ensuring fair competition. The country has become the leader in the development of broadband networks and succeeded in joining the ranks of advanced countries in terms of overall informatization level. Korea also has seen rapid increase in the use of ICTs, with ICT expenditures increasing from 6.4 percent of GDP in 2001 to 6.9 percent in 2005. As seen in figure 5.1, Korea's ICT expenditure now ranks seventh among the OECD countries.

> Korea's ICT-related polices have spanned three areas: building information infrastructure; promoting ICT industrial activities, including capacity building of the ICT industry; and ensuring fair competition.

Figure 5.1 ICT Expenditure (Share of GDP), Selected OECD Countries, 2005

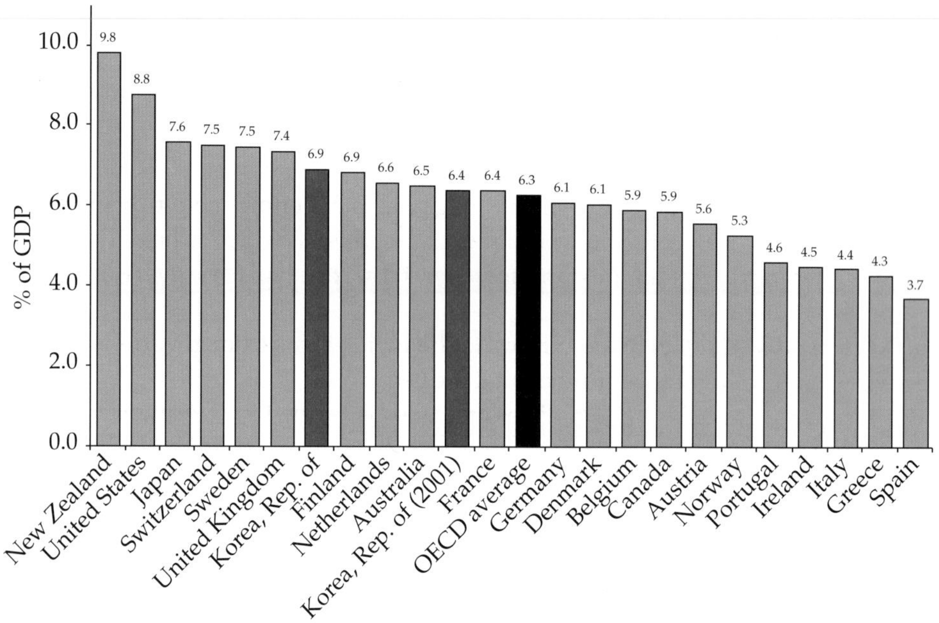

Source: World Bank SIMA database.

The primary objectives of the Korean government were to provide a vision of the future and increase awareness of the benefits and usage of ICTs while minimizing market intervention. For example, the e-government initiative, apart from improving the efficiency of delivery of government services, encouraged Koreans to use ICTs, thereby narrowing the digital divide.

On the supply side, the government took the initiative by providing the seed money for infrastructure development and ardently adhered to the best global standards in privatization, market liberalization, and competition policy. In particular, Korea's vision of creating the virtuous cycle, initiated by facility-based competition, had remarkable success. Availability of affordable and modern information infrastructure promoted growth of the service sector, which, in turn, created more demand for high-end equipment and terminals and promoted the manufacturing sector. This virtuous cycle continued improving with the underlying, procompetition regulatory measures.

Korea's ICT industrial policy has focused on three main areas: R&D, human resource development, and ensuring the availability of venture capital. The public sector finances less than 10 percent R&D expenditure in ICT, but it plays an important role in coordinating private and public efforts in R&D, with emphasis on supporting small and medium-size enterprises (SMEs) through its ICT promotion funds.

> Korea's ICT industrial policy has focused on three main areas: R&D, human resource development, and ensuring the availability of venture capital.

With the accelerating employment growth in the ICT industries from 1997 to 2000, Korea's human resource development policies focused mainly on expanding the number of potential entrants to the labor market who were equipped with ICT skills. After undergoing the decline of ICT sector employment in 2001, however, the emphasis of the policies shifted from quantitative expansion to qualitative improvement of ICT workers. Fostering ICT professionals who meet the industry's rapidly changing skill requirements became the top policy priority.

The Korean government has also been an important player in domestic venture capital fund-raising. In the short run, government efforts help to stabilize the amount of funds raised for the venture capital industry, which is heavily focused on the ICT sector. In the long run, however, it might displace private efforts for fundraising and impede the development of the industry. Because of this effect, the Korean government has been moving the policy focus from government fund-raising to promoting the venture capital industry.

This chapter examines ICT policies and lessons learned in informatization promotion, R&D, human resource development, promotion of SMEs in ICT, venture businesses development, and deregulation. It also reviews the development of the Korean ICT industry in terms of output, export, and employment.

Developing an Advanced Information Infrastructure

Modern information infrastructure is a key foundation of a KBE. Korea has built one of the most sophisticated information superhighways in the world. One reason for Korea's success was a comprehensive policy approach that strived to create a virtuous cycle, where a modern information infrastructure enables advanced applications and content sharing—which, in turn, creates even more demand for infrastructure.

> Korea's approach to developing information infrastructure includes the creation a virtuous cycle, where a modern information infrastructure enables advanced applications and content sharing—which leads to even more demand for infrastructure.

Korea took a methodical path of developing its telecommunications market by means of privatization, liberalization, and encouragement of competition. The principal objective was to expand and improve the infrastructure and provide quality services at lower rates, hence increasing consumer and social welfare. This foundation turned out to be the essential market and regulatory element for building a thriving telecommunications market in Korea.

> To increase efficiency in the information infrastructure sector, Korea introduced competition by deregulating and liberalizing the sector and privatizing government-owned telecom operators.

The Early Stages: Separation of Business and Policy Functions

During the 1970s, the Korean telecommunications sector struggled to keep pace with the rapid economic growth, which revolved around industrial sectors. The existing telecommunications infrastructure and capacity were well short of meeting the increasing demand for subscriber lines and call traffic. The result was serious congestion in voice telephony services. Teledensity in 1980 was at only 7.3 percent (figure 5.2). Users had to wait for months for connection, and the tariffs were very high. The government set new policy objectives that included developing and expanding telecommunications infrastructure and capacity to relieve the congestion, improving the efficiency of telecommunications services, and accumulating technology for equipment and terminal manufacturing.

Telecommunications service is a natural monopoly that exhibits economies of scale. Another noneconomic consideration, safeguarding national security, was also a factor. As such, it was natural that the government provided telecommunications services directly to the public. However, as with many government operations, it was inefficient, and so the government established the government-owned Korea Telecommunication Authority (KTA) in December 1981 to separate the policy and operational functions. The establishment of the KTA marks the beginning of moving the market environment toward liberalization and increased competition. Before this, the Ministry of Post and Telecommunication carried out the integrated functions. The separation aimed at improving the efficiency of the services provided by allowing flexibility in business decisions and by reducing red tape. It allowed more freedom in the compilation and execution of the budget and in human resource management. The government, however, concentrated on the role of regulating the monopoly operator and began implementing promotion policies.

Figure 5.2 Teledensity in Korea, 1975–2005

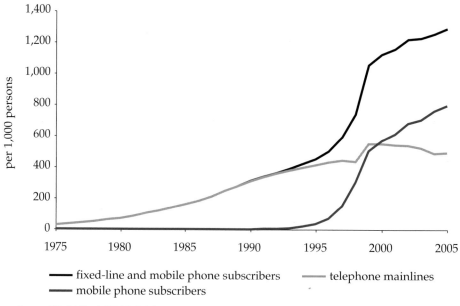

Source: World Bank SIMA database.

Privatization of Telecom Operators

Korea was one of the early movers to fully privatize an incumbent monopoly operator. Before 1990, three monopoly firms served each telecom subsector: Korea Telecom (KT) for fixed-line services, Korea Data Communication Corporation (Dacom) for data services, and Korea Mobile Telecom (KMT) for wireless services. In 1990, the government's share of KT was reduced to 49 percent; KT became a fully private company in 2002. Dacom and KMT (which became SK Telecom), were fully privatized in 1993 and 1997, respectively.

Privatization provides profit incentive for stockholders and management, which, in turn, increases productive efficiency. Privatization also makes the regulatory process more transparent and unbiased because the regulatory body becomes independent from the operators.

Liberalization of Telecommunication Services

Korea took a sequential but rapid path to liberalization of the ICT services sector. During the Basic Telecom Negotiation of the Uruguay Round WTO negotiations in 1994, Korea committed to the full liberalization of the resale-based sector and partially committed to the schedule of step-by-step reduction of the limit of foreign ownership of facility-based operators. In addition, the Reference Paper of the WTO Basic Telecommunication Agreement was also adopted by the Korean government. The paper guided governments in the implementation of various regulatory measures concerned with competitive safeguards, and ensured interconnection, allocation of scarce resources, provision of universal services, and transparent licensing. Korea's policies and regulatory framework were notable in their pursuit of this textbook method of the global standard. The well-designed liberalization policies resulted in the transfer of technology and innovation and investment funding from foreign operators, resulting in faster growth of the market and providing proper incubation of competitive domestic operators.

Introduction of Market Competition

The government's next task in the telecommunications sector was to improve efficiency by introducing competition and market mechanisms. World trends suggested this course. In the United States, American Telephone and Telegraph Company (AT&T) had been structurally separated. In the United Kingdom and Japan, British Telecom (BT) and Nippon Telegraph and Telephone Corporation (NTT) had been privatized. In a number of countries, competition was being introduced and markets were being liberalized.

Step-by-step entry of new telecommunications operators and gradual fomenting of a more competitive market environment constituted the basic framework of Korea's competition policy (table 5.1). Another objective was the diversification of services, which included fixed-line voice telephony, data communication, and mobile communication.

The first phase of the market structure reform began in 1990. Dacom's entry into the international call market in 1990 was the first form of competition in telecommunications services. Shinsegi Telecom's entry into the mobile market in 1994 and

> Step-by-step entry of new telecommunications operators and gradual fomenting of a more competitive market environment constituted the basic framework of Korea's competition policy.

Dacom's entry into the long-distance market in 1995 opened those markets for competition. Multiple licenses were granted for trunked radio and paging services. After this first phase, except for local telephony, every subsector of telecommunications services had at least a duopoly market structure. The second phase in inducing competition began in 1996, when 27 new licenses in seven subsectors were granted, including three personal communication services licenses. In 1997, the entry of Hanaro Telecom finally provided competition in the local telephony market. In the same year, resale-based operation in the fixed-line voice market was allowed.

The government also implemented institutional measures. The Korea Communication Commission (KCC) was established in 1992 to oversee the market and monitor any anticompetitive practices. The KCC's other regulatory functions included resolution of disputes among operators, consumer protection, and interconnection. To achieve a healthy competitive environment in telecommunications, an interconnection scheme must be fair and transparent. In particular, switching the tariff scheme from a rate-of-return method to a cost-based method was a significant step. Unbundling network components in the interconnection contract was another measure to ensure fair competition.

The efforts of the Korean government in developing the telecommunications sector and making it more efficient resulted in a significant decrease in the cost of telephone calls. In particular, the cost of a three-minute phone call to the United Sates dropped by 84 percent, from US$4.88 in 1996 to US$0.76 in 2004 (figure 5.3).

Facility-Based Competition for the Information Age

The key feature that distinguishes Korea's deregulation and competition policy in the telecommunications services sector from other countries was its reliance on

Table 5.1 Developing Competition in Telecommunications Services

1981	Establishment of KTA
1990	Competition introduced in value added services
	Entry of Dacom into international market
1992	Competition introduced in paging services (10 new operators)
1994	Second cellular license issued (Shinsegi Telecom)
1995	Competition introduced in long-distance market (Dacom)
1996	26 new licenses granted: 3 personal communication services; 6 trunked radio systems; 11 second-generation cordless telephone; 2 dedicated line; 1 paging, third international operator (Onse); and 3 wireless data transmission
1997	10 new licenses granted: 1 local operator (Hanaro), 1 long-distance (Onse), 6 trunked radio systems, 1 paging
	Resale-based competition introduced

Source: Authors.

Figure 5.3 Average Cost of Telephone Call to the United States (US$ per three minutes)

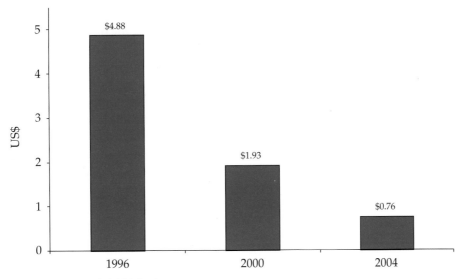

Source: World Bank SIMA database.

facility-based competition. Facility-based competition between telecom service providers results when new entrants into the sector build their own facilities to provide services, as opposed to service-based competition, where the entrant uses the facilities of the incumbent. In contrast to Korea, the United States and Europe used service-based competition efforts to encourage competition and were successful only in the long-distance and international markets, but not local markets.

> The key feature that distinguishes Korea's deregulation and competition policy from other countries is its reliance on facility-based competition.

Korea is one of the few countries that use multiple operators in all markets of the telecom services sector. For local telephony networks, there are KT and Hanaro. In mobile services, five network-based operators were licensed, of which three remain in competition: SK Telecom, Korea Telecom Freetel (KTF), and LGTelecom. The astonishing success in the broadband Internet service market was also credited to facility-based competition, where KT's and Hanaro's xDSL and Thrunet's cable modem services provided fierce competition. The government's laissez-faire approach, with minimal regulation, also contributed to the sector's growth.

Facility-based competition has proven to be viable even though there was a concern that the large fixed costs of constructing multiple broadband networks would incur high social cost and reduce profitability. The economic value created from the competition far exceeds the cost of network construction when effective network competition fosters successful competition in the content sector as well. Indeed, facility-based competition has many advantages.

First, regulations that encourage network competition are more effective in inducing true competition, and network competition will accelerate network enhancements for each end user's full satisfaction in the delivery of the content and applications.

Second, facility-based competition provides incentives for the profit-maximizing operators. It facilitates achievement of the optimal level of investment, because each operator chooses its own optimal network size and appropriates the return from the investment in the additional facilities.

Third, the network and service in telecommunications form a virtuous cycle in which the network competition promotes the service and content industries, which in return would attract more network subscribers. As a result, such industries as e-commerce, online gaming, and Internet broadcasting have flourished in Korea. This virtuous cycle becomes a key driver and the objective of telecom policy in the information age.

In the absence of facility-based competition, the vertical structure would allow the incumbent monopoly network operator to extract the downstream rent. It could be prohibitive for content providers to have proper incentives in such an environment. Korea's experience indicates that for effective competition in both the network and content sectors to be realized, facility-based competition should be in place, along with proper regulatory safeguards against market failure. Also, as the source of economic value shifts from network to content and application, a competitive environment in the content and application sectors becomes pivotal and should attract more regulatory attention.

Development of Special-Purpose, High-Speed Networks

Korea's investment in the advanced networks began with the first Korea Information Infrastructure (KII) Plan of 1994 (see table 5.2), which has since been updated several times. The KII Plan includes the completion of the Test-Bed Network, the Korea Information Infrastructure–Government (KII-G), and the Korea Information Infrastructure–Public (KII-P) Plans. KII-G is the backbone network predominantly for government agencies; it was developed by telecommunications service providers using public funds. KII-P is the advanced network for the public at large; it was developed by telecom providers using private funds. The Korean government also built the Test-Bed Network to encourage the development of state-of-the-art network technologies and applications and accumulate premarket testing experience in building, operating, and managing high-speed information networks.

For the three stages of the KII projects, the Korean government invested US$620 million, which amounted to 3.6 percent of the total investment for the whole KII Plan from private and public investment. As a result, Korea could acquire a national information infrastructure with state-of-the-art technology and supreme speed and bandwidth on the local loop, not to mention on the national backbone.

The KII-G project initiated investments in the national information superhighway. As of April 2004, a total of 31,632 governmental organizations, such as national and local administrative offices, educational institutes, research institutes, and medical institutions, use this network at a discounted price. The approach, called

Table 5.2 Accomplishments of the KII-Projects, by Stages

KII		1st stage (1995–97)	2nd stage (1998–2000)	3rd stage (2001–03)
KII Test-Bed Network		• 2.5 gbps test: backbone between Seoul and Taejon	• 2.5 gbps test: backbones in five cities	• 40 gbps test: backbones in six cities
KII-G	Backbone networks	• 80 local call areas (up to 5 gbps)	• All 144 local call areas (up to 5 gbps)	• Upgrade band-width up to 40 gbps
	ATM switches	• ATM test-beds in 5 areas	• ATM networks in all 144 local call areas	• Ensuring quality of service of the network (multi-protocol label switching)
KII-P	Backbone	• Optical cables to all cities and counties (up to 40 gbps)	• Optical cables to rural villages (up to 40 gbps)	• Upgrade band-width up to 320 gbps
	Local loops	• Fiber to the office to major buildings	• ADTV, CATV (FTTC: 10% of all local call areas)	• ADTV, CATV, fiber to the home (FTTC: 90% of all local call areas)

Source: MIC 2004, p. 25.

Note: ADTV = advanced-definition television; ATM = automated teller machine; CATV = cable television; FTTC = fiber to the curb; FTTH = fiber to the home; gbps = gigabits per second.

"Invest First, Settle Later," was a win-win strategy in which private companies could undertake a large-scale investment in the new and unproven broadband technology using public funds; it also enabled the public sector to attain lower network costs. The KII-G project also created the physical infrastructure necessary for the e-government projects undertaken in the early 2000s. With the completion of the KII-G project, most of the national and local administrative offices could rationalize the formation of their own information networks. In addition, all the elementary, middle, and high schools in Korea (10,432 schools) would have two megabits per second (mbps) access, regardless of their location, on which to build their individual educational information systems.

The KII-P project proceeded on the basis of experience gained in the establishment and operation of the KII-G. It was built using private funds raised by the telecommunications service providers to meet the demands for high-speed information and communications services. The KII-P project placed particular emphasis on building advanced local loops, and to build the infrastructure efficiently and economically while actively responding to technological developments and changing demands, diverse implementation methods were used. For example, networks in commercial and densely populated areas were built with optical cables, and networks extending to subscriber premises were built partly using optical cables and partly by digitizing and enhancing the speed of existing telephone lines or CATV networks or by building new wireless local loops.

Figure 5.4 shows that Internet penetration in Korea, measured by the number of Internet users per 1,000 persons, has increased dramatically since 1990. In 1990, only 0.23 person of every 1,000 persons was using the Internet. By 2005, this number had increased to 684 persons per 1,000. In addition, since 1999, Korea's Internet penetration rates have been higher than the OECD average and also have the highest rate among the East Asian newly industrializing economies (NIEs), a good indication that the Korean government's proactive efforts in encouraging Internet use are paying off.

Promoting Broadband Internet Access

As of June 2004, the number of subscribers to Korea's broadband Internet service reached 36 million, implying that broadband Internet is accessible in 24 percent of the population, the highest in the world (figure 5.5). Many facilities-based service providers are now operating in the market, driving down the tariffs. Users of xDSL accounted for 57.3 percent of broadband Internet services, 34.3 percent are cable modem users, and local area network (LAN) users' share is 8.2 percent.

Four factors account for the successful takeoff and continued growth of the broadband Internet service market in Korea.

First is the competition among the different technologies. Broadband Internet service was classified as a value added service, free of regulation regarding entry

Figure 5.4 East Asian Newly Industrializing Economies and OECD Average—Internet Users, 1990–2005

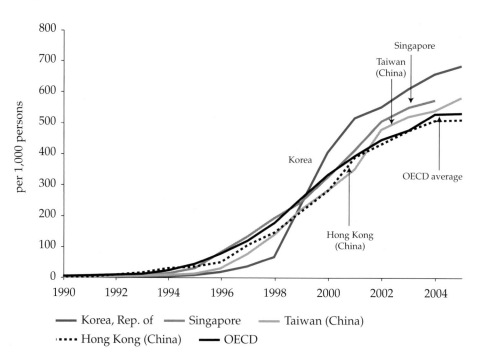

Source: Constructed based on data obtained from World Bank SIMA database.

Figure 5.5 Broadband Subscribers by Technology per 100 Inhabitants, Selected Countries, 2004

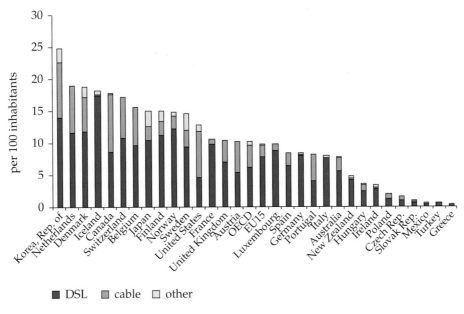

Source: OECD 2005b.

and pricing.[1] Almost concurrently, full service providers (FSPs) entered the market, setting flat-rate retail charges at levels low enough to induce dial-up users to switch to broadband. Also, facility-based competition encouraged the expansion and upgrading of access networks, including fiber to the curb, fiber to the office, and fiber to the home, which was an indispensable part of the advancement of the information society.

The second factor is the urban geography of Korea, which allowed households to be efficiently wired for broadband Internet connections. Nearly 48 percent of total households live in apartment complexes that allow economies of scale in the market operations of FSPs. Also, in the case of the asymmetric digital subscriber line (ADSL), the issue of distance does not apply, because more than 90 percent of households are located within a radius of four kilometers around KT's wire centers. One of the key reasons why ADSL subscription rates rapidly caught up with that of cable modems is that Hanaro Telecom used a preemptive strategy that targeted densely populated apartment complexes with more than 300 households. Similarly, KT extended its existing copper local loops in anticipation of a large number of new potential customers.

The third factor is the government's early commitment to building an extensive and modern information infrastructure. Beginning in 1999, the government provided FSPs with public loans at prime rates to reduce their financial burden of

---

1. Although in July 2004, broadband Internet service was classified as a facility-based service.

investing in such access networks. To further promote the penetration of the broadband network, the government coined the unique Cyber Building Certificate system in 1999. The idea originated from the concept of the "cyber apartment," which was created by Hanaro Telecom as a new marketing strategy. Certificates are being issued to buildings equipped with high-speed telecommunications capacity (LAN), depending on their bandwidth. As of May 2003, 2,146 certificates have been issued to cyber apartments or cyber buildings.

The fourth factor is the voice over Internet protocol and other services that have greatly increased versatility and attractiveness of the broadband connection.

Promoting ICT Literacy, Content, and Applications

To promote and take advantage of development of advanced telecommunications networks, the Korean government has exerted enormous effort to providing public services through the Internet. This stimulated the demand for the newly rolled-out high speed networks among citizens and businesses.

At the beginning of 2001, the government established a special committee for implementing e-government initiatives, which was under the direct control of the president of Korea. Since then, the government has invested more than US$250 million over two years and selected 11 major e-government projects for implementation (table 5.3). The committee led these cross-agency projects, thus providing a solid basis for a successful e-government implementation.

The Special Committee for e-Government set these principles and the direction for the e-government initiatives: (a) focus on national priorities, (b) integrate interagency-related initiatives into a single government-wide initiative, (c) maximize the sharing of information across agencies and eliminate overlap of duties, and (d) promote the use of IT based on business process reengineering. Under the principles and direction formulated by the special committee, extensive administrative processes have been refocused to provide citizen-centered government services via the Internet through the expansion of information sharing across government agencies.

> The Special Committee for e-Government had these principles for implementing e-government initiatives: (a) focus on national priorities, (b) integrate interagency-related initiatives into a single government-wide initiative, (c) maximize the sharing of information across agencies and eliminate overlap of duties, and (d) promote the use of IT based on business process reengineering.

The Government for Citizens (G4C) system has been established to connect the database networks of many government agencies and streamline government processes for delivering services to citizens. For example, the Home Tax Service through the Internet allows taxpayers to file tax returns, receive electronic bills, and process payments from their homes via the Internet. The database networks for health insurance, pension insurance, industrial accident compensation insurance, and unemployment insurance policies, which are the four major social insurance systems in Korea, have been interconnected into a seamless network.

Table 5.3 Major e-Government Initiatives

Objectives	e-government initiatives
Upgrade government-wide services for citizens and private businesses	1. Set up information sharing in five major government services, including resident registration, real estate, and vehicle records. 2. Created a G4C system to establish a government-wide service processing system Established a Social Insurance Information Sharing system for health, pension, unemployment, and industrial accident compensation 3. Built a Home Tax Service system that enables online filing of tax returns, electronic bill payment, tax consultation, and issuance service for tax-related certificates 4. Established a government e-procurement system to achieve transparent procurement processes
Improve the effectiveness of administration	5. Built a National Finance Information System for budget planning and allocation, accounting, and settlement of accounts and made financial information available through an interagency network 6. Built a National Education Information System for the electronic distribution and management of records across schools, offices of education, and the Ministry of Education and Human Resources Development 7. Proceeded with the Local Government Information Network System project for 21 service areas 8. Built a Personnel Policy Support System to manage the hiring, promotion, and compensation of civil servants in a fair and systematic way
Establish an infrastructure for e-government	9. Expanded the use and distribution of e-approvals and e-documents between agencies 10. Expanded the use of electronic signatures and seals to establish a reliable e-administration 11. Constructed a government-wide integrated computer network in project-specific stages (since November 2002, the redesign plan for work processes and the strategic plan for IT has been formulated)

Source: Special Committee for e-Government 2003, p. 13.

The government has also heavily invested in public awareness programs to rapidly increase the number of Internet users. Between 2000 and 2003, 13.9 million people benefited from a basic ICT education program, and an additional 5 million people are expected to benefit from the program from 2004 to 2008. This campaign has particularly targeted information have-nots—the disabled, the elderly, housewives, manual workers, and those engaged in agricultural and fishing industries. In parallel, KT committed to provide broadband Internet service (one mbps) to all farming and fishing villages by 2005.

Universal ICT literacy is a national priority. Korea completed LAN installation and Internet connection in all of the nation's 10,064 schools by the end of 2000. The next step was to improve teachers' ICT literacy, develop new curriculum and teaching methods using ICTs, and produce new educational content using ICTs. At least once every four years, every teacher now participates in a training program on ICTs, which takes place at the Information and Communication Officials Training Institute established to provide ICT education for government officials.

Flexible Financing Mechanisms for Informatization Initiatives

The promotion of informatization requires large-scale investment and calls for the long-term cooperation of various organizations, thus it is difficult to carry out the projects within the general budget. The Informatization Promotion Fund (IPF) was established in 1996 as a special vehicle to overcome the budgetary restrictions and promote informatization projects.

> Because the promotion of informatization requires large-scale investment and the long-term cooperation of various government organizations, the Informatization Promotion Fund (IPF) was established to overcome the budgetary restrictions and provide the necessary long-term financing for informatization projects.

The goals of the IPF are to roll out broadband networks, promote e-government, support R&D and standardization, and educate workers in ICTs. The fund, based on government budgetary and private sector contributions, allows profits from ICT fields to be reallocated into the ICT sector. From 1993 to 2002, the IPF reached a total of US$7.78 billion. About 40 percent of the fund (US$3.06 billion) came from the government budget, 46 percent (US$8.95 billion) came from private firms, and 14 percent (US$1.13 billion) came from miscellaneous profits and interest receipts. A total of US$5.33 billion was invested between 1994 and 2003. Of that, 38 percent was invested in ICT R&D, 20 percent into informatization promotion, 18 percent in ICT human resource development, 15.1 percent in broadband infrastructure and promotion, 7 percent in infrastructure in the ICT industries, and 3 percent in standardization.

The fund is managed by the MIC (overall management), the Institute of Information Technology Assessment (specific project management), and the Fund Management Council (evaluation). The chair of the council is vice minister of the MIC, and its members are directors general of related ministries.

The IPF played a key role in the balanced promotion of informatization policy to create demand and in the ICT industry policy for expansion of the supply base.

Outcome of Information Infrastructure Development

Figure 5.6 displays the KAM spidergram for ICT indicators using data for Korea and the average for the G7 and High Income countries for the most recent year. As expected, Korea's performance in the ICT pillar of the knowledge economy is very balanced and very strong, with a number of the indicators being at par with and

Figure 5.6 ICT Indicators—Republic of Korea, G-7, and High Income Countries

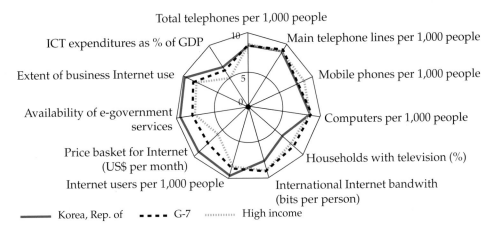

Variable	Korea, Rep. of		G-7		High income	
	Actual	Normalized	Actual	Normalized	Actual	Normalized
Total telephones per 1,000 people, 2004	1,302.80	8.11	1,350.06	8.3	1,374.27	8.52
Main telephone lines per 1000 people, 2004	541.90	8.94	562.34	9.13	496.11	8.61
Mobile phones per 1,000 people, 2004	760.90	7.42	787.71	7.55	878.15	8.3
Computers per 1,000 people, 2004	544.90	8.73	564.86	8.85	479.61	8.31
Households with television (%), 2004	93.00	6.36	97.3	8.18	96.35	7.54
International Internet bandwidth (bits per person), 2004	1,484.50	7.74	5,207.33	8.9	5,475.39	8.93
Internet users per 1000 people, 2004	656.80	9.62	555.16	8.83	480.68	8.43
Price basket for Internet (US$ per month), 2003	9.70	9.32	16.76	7.39	21.21	5.8
Availability of e-government services (1–7), 2006	5.46	9.36	4.58	7.87	4.55	7.77
Extent of business Internet use (1–7), 2006	6.10	9.83	5.36	8.61	4.93	7.94
ICT expenditure as % of GDP, 2005	6.91	6.35	6.65	6.01	6.05	4.93

Source: KAM, December 2006 (www.worldbank.org/wbi/kam).

even exceeding that of the G7 and High Income country averages. Korea is particularly strong in internet penetration, cost of internet access, e-government services, and extent of business Internet use, with these variables scoring above the 90th percentile.

ICT Adoption and Economic Growth

ICTs can be viewed as general purpose technologies that can affect economic growth of the whole industry through two channels. First, the rise in ICT investments leads to capital accumulation, which is directly linked to economic growth. Second, ICT investments can enhance productivity growth within industries. Changes in production, management, and organization that are accompanied by ICT investment further improve productivity.

Bank of Korea statistics show that ICT investments, including computers, peripherals, networking, and software, sharply increased their share in overall facility investments from 24 percent in 1995 to 34.5 percent in 2004. According to Hong and others (2003a), the contribution of ICT investments to overall GDP growth was about 3.5 percent for the period 1990–95; that contribution rose to 17.7 percent of economic growth from 1995 to 2000.

The effects of ICT investments on productivity growth cannot be easily identified across the industry as a whole. Some researchers have categorized industries into ICT high-use industry and ICT low-use industry and found that the productivity of the former was higher than that of the latter (see table 5.4).

According to Bresnahan, Brynjolfsson, and Hitt (2002), the effects of ICT investments on productivity may differ among businesses, because complementary changes in organizational structure and job process may be incurred differently. In other words, in addition to the ICT investment, complementary changes such as human resource investment, incentives, and decentralization play a pivotal role in enhancing productivity. Hong (2004) pointed out that ICT investment could have only limited effects on productivity because of the partial correlation between ICT investments and changes in job processes and internal organization in Korea.

Challenges Ahead: Convergence and Effective Competition

Korea's current tasks are to balance continued network enhancement and ensure effective competition. There is a trade-off between network enhancement, which helps achieve production efficiency, and effective competition, which helps distribution efficiency. Because convergence is a trend in telecommunications, the network becomes more sophisticated as well as faster. It becomes unavoidable that, even without anticompetitive practices, the incumbent operator has a greater advantage in supplying convergent services. This has a detrimental effect on com-

Table 5.4 Productivity Growth of ICT High-Use and Low-Use Industries
(percent)

Labor productivity growth[a]	1994–98	1998–2001		1994–2001
ICT high-use industry	9.1	5.6		8.0
ICT low-use industry	4.0	2.6		0.9
TFP growth[b]	*1993–97*	*1998–2001*	*2002–04*	*1993–2004*
ICT high-use industry	2.0	1.2	3.1	1.2
ICT low-use industry	0.6	0.9	0.8	0.1

Sources: a. KISDI 2004; b. Park and Ha 2005.

petition, so that the dominant operator in the market tends to gain market share. The convergent trend also makes the design and implementation of competition policy more complicated. Thus, another challenge for the Korean government is to keep the regulatory framework up to date in a rapidly changing telecommunications market.

The possible directions in the era of convergence are as follows: New market definitions for and classification of telecommunications services are needed to accommodate convergence. The regulatory framework for the market structure and effective competition, such as licensing, cross-subsidization, and bundling, needs to be more sophisticated. During the transitional phase, traditional regulatory measures still need to be implemented; however, uniform regulation should be avoided. Careful analysis of market conditions and relevant effects should precede each policy or regulatory measure to allow flexibility.

Development of the ICT Industry in Korea

Enthusiastic adoption of ICTs by Korean industries and rapid emergence of a competitive ICT production sector helped Korea to recover from the economic crisis and take off on a new phase of development. Although the ICT industry in Korea underwent a stagnant period after 2001, the value of ICTs as a future growth engine should not be underestimated. Especially as the boundary between industry and products collapses because of broadband networking and convergence, a second momentum is being formed. This second part of this chapter analyzes the development of the Korean ICT industry as a high-value-added sector with substantial export potential.

> Intensive and rapid adoption of ICTs by Korean industries and rapid emergence of a competitive ICT production sector helped Korea to recover from the economic crisis and take off on a new phase of development.

Growing Importance of the ICT Industry

In the 1990s, the ICT industry in Korea had the highest growth rates of any major industry and became the new engine for growth. The Bank of Korea estimates that the share of the ICT industry in Korea's GDP rose from 7.7 percent in 1997 to 16.2 percent in 2006. A better way to evaluate the importance of the ICT industry is to look at its contribution to real GDP growth. Since 1998, the ICT industry has contributed more that more than a 1 percentage point increase to GDP annually. Table 5.5 shows that the growth rate of the ICT industry has been much higher than that of the overall economy, and its contribution to GDP growth remains high.

The main driver for the rapid growth of the ICT industry was the enhancement in productivity attributed to continuous technology development. As table 5.6 shows, researchers have consistently reported that TFP growth in the ICT industry, more than 10 percent in the 1990s, exceeded TFP growth in other industries by a large margin during that decade. In particular, the difference between TFP growth

Table 5.5 Contribution of the ICT Industry to Economic Growth, 1997–2006
(percent of GDP)

	1997	1998	1999	2000	2001	2002	2003	2004	2005	2006
Growth rate of the ICT industry	11.6	23.0	35.3	33.8	10.5	17.6	14.2	17.5	13.5	13.3
Growth rate of GDP	4.7	−6.9	9.5	8.5	3.8	7.0	3.1	4.7	4.2	5.0
ICT industry share of GDP	4.7	6.2	7.7	9.5	10.1	11.1	12.3	13.8	15.0	16.2
ICT industry contribution to GDP growth	0.5	1.1	2.2	2.6	1.0	1.8	1.6	2.2	1.9	2.0

Source: Bank of Korea 2006.
Note: 1997–2006 statistics were calculated at 2000 constant prices.

in ICTs and in other industries is estimated to have widened after the financial crisis of 1997, partly because the TFP growth in non-ICT industries has fallen since the crisis.

> The main driver for the rapid growth of the ICT industry was the enhancement in productivity attributed to continuous technology development.

The ICT Industry and Korea's International Trade

The significant contribution of the ICT industry to the growth of the national economy was mainly attributed to rapidly expanding ICT exports. The share of ICTs in Korea's total exports rose from 23.1 percent in 1998 to 29.4 percent in 2004. The quality of key ICT products such as dynamic random access memory (DRAM), mobile handsets, liquid crystal display (LCD) monitors, and set-top boxes has risen to the global standard.

Improvements should be made in two areas of ICT trade for Korea's ICT exports to continue to lead the national economy. First, trading partners for ICT products should be diversified. Korea's exports and imports in the ICT industry depend heavily on five major trading partners: China, Hong Kong (China), the United States, Taiwan (China), Japan, and Germany. As of 2004, those nations accounted for 65.1 percent of total ICT exports and 75.9 percent of total ICT imports. This heavy reliance on five major trading partners implies that the future of Korea's ICT

Table 5.6 Estimates of TFP Growth in the ICTs and All Manufacturing Industries in Korea
(percent)

Period	1991–97	1998–2000	1991–2000
All manufacturing industries	2.8	1.5	2.3
ICT industry	11.5	7.0	10.0

Source: Hong and others 2003.

industry depends on the economic situations of those nations. Increasing the number of trading partners is necessary to sustain the growth of the ICT industry and diversify the risks.

Second, Korea needs to diversify export products. Key products leading Korea's ICT exports include mobile communications handsets, memory semiconductors, and LCD monitors. These products represented more than 50 percent of ICT exports (27.7, 22.8, and 6.9 percent, respectively) in 2004, reflecting their high contributions to Korea's exports. However, too much reliance on several items in exports should be relieved.

Composition of the ICT Industry

In 2004, the total production of the ICT industry in Korea was W 230 trillion, Yet the sector development is very unbalanced. *Polarization* is the term used in Korea to explain the widening gap between advanced and underdeveloped sectors in the economy.

First, the software and computer service industry is underdeveloped in contrast with the world-class ICT manufacturing industry. As shown in table 5.7, ICT hardware accounts for 72 percent of total ICT production as of 2004. The Korean economy has been globally competitive in assembly and mass production operations, and this traditional strength has again surfaced in the ICT manufacturing industry.

Table 5.8 compares ICT industries in Korea and the United States in terms of value added and employment. The value added by the software and computer service industry accounted for about 6 percent of the total value added in Korea's ICT industry in 2004, whereas it accounted for 39 percent in the United States in 2002. The proportion of value added of the ICT equipment industry shows a greater difference: 72.2 percent in Korea compared with 28.4 percent in the United States. Differences between the two nations in the software employment share of the ICT industry were smaller than those of value added, reflecting Korea's low labor productivity in that sector.

Second, a weak ICT components and materials industry, in comparison with the final ICT goods industry, poses some problems for the Korean ICT industry's long-

Table 5.7 Composition of ICT Industry Production, 1997–2004
(trillion won)

	1997	1998	1999	2000	2001	2002	2003	2004
ICT service	17.0	19.6	24.5	31.6	36.3	43.0	41.6	46.0
	(22.6)	(21.8)	(20.8)	(21.3)	(24.2)	(22.7)	(20.6)	(20.0)
ICT hardware	55.0	65.6	86.8	105.9	99.1	127.7	141.6	164.9
	(72.8)	(72.9)	(73.7)	(71.4)	(66.0)	(67.6)	(70.2)	(71.8)
Software	3.5	4.7	6.5	10.7	14.7	18.2	18.4	18.7
	(4.6)	(5.2)	(5.5)	(7.4)	(9.8)	(9.7)	(9.1)	(8.1)
Total	75.5	89.9	117.8	148.2	150.1	188.9	201.6	229.6
Growth rate	27.1	19.0	31.1	25.8	1.3	25.8	6.7	13.9

Source: KAIT 2005.

Note: ICT service includes telecommunications and broadcasting services. Software includes packaged software and computer-related services. Numbers in parentheses denote percentage of total ICT production.

Table 5.8 Comparison of the Structure of ICT Industries

	Korea (2004)				United States (2002)			
	Value added (billion won)	Share of industry total (%)	Employ-ment (persons)	Share of industry total (%)	Value added (US billion)	Share of value added (%)	Employ-ment (100 persons)	Share of industry total (%)
ICT equipment	80,903	72.2	444,177	66.1	235.9	28.4	16,248	34
ICT service	24,544	21.9	118,198	17.6	272.1	32.7	11,931	25
Software and computer services	6,551	5.8	109,970	16.4	323.7	38.9	19,610	41
Total	111,997	100.0	672,345	100.0	831.6	100.0	47,790	100.0

Source: KAIT 2005; U.S. Department of Commerce 2003.

term growth. The import-inducing coefficients of key ICT components range from 0.45 to 0.55, about four times larger than that of Japan's electric and electronics industry (0.13). About 70 to 80 percent of the trade deficits with Japan are from the components and materials industry, 40 percent of which are occurring in the ICT industry (Kim 2004).

Because intermediate components need to be obtained from abroad and at a higher cost, the immature components and materials industry tends to imply that the ICT final goods industry may eventually become less competitive, which would hamper economic growth. Rodrik (2004) has emphasized the role of the intermediate goods industry (components and materials) in economic growth and technology development. There also is a strong mutual dependence between the final and intermediate ICT goods industries. The specialization and diversification of the components and materials industry lead to the enhancement of the productivity of the finished goods industry, which in turn increases demand for components and materials. The failure to establish a virtuous cycle results in a lack of mutual reliance and can cause the ICT industry, and hence the economy, to suffer from low growth in the long run.

Third, a sizable gap exists between large ICT firms and ICT SMEs in Korea. Table 5.9 illustrates that employment, revenue, value added, and labor productivity of the ICT-manufacturing SMEs are lower than those of non-ICT SMEs. In 2005, the share of large conglomerates in the whole manufacturing industry in terms of the number of establishments is just 0.6 percent; their shares in the ICT manufacturing industry and in the components and materials industry are 2.1 percent and 2.6 percent, respectively. As a result, the share of large businesses in terms of employment and sales is much higher in the ICT manufacturing industry and ICT components and materials manufacturing industries than in the manufacturing industry as a whole. The same is true for value added. The labor productivities of large firms are 3.0 times, 3.6 times, and 3.2 times larger than those of the SMEs, in the manufacturing, ICT manufacturing, and ICT components and materials industries, respectively.

Besides the higher productivity of large ICT companies, the disparity can be partially explained by the fact that the Korean ICT industry is capital intensive as well as R&D intensive. Therefore, it is easier for large firms to run ICT industries because they have more access to financial resources. For example, Dedrick and

Table 5.9 Distribution of ICT Components and Materials Businesses, 2005

Classification		Number of establish-ments	Employ-ment (persons)	Revenue (million won)	Value added (million won)	Labor produc-tivity
Manufacturing	Large business	662 (0.6)	683,200 (23.7)	428,252,729 (50.1)	151,564,208 (48.2)	221.8
	SME	117,156 (99.4)	2,197,803 (76.3)	425,981,059 (49.9)	162,876,715 (51.8)	74.1
	Total	117,818	2,881,003	854,233,788	314,440,923	109.1
ICT manufacturing	Large business	172 (2.1)	239,190 (50.3)	121,636,898 (74.4)	56,640,876 (78.3)	236.8
	SME	8,116 (97.9)	236,640 (49.7)	41,764,288 (25.6)	15,731,339 (21.7)	66.5
	Total	8,288	475,830	163,401,186	72,372,215	152.1
ICT component and materials manufacturing	Large business	126 (2.6)	172,086 (55.5)	71,858,281 (74.3)	38,022,730 (79.8)	221.0
	SME	4,779 (97.4)	137,902 (44.5)	24,812,638 (25.7)	9,635,824 (20.2)	69.9
	Total	4,905	309,988	96,670,919	47,658,554	153.7

Source: National Statistical Office 2006.
Note: Numbers in parentheses indicate percentage share in category.

Kraemer (1997) analyze how the management style of some large firms (chaebols) work in their favor. The president of a chaebol has full authority over the company and can take it into a risky new business without worrying about the threat to stock prices or about achieving consensus among the management team. In contrast, SMEs, especially high-tech start-ups, usually do not have sufficient cash or tangible assets to be taken as collateral, so the (usually conservative) commercial banks are cautious about extending loans to start-ups.

The polarization in the ICT industry by firm size may also be partially attributed to unfair trade practices—such as the unilateral request by large conglomerates to lower unit prices or unfair contracts that prohibit SMEs in the components industry from contracting with competing companies that assemble finished goods. If this is the case, it may limit technology innovation in SMEs.

Capacity-Building Initiatives for the ICT Sector

Research and Development

R&D in ICTs has been one of the key factors contributing to the growth of the ICT sector in Korea. Keeping pace with technological change and remaining globally competitive, Korea's ICT sector has continuously increased its investment in R&D. During the period 1994–2005, the average annual growth rate of R&D expenditure on ICTs was about 22 percent. In 2005, R&D investment in ICTs accounted for about 47 percent of total R&D spending in Korea (see figure 5.7). Business enterprises had the largest share of R&D spending in the ICT sector: about 89 percent in 2005 (table 5.10).

Figure 5.7 ICT R&D Expenditure in Korea, 1993–2005

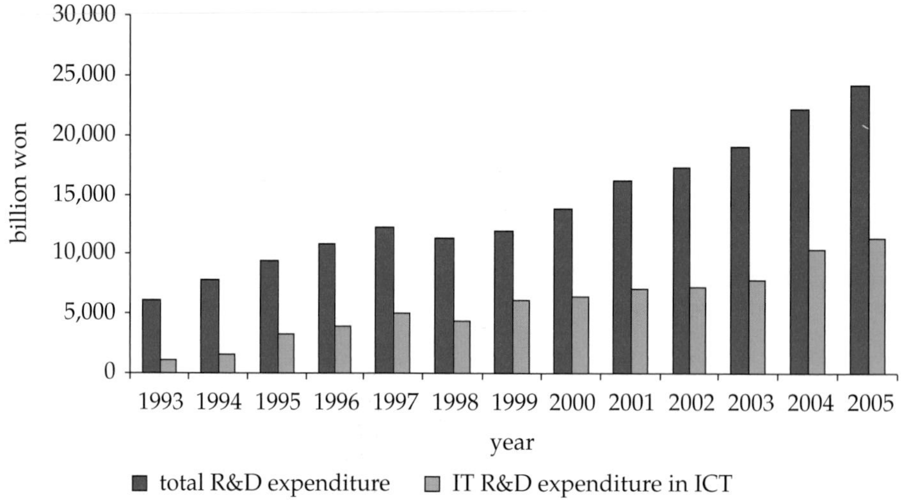

■ total R&D expenditure   □ IT R&D expenditure in ICT

Source: MOST, Electronics and Telecommunications Research Institute (ETRI), Korea Information Strategy Development Institute (KISDI).

Because of the private sector's aggressive investment in R&D for ICTs, the government has been able to focus on a few strategic ICT areas that are expected to bring higher social return. As of 2003, the government's ICT development programs were composed of three priority areas.

The Leading Technology Development Program focuses on strategic R&D projects that require long-term investments that the private sector would not engage in without the government's support. The list of technologies under the program includes next-generation mobile communications, digital television and broadcasting, optical subscriber networking, and embedded software. In general, about half of the government's R&D resources for the development of leading technologies is given to national research institutes (Yoon and others 2002), but cooperative research with private enterprises and universities is highly encouraged.

The Industrial ICT Development Program provides financial assistance to private ICT firms that focus on the development of applied technologies that can be commercialized within a short time. To facilitate the commercialization of R&D results, the government gives higher priority to proposals for joint R&D projects between public research institutes and private enterprises.

Table 5.10 Composition of R&D Expenditure in ICT, 1997–2005
(percent)

	1997	1998	1999	2000	2001	2002	2003	2004	2005
Business R&D	86.5	90.9	94.5	94.9	89.1	84.5	87.7	89.0	89.3
Public R&D	13.5	9.1	5.5	5.1	10.9	15.5	12.3	11.0	10.7

Source: MOST, ETRI, and KISDI.
Note: All values appear as a percentage of total R&D expenditure in ICT.

The New Technology Support Program is designed to help new SMEs in the ICT sector. SMEs often face financial difficulty in developing innovative ideas and technologies. Firms with innovative ideas or patents and in business for fewer than three years may participate in the program. If the technology development supported by the program is successful, the program also provides management assistance and helps find investors to bring the products or services to their full market potential.

Human Resources

The rapid expansion of the ICT sector in the Korean economy has increased demand for R&D personnel. To increase the number of researchers in the IT field, the Korean government has designed a long-term support program that provides funds for the development of ICT research centers at private and public universities. To foster qualified researchers, the government offers fellowship programs that give students and researchers opportunities to study abroad in distinguished academic institutions.

> To accommodate the rapidly increased demand for R&D personnel, in terms of both quantity and quality, in the ICT sector, the Korean government facilitated the development of ICT research centers at universities and provided scholarships to distinguished foreign academic institutions.

In 2003, the government introduced a supply chain management model into its program of fostering ICT professionals. The program focuses on fostering professionals who will be able to meet the rapidly changing ICT skill requirements. The government also helped ICT-related schools improve their equipment and education curricula. Assistance was provided for ICT internships so that more students could gain on-the-job experience.

ICT Venture Enterprises and Venture Capital

The number of venture business firms in Korea has rapidly increased since the financial crisis. Although the number of certified venture businesses decreased drastically after 2001, they still take a large share of overall ventures. ICT start-ups accounted for about 42 percent of the certified ventures at the end of 2003.

Start-up investment companies (SICs), account for the majority of venture capital industry in Korea.[2] Unlike a typical U.S. venture capital firm, which is a limited partnership operating a small amount of partnership funds at any given time, Korean venture capital firms are incorporated joint stock companies with their own

---

2. The venture capital industry in Korea is composed of two kinds: SICs and new technology financing companies (NTFCs). NTFCs are registered with MOFE and are engaged in broader areas of financing activities, such as leasing, factoring, consumer credit, and private equity investment.

financial resources for investment. However, they can also form investment funds with outside money, which comes mostly from the government, institutional investors, and corporations.

Both the number of SICs and the amount of funds the SICs manage have increased significantly since 1998. The IT industry is the single most important area of investment for venture capital. As figure 5.8 shows, venture capital investment in IT-based firms reached up to 70 percent of total venture capital investments during the IT boom (1999–2000). As in the United States, many venture capital companies claim IT investment as their specialty and continue to focus on the IT industry despite the market's recent sluggishness.

Since the Korean economy experienced a downturn, venture businesses have had difficulties. However, recent evidence shows that venture businesses in some sectors are doing better than others. Specifically, the profits of firms in Internet service and parts manufacture have increased, whereas those in software, computing service, and semiconductor equipment have decreased and are even experiencing losses. Software and computing service ventures suffer from chronic deficits because most governmental procurement processes award contracts to the lowest bidder, and usually it is the incumbent firms that are able to offer the lowest bids.

Despite overall dynamic development of venture capital fund-raising, there are some problematic outcomes. First, because the business environment has not been favorable for the start-ups since 2001, the return on investment for start-ups has also decreased. Thus, the size of start-up funding was greatly reduced, and fund-raising had to depend heavily on the government. The SMBA shows that the portions of the public sector funding for the start-up investment fund increased from

Figure 5.8 SIC Investment by Industry, 1998-2005
(billion won)

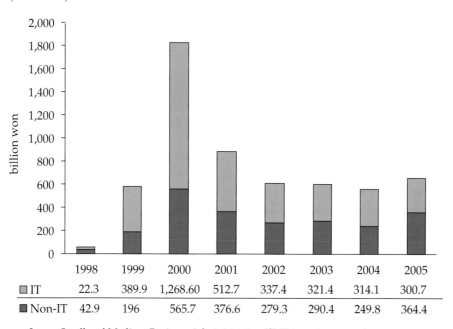

	1998	1999	2000	2001	2002	2003	2004	2005
☐ IT	22.3	389.9	1,268.60	512.7	337.4	321.4	314.1	300.7
■ Non-IT	42.9	196	565.7	376.6	279.3	290.4	249.8	364.4

Source: Small and Medium Business Administration (SMBA; various years).

2004 to 2005, which were 34.1 percent and 46.5 percent, respectively. Second, the policy has been one dimensional, failing to consider the different characteristics of industries and different developmental stages of firms. For example, business performance by industries differs because of sectors' individual characteristics. And in various ways, the government has been supporting even the firms for which venture capital firms play a role. Such government actions may impede the development of the venture capital industry. Finally, venture capital fund-raising has focused only on providing assistance for start-up firms, and it does not provide any assistance for the restructuring of existing firms. Thus, many inefficient start-up firms are unable to restructure.

Hence, a new paradigm is needed for setting policy to promote start-up ventures. The government can play an important role for some ventures, but not all. It would be enough for the government to focus on the early-stage firms; then it could give venture capital firms opportunities in the ventures in the expansion stage.

Conclusion and Further Challenges

Since the mid-1990s, Korea has pushed nationwide informatization. The government has consistently tried to take balanced approaches to three policy areas: building information infrastructure; promoting industrial activities, including expanding the ICT knowledge base; and ensuring fair competition. As a result, Korea now has one of the world's top broadband Internet infrastructures.

However, despite the relatively well-advanced information infrastructure, Korea has yet to translate the rapid diffusion of informatization into qualitative results, such as enhancement of labor productivity and industrial competitiveness. For example, although Korea is top among OECD countries in terms of informatization, its use of ICT is not comparable to such information infrastructures (Figure 5.9).

In general, Korea's ICT sector is characterized as hardware-oriented in that it has grown with massive capital investment by large firms. Hence, the sector shows industrial competitiveness in mass-producible products such as semiconductors and displays, but shows weaknesses in generic technologies and in core parts and components that are segmented in markets. Korea needs to build on its strengths and correct its weaknesses to make its ICT industry more competitive.

The ICT sector is expected to continue to lead global economic growth in the future; therefore, enhancing the competitiveness of the ICT industry is critical to national economic growth. Foremost, the government must emphasize continuing informatization and building up next-generation information and communications infrastructure, thus strengthening the foundation for Korea as a leading information economy. More important than investment in physical infrastructures, Korea should effectively address the polarization issue in the ICT sector. In relation to the divergent performances between the ICT and non-ICT industries, more effective use of ICT and infrastructures by non-ICT industries is very important to enhance the productivity of other industries.

With regard to the divergence of productivity growth between large enterprises and SMEs in the ICT industry, it is important to strengthen the innovative capabilities of smaller firms that fill the gap left by the large firms. One specific area of significant policy importance is the intermediate goods sector in the ICT industry. A

Figure 5.9 Business Usage of ICT, June 2004

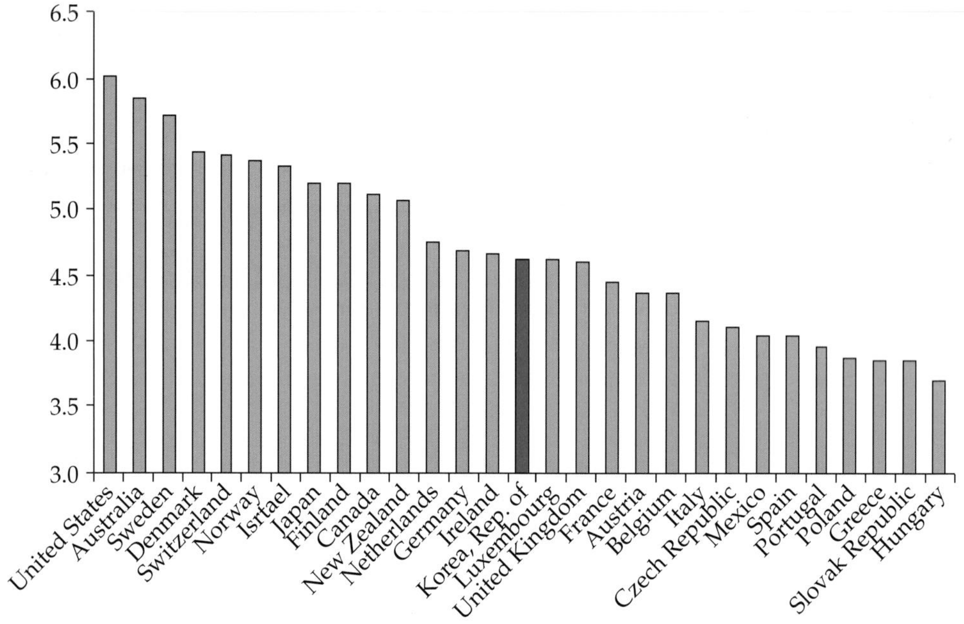

Source: OECD 2005a.
Note: Chart indicates the score on the business usage subindex of the World Economic Forum Networked Readiness Index 2003–04.

strong mutual dependence exists between final ICT products for which Korea has competitive advantages and ICT components and parts for which Korea is relatively weak. Korea's entry into ICT services and software, which necessitates many years for Korean companies to accumulate core competencies, will remain the country's most daunting long-term challenge.

The future of Korean ICT policy may be summarized in its IT 839 policy. Telecommunications services, infrastructure, equipment, software, and content are the elements that make up the vertical and horizontal value chains of the IT industry. Under the value chains, the introduction of new-generation broadband services will prompt investment in the building of three essential networks. And these networks will pave the way for the rapid growth of nine new sectors, creating a synergistic effect (MIC IT 839 strategy). By launching nine flagship R&D projects, Korea plans to change its ICT sector from a fast follower to a world-leading innovator. The broadband convergence network, the Korean version of a next-generation network, will link 90 percent of the population with at least a 20-mbps broadband network.

With this plan, Korea may become the first country to set the broadband Internet as a universal service. Korea is the leading country in launching many new services, including satellite and terrestrial digital multimedia broadcasting and wireless broadband. Users in Korea will soon embrace an era of convergence that is characterized by the seamless interoperability of many different advanced networks.

Government continuously adjusts the IT 839 strategy to reflect changes in technology and market environments. For example, recently adjusted strategy emphasizes the software sector, reflecting the growing importance of the software sector for job creation and balanced growth. The government's role as the facilitator of different market elements will be extended to that of a vision provider under IT 839. The IT 839 strategy is expected to shape the future of the IT industry and make a great contribution to laying the foundation for Korea's new growth momentum. It will transform the Korean IT industry, moving it away from a "catch-up" development model of the past to become a world market leader.

6

Meeting Skill and Human Resource Requirements

Anna Kim and Byung-Shik Rhee

Education has been a key factor in the rapid economic growth of Korea over the past four decades. Since the 1960s, the government-led economic development plans have been directly reflected in education policy and planning. The government has been generally successful in providing and expanding the education system based on the industrial needs of human resource. As a result, Korea's education system developed in tandem with the various stages of economic development, complementing the other pillars of the knowledge economy. The focus of the government's educational plan has moved from primary to secondary education and finally to the tertiary level, according to the nation's economic advancement. The rapid expansion of education in terms of quantity and, to a lesser extent, quality is the most salient feature of Korean educational development during the country's industrialization.

> Korea's education system developed in tandem with the various stages of economic development, complementing the other pillars of the knowledge economy.

However, the recent transition to an advanced KBE and the problems in the educational system that originated in the industrialization process require a new policy framework in education. Until now, the full potential of Korea's human resources has not been fully realized because of the rigidity and inflexibility of the education and training systems. The pool of human resources in Korea is large enough, because of efforts to expand educational opportunities, but the availability of adequately and appropriately trained human resources is limited. From this point, Korea's education and training systems have failed to play their required roles. Therefore, establishing a new system of education and training that meets the skill requirements for a KBE is a new challenge for Korea.

This chapter characterizes the Korean education model during the industrialization process. It contrasts the developmental model that Korea had implemented during the high-growth era before the financial crisis of 1997 and the human resource development model aimed at a KBE, which Korea has pursued to overcome the crisis and sustain economic growth afterward. This chapter discusses Korea's achievements in education, as well as remaining tasks, with the common theme of this report—how Korea has narrowed the institutional and knowledge gaps compared with other countries that are considered to be global leaders.

The Korean Education System

Since Korea launched an economic development program early in the 1960s, industrialization and urbanization have accelerated. With the poor natural resources available, Korea's strong family structure and high respect for education have been the driving force behind the country's rapid economic development. Koreans' strong belief in education is attributed in large part to the emphasis on credentials that prevails in Korean society. Education has also played a major role in laying the foundation upon which democratic principles and institutions are based. It has promoted political knowledge, changed political behavior patterns, and shaped political attitudes and values. At the same time, education has imbued the people with commitment to modernization and citizenship. Increased educational opportunities have made upward social mobility possible, and the middle class has expanded as a result (Kim, A. 2003).

The formal education system in Korea follows a single track of six years in elementary school, three years in middle school, three years in high school, and four years in college or university. Elementary education is free and compulsory. Upon reaching the age of six, children receive a notification of admission to a school in their residential area. Upon entrance to elementary school, children automatically advance to the next grade each year. Free, compulsory middle-school education began in 1985 in farming and fishing areas and gradually was expanded nationwide. Middle-school graduates have two options: to attend an academic general high school or a vocational high school. Those who are admitted to a vocational high school cannot transfer to an academic high school. But there is no restriction on vocational high-school graduates entering higher education institutions. Therefore, overall student selection and screening in Korea are reserved until candidates are selected for universities and colleges. Everyone is encouraged to participate in the competition for higher education. This system of contested mobility resulted in a continuous increase in the demand for educational opportunities and thus pushed the government to extend the provision of such opportunities.

Educational Expansion in Elementary and Secondary Education

> The rapid expansion of education in terms of quantity and, to a lesser extent, quality is the most salient feature of the Korean educational development during the country's industrialization.

The Korean education system has been successful at the primary and secondary levels in providing equal educational access to students, irrespective of their gender, geographical location, and socioeconomic background (see figures 6.1 and 6.2). The rate of pupil retention is nearly 100 percent in the lower grades. The school-age population is now forecast to grow at a slower pace, thus easing the tax burden of financing education. This outlook suggests a strong likelihood that public resources will be available for upgrading the provision of educational services.

Expansion of Higher Education

The rate of educational expansion is more remarkable at the tertiary level (see figure 6.1 and table 6.1). Until the 1970s, the college admission quota was strictly

Figure 6.1 Educational Expansion in Korea, Gross Enrollment Rates

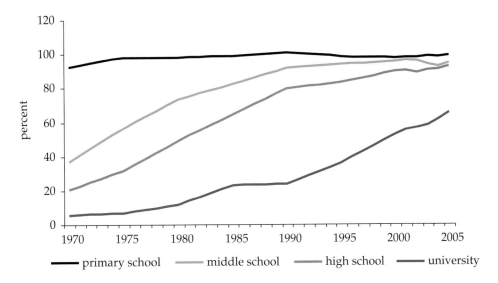

Source: Ministry of Education, Statistical Yearbook, various years.

Figure 6.2 Korea—Gross School Enrollment Rates by Sex, 2005

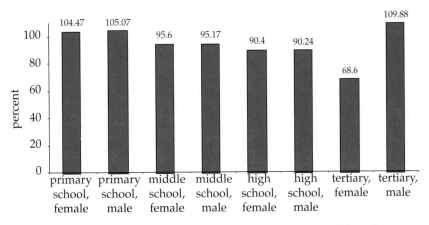

Source: World Bank Edstats database (www1.worldbank.org/education/edstats/).

Table 6.1 Number of Higher Education Institutions, by Institution Type, 2005

Institution type	Number of institutions		
	National/Public	Private	Total
University (4 years)	26	147 (85)	173
Junior college (2- and 3-year vocational college)	14	144 (91)	158
University of education	11	—	11
Industrial university	8	10 (56)	18
Technical university	0	1 (100)	1
Air and correspondence university	1	—	1
Cyber college and university	0	17 (100)	17
Corporate university	0	1 (100)	1
Misc. school (college & university)	0	5 (100)	4
Total	60	359 (86)	419

Source: KEDI/MOE & HRD 2005.
Note: Percentage of total that is private is in parentheses.
— = n.a.

regulated by the government, which set up the quota based on the analysis of demand for human resources. However, in 1980, the government abolished college entrance examinations and expanded educational opportunities for higher education. During the 1990s, the government initiated diversification and specialization of higher education institutions to accommodate the diverse needs of society. For this purpose, standards and conditions for granting university charters were loosened, and the numbers of institutions and of students increased steeply after 1996.

Quality Performance

Korea's education system has achieved quality improvements in tandem with quantitative expansion, though to a lesser extent for the former. For example, the most recent published results (2003) of periodic international tests in mathematics and science, such as the OECD's PISA (Programme for International Student Assessment) and TIMSS (Trends in International Mathematics and Science Study), showed the qualitative evidence for the highly competitive knowledge and skills of 15-year-old students of Korea (see figures 6.3a and 6.3b).

Similarly, the efficiency index shows that the efficiency of secondary education in Korea ranks second, following Finland, among OECD countries. The index was calculated by running the regression of reading literacy of the 15-year-old students on the cumulative expenditure per pupil for children ages 6 through 15 (see figure 6.4). This result indicates that Korean students show relatively high performance, although Korea's cumulative expenditures per pupil are below the OECD average (OECD 2004c).

However, the PISA survey results unveil an interesting feature of Korean students: individually they show high performance in academic achievement, but they have a relatively low sense of affiliation with their schools. This lack of affilia-

Figure 6.3a PISA 2003 Mathematics and Science Scores, Selected Countries

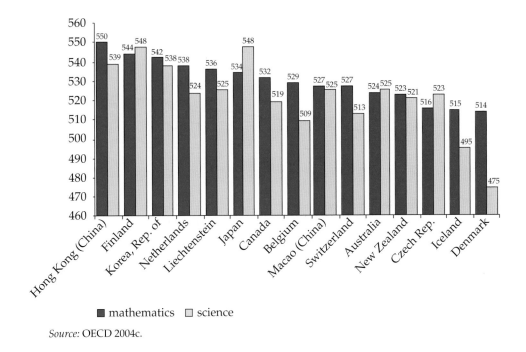

Source: OECD 2004c.

Figure 6.3b TIMSS 2003 Mathematics and Science Scores, Selected Countries

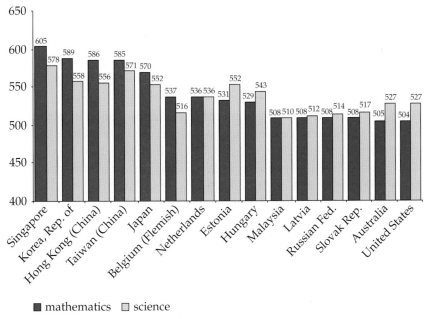

Source: Gonzales et al. 2004.

Figure 6.4 Student Performance and Spending per Student, 2003

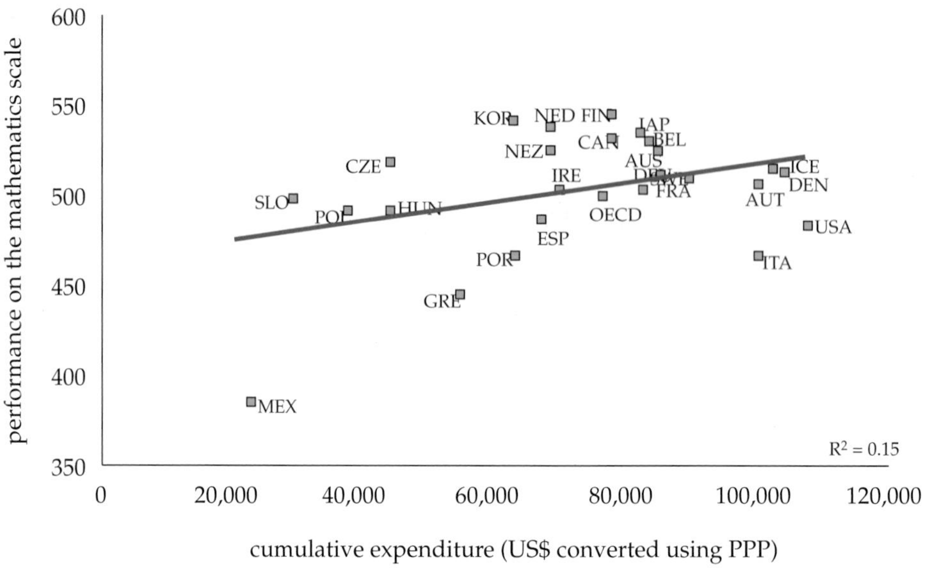

Source: OECD 2006. Education at a Glance. Paris: OECD
Note: Relationship between performance in mathematics and cumulative expenditure on educational institutions per student between ages of 6 and 15 years, in U.S. dollars, converted using purchasing power parity (PPP).

tion is partly attributable to the low credibility of the public education system. Moreover, Korean students show relatively low scores in all of the 13 affective characteristics and particularly low scores in motivational preferences and volition, self-related beliefs, and preference for cooperative learning. This indicates that the high performance of Korean students is driven not by their internal motivation but by external factors, and it explains why Korean students lose the positive learning attitude that generates consistent and creative learning and research during their college years, as soon as they finish the college entrance exam.

Korea's overall performance in the education arena can be seen in figure 6.5, which displays the KAM spidergram for education indicators using data for the Republic of Korea and the average for the G7 and high-income countries for the most recent year. Korea's performance in the education pillar is relatively strong, with 6 of the 14 indicators ranking in the 80th percentile and above. These are the average years of schooling, tertiary enrollment, Internet access in schools, eighth-grade achievement in science and mathematics, and extent of staff training. In addition, the performance is well balanced, with all but one of the indicators, professional and technical workers, ranking above the 50th percentile.

When compared to the average G7 or high-income country, Korea also stands up relatively well. Korea performs relatively better than the the average G7 or high-income country in terms of the quality of mathematics and science education, internet access in schools, tertiary enrollment, and average years of schooling. On the other hand it is relatively weaker in the quality of management schools, brain drain and as mentioned, the availability of professional and technical workers.

Figure 6.5 Education Indicators

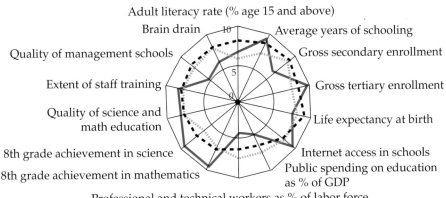

Adult literacy rate (% age 15 and above)

Brain drain

Average years of schooling

Quality of management schools

Gross secondary enrollment

Extent of staff training

Gross tertiary enrollment

Quality of science and math education

Life expectancy at birth

8th grade achievement in science

Internet access in schools

8th grade achievement in mathematics

Public spending on education as % of GDP

Professional and technical workers as % of labor force

———— Korea, Rep. of   ▪ ▪ ▪ ▪ G-7   ·········· High income

Variable	Korea, Rep. of		G-7		High income	
	Actual	Normalized	Actual	Normalized	Actual	Normalized
Adult literacy rate (% age 15 and above), 2004	97.90	6.59	99.77	8.22	96.68	5.95
Average years of schooling, 2000	10.84	9.26	9.68	8.67	9.20	7.38
Gross secondary enrollment, 2004	90.90	6.28	102.73	8.80	102.18	8.72
Gross tertiary enrollment, 2004	88.50	9.84	60.84	8.28	56.19	7.64
Life expectancy at birth, 2004	77.10	7.58	79.46	9.12	78.57	8.26
Internet access in schools (1–7), 2006	6.40	9.66	5.53	7.09	5.61	8.02
Public spending on education as % of GDP, 2003	4.60	5.04	5.14	6.42	5.59	7.17
Professional and technical workers as % of labor force, 2004	17.98	4.20	24.71	6.38	26.25	7.35
8th grade achievement in mathematics, 2003	589.00	9.39	517.00	7.18	513.48	6.86
8th grade achievement in science, 2003	558.00	9.39	528.20	7.35	516.24	6.02
Quality of science and math education (1–7), 2006	5.10	7.84	4.96	7.52	4.94	7.46
Extent of staff training (1–7), 2006	5.20	8.36	5.17	8.25	4.99	7.80
Quality of management schools (1–7), 2006	4.30	5.09	5.36	8.19	5.10	7.67
Brain drain (1–7), 2006	3.70	6.09	4.70	8.22	4.67	7.96

Source: KAM, December 2006 (www.worldbank.org/wbi/kam).

Main Features of Educational Development

The Korean Model of Educational Development

In the late 1940s and the 1950s, education policy focused on establishing educational infrastructure and expanding primary and secondary education, which are critical to supplying industry with a skilled workforce. The most conspicuous feature of educational development in the 1960s was the quantitative expansion of student enrollment and the number of schools. Vocational high schools were established in the 1960s to provide training in craft skills for the growing labor-intensive light industries. During the 1970s, one of the priority areas of economic development plans was the strengthening of vocational education. Vocational junior colleges were set up to supply technicians for the heavy and chemical industries (HCIs).

During the 1970s and 1980s, higher education was expanded in two ways: increased student enrollment and diversified institutions of higher education. As junior colleges took a larger share of tertiary education, their programs were diversified to meet industrial needs. Education reform in the 1980s included such measures as abolishing university entrance examinations, renovating school facilities, and introducing incentives for teachers. The availability of human resources became increasingly strained in the 1980s. The increased rate of the economically active population dropped sharply in that decade compared with the previous decade, and labor demand continued to increase as the economy grew at a high average annual rate of 10 percent in the second half of the 1980s. The changes in labor demand toward a more skilled and high-caliber workforce in the 1980s—brought about by the rapid economic growth—called for strengthening science and engineering education in universities.

The rapid economic growth had a strong effect on human resource development in two ways. On the industrial side, rapid industrialization affected skill formation in workplaces; in particular, industrial deepening in a short time required substantial effort to upgrade workforce skills and knowledge. On the supply side, the education and training system needed to change to meet the new requirements of the industry. Hence, Korea's education and training system responded to the growth of the Korean economy through rapid expansion of student enrollment capacity, which caused the imbalance between quantitative expansion and qualitative improvement of education and the skill mismatch between public training and industrial needs. Korea's education system is a good example of a transformation for national development. The main features of the changes in the Korean educational development model are shown in table 6.2.

Key Success Factors and Limitations of Previous Development

As discussed in the previous section, education has played an important role in Korea's successful industrialization. The government was right to expand the education system based on the needs of the industry and mobilize private resources for this purpose. However, the government-led, supply-side educational policy and planning caused rigidity in the education and training systems and an imbalance between quantitative expansion and qualitative improvement, which turned out to be restraints on Korea's transition to a KBE.

Government's Strategic Approaches to Educational Expansion

After the provision of universal primary education, secondary and tertiary enrollment were expanded in accordance with the human resource needs at the various stages of economic development.

Table 6.2 *Korean Educational Development Model, 1948–2004*

Year	1948–60	1960–80	1980–2000	2000–04
Challenges at the national level	Establishment of national infrastructure	Educational planning for economic development	Enhancement of lifelong learning	Human resources innovation
Strategy	• Implementing a government-initiated approach	• Focusing on traditional institutions of higher education • Continuing the government-initiated approach	• Reaching out to the non-traditional education sector • Using a government-led, partial market approach	• Tightening up the loosely connected system of human resource development • Implementing a government- and market-coordinated approach (market influence increased)
Primary tasks and activities	• Building elementary schools • Developing vocational schools • Developing human resources in medicine, engineering, agriculture, and teacher education	• Improving teaching quality (elementary and secondary education) • Increasing college graduates with engineering majors • Developing medium-skilled human resources	• Developing highly skilled human resources in national strategic fields (information technology, biotechnology, S&T, and so on) • Developing a system of lifelong learning	• Improving quality or relevance of university education • Increasing research productivity • Enhancing the efficiency of the human resource development system • Focusing on regional development and innovation
Resources (tools)	• Seeking foreign assistance (UN Korean Reconstruction Agency, Office of the Economic Coordinator, USOM = U.S Operations Mission, and so on)	• Increasing educational period for new elementary and secondary teachers (2 to 4 years) • Creating vocational colleges • Mobilizing private resources for expansion of the education sector	• Increasing research funds in S&T • Creating diverse types of higher education institutions • Introducing credit-bank system	• Restructuring at government, system, and institutional levels • Infusion of financial support from the government (BK21, post-BK21, NURI)

Source: Author's compilation.
Note: BK21 = Brain Korea 21; NURI = New University for Regional Innovation.

115

The Korean government emphasized primary education at a very early stage of its educational development, before its high-growth phase. In 1954, the government established the six-year plan for accomplishing compulsory education. After achieving universal primary education, the government shifted its investment emphasis to secondary education in the 1960s and 1970s and then to higher education in the 1980s. As the social demand for secondary education increased because of universal primary education, and as the demand for skilled human resources increased with the shift to HCIs, the government had to invest more in secondary education for constructing school buildings and hiring more teachers. And as the number of high-school graduates increased and the average income of households rose, the social demand for higher education increased dramatically.

In 1968, the government abolished the middle-school entrance examination and instead introduced a system of student allocation in which primary-school graduates were assigned to a middle school through a lottery system. With the elimination of the middle-school entrance exam, the flow of students into and out of the middle-school system greatly increased, and, consequently, competition for entrance into the elite high schools became severe. In 1974, the government again responded by adopting the High School Equalization Policy, which was intended to make every high school equal in terms of the students' academic background, educational conditions, teaching staff, and financing. A new admissions policy, which is still in effect in most metropolitan areas, replaced each individual high school's entrance exam with a locally administered standardized test and a lottery system. The abolition of the secondary entrance examinations brought about a great increase in secondary education opportunities.

Higher education expanded rapidly in the mid-1950s because of the government's laissez-faire policy regarding increases in enrollment quotas. The aim of the policy was to accommodate the demand for higher education, which was suppressed during Japanese rule. However, the laissez-faire policy resulted in the oversupply of college graduates and high unemployment rates among the graduates. Thus, the government exercised tight control over the enrollment quotas for each college and university. As a result, college enrollment increased slowly until the 1970s. During the 1970s, the government selectively expanded the enrollment quotas in the fields of engineering, natural sciences, business and commerce, and foreign languages, but it basically maintained the policy of slow expansion. Higher education greatly expanded during the first half of the 1980s under a policy of adopting a graduation enrollment quota system and expanding enrollment quotas. Higher education continued to expand during the 1990s. The main areas of expansion were two-year vocational colleges and the fields of engineering and natural sciences at four-year colleges and universities.

In general, the government's expansion policy for higher education has been effective in terms of supplying high-quality white-collar workers and R&D personnel according to each stage of economic development. Specifically, the government's control over the enrollment quotas during the 1960s and 1970s played a key role in balancing the demand and supply of college graduates in the labor market, consequently reducing inefficiency in the national economy and social problems that resulted from the oversupply and underemployment of college graduates.

The government's expansion policy for higher education effectively supplied high-quality white-collar workers and R&D personnel in line with industrial needs at each stage of economic development.

The Steady Increase of the Education Budget and Efficient Public Funding

The growth rates of the education budget have outpaced those of the GDP, and the government has put a high priority on education spending over the years. From 1963 to 2005, the government's spending on education increased more than 29 times in real terms, and the GDP and the government's overall budget increased 20 times.

As shown in figure 6.6, the share of education budget out of total government budget had remained around 15 percent in 1960 but it has increased over the years, reaching more than 20 percent in 2000s.

The share of in-school expenditures for primary education has steadily decreased since 1963, and those for middle and high schools have increased slightly since 1982. The share of in-school expenditures for higher education increased from 14.3 percent in 1963 to 31.2 percent in 1982, decreased to 27.3 percent in 1990, and increased again to 30.2 percent in 1994. For secondary and higher education, a substantial amount of funding came from the private sector, such as households and private foundations. At the secondary level, the private share is more than 40 percent, and at the tertiary level, it's over 70 percent. Because of budget constraints, the government encouraged private foundations to establish secondary schools and higher education institutions. Expenses for school operation were funded through user fees. Private financing therefore accounts for about two-thirds of total direct costs in education. Also, households in Korea cover much more of education costs (76.7 percent) than do their counterparts in most European countries (see figure 6.7), which is on average about 21.4 percent (MOE and KEDI 2004a).

Figure 6.6 Amount and Share of Education Budget, 1963-2005

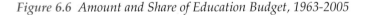

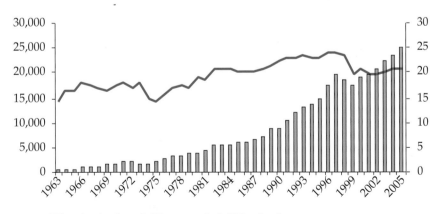

    ▫ Eduation budget (billion won in 2,000 prices)
    — Share of education budget out of total government budget (%, right axis)

Source: Ministry of Education & Human Resource Development and Korea Educational Development Institute, *Statistical Yearbook of Education,* various issues.

Note: GDP deflators were used to change nominal education budgets into 2000 prices.

Figure 6.7 Education Spending as a Percentage of GDP, 2003

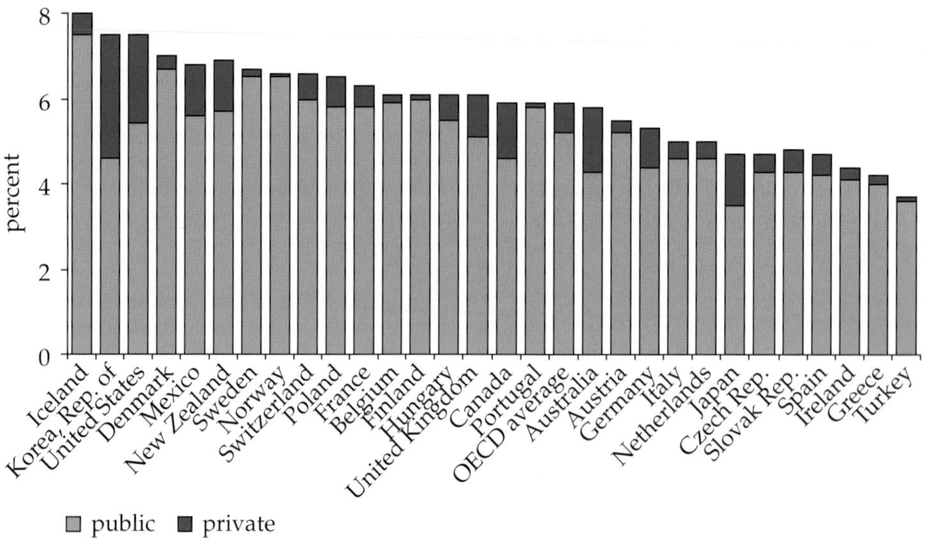

☐ public ■ private

Source: OECD. 2006. *Education at a Glance.* Paris: OECD.

The net effect of educational expansion between 1965 and 1990 showed that secondary school enrollment and investment in education had a positive relationship to Korea's economic growth (McMahon 1995). Expansion of secondary school enrollment and public investment in secondary education were very important in offsetting diminishing returns on investment in physical capital; thus, the investment in education contributed significantly to sustaining the growth of per capita income. Human capital investment has been successful from an economic point of view: it has enabled the timely supply of human resources and offset the diminishing returns to physical capital investment (Paik 1999).

Private Funding for Education

Primary education in Korea has been treated as a collective good, and it has been mostly publicly funded (see figures 6.8 and 6.9). For secondary and higher education, a substantial amount of funding came from the private sector, such as households and private foundations, as mentioned above. The heavy reliance on private funding in secondary and higher education has an important policy implication. Inducing the private sector to play a more active role in providing educational services at the secondary and higher education levels would offer a leverage effect, allowing limited government resources to be spent on prioritized areas. Until recent years, by leaving higher levels of education to the private sector and targeting public resources for primary education, Korea has been able to address one of the main equity issues: basic education for all.

> By encouraging the private sector to shoulder a significant portion of total education costs, Korea has been able to offer universal primary education.

Figure 6.8 Ratio of Private to National/Public Schools, 2005

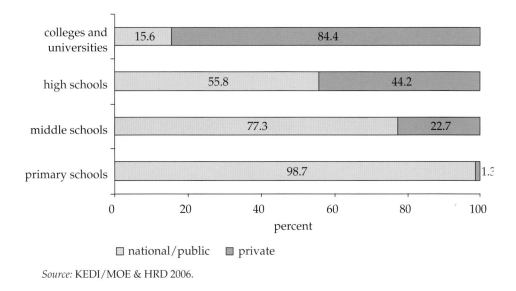

Source: KEDI/MOE & HRD 2006.

Figure 6.9 Enrollment Ratio of Private to National/Public Schools, 2005

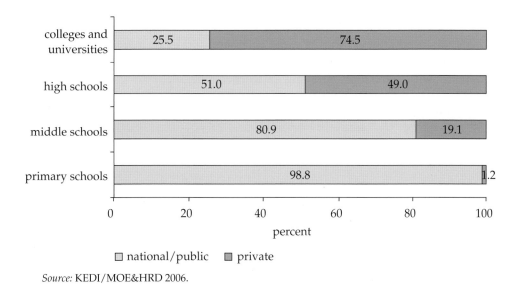

Source: KEDI/MOE&HRD 2006.

However, the central government has also supported private-school foundations through tax benefits. For example, private-school foundations are regarded as
nonprofit organizations, so they can save on corporation tax, which for-profit
organizations cannot do, and they are allowed to receive tax-exempt donations and
endowments. In addition to these benefits, governments have promoted private
schools through loan systems. The Korean Foundation for the Promotion of Private
Schools was established in 1989 to support private schools in improving the educational environment. Long-term loans with low interest rates are provided for pri-

vate schools at any level. Table 6.3 summarizes some statistics of school loans requested and provided for the past 15 years. The Foundation and its loans have turned out to be so successful that even given the limited financial resources at the government level, the education sector has expanded dramatically with the help of private resources.

> The Korean Foundation for the Promotion of Private Schools extended long-term loans with low interest rates to private schools at any level.

Quality Teaching for High Performance

Despite larger class sizes, Korean pupils' achievement levels have been very high compared to those in other OECD countries, as shown in international comparisons of student achievement such as PISA and TIMSS (see figures 6.3a and b). Considering that the numbers of students per teacher and per class in Korea are higher, the Korean education system can be judged to be efficient, at least at the primary and secondary levels. This implies that Korean teachers were able to provide high-quality education according to international standards, despite larger class sizes and, therefore, much lower cost per student. The Korean government has provided diverse incentives to recruit competent people for the teaching profession. Until 1990, public colleges charged no tuition for students training to become teachers. Students were also supported for boarding and other educational expenses. Job security was another factor in recruiting high-quality young people for the teaching profession, especially in times of rapid economic and labor market restructuring. This phenomenon can be clearly observed in the increasing number of high-school graduates with high scores applying for teacher colleges.

However, qualitative achievements of the Korean students are viewed more skeptically. That is, although the Korean school system has successfully responded

Table 6.3 Size of Loans to Private Schools, 1990–2004

Year	Requested No. of schools	Requested Amounts (million won)	Provided No. of schools	Provided Amounts (million won)	Percentage of loans granted No. of schools	Percentage of loans granted Amounts (million won)
1990–94	673	475,447	403	150,900	59.9	31.7
1995	139	156,139	126	65,000	90.6	41.6
1996	148	236,360	142	100,400	95.9	42.5
1997	141	341,165	136	123,050	96.5	36.1
1998	172	492,070	167	126,000	97.1	25.6
1999	130	283,230	120	110,200	92.3	38.9
2000	106	250,030	98	113,940	92.5	45.6
2001	78	198,700	72	114,420	92.3	57.6
2002	87	218,390	80	132,420	92.0	60.6
2003	76	235,060	71	99,930	93.4	42.5
2004	88	302,374	82	124,940	93.2	41.3
Total	1,838	3,188,965	1,497	1,261,200	81.4	39.5

Source: MOE & KEDI 2005.

to the changes in social demand, the very purpose of education—to cultivate students' innate abilities, interests, and creativity and to educate them as a whole person—has been neglected. This neglect has come about mainly because education has been preoccupied with preparing students for the entrance exams to higher levels of school, especially college level. Teacher-centered one-way teaching, rote memorization, and the lack of diversity of educational programs have had a negative impact on the development of individual students' innate abilities and creativity.

> Although the Korean school system has successfully responded to the changes in social demand, the very purpose of education—to cultivate students' innate abilities, interests, and creativity—has been neglected.

Koreans' Meritocratic Values and Strong Educational Zeal

Besides the success factors explained in the preceding section, Koreans' sociocultural and educational values should be emphasized as driving forces for their country's educational development. Koreans' educational attitude is more than enthusiastic, and it is almost obsessive, regardless of socioeconomic status. Korean parents are willing to sacrifice for their children's education, which is expressed as a high propensity to spend for education (table 6.4). Educated Korean mothers do not hesitate to take on drudgery to make more money for their children's tutoring. They wait in front of the cram schools (private institutes to prepare students for college entrance exams) at midnight to pick up their children and stay up all night with their children while they study for exams. Their lives are stopped temporarily until their children go to college. This phenomenon has often been called "education fever" in Korea.

Many factors explain education fever and the intense competition for education, especially for higher education. Among them are historical factors such as the Con-

> Education has an intrinsic social value in the Korean culture. This cultural factor has contributed significantly to the high propensity for private spending in education.

Table 6.4 Divisions of and Trends in of Educational Expenditures, 2003
(percentage of GDP)

| | Public versus. private educational expenditures | | | | | | |
| | Total expenditures on education | | | Primary and secondary education | | Higher education | |
	Total	Public	Private	Public	Private	Public	Private
Korea	7.5	4.6	2.9	3.5	0.9	0.6	2.0
United States	7.5	5.4	2.1	3.9	0.3	1.2	1.6
United Kingdom	6.1	5.1	1.0	4.0	0.6	0.8	0.3
Japan	4.8	3.5	1.2	2.7	0.3	0.5	0.8
Average of OECD countries	5.9	5.2	0.7	3.6	0.3	1.1	0.4

Source: OECD. 2006. *Education at a Glance.* Paris: OECD.

fucian tradition and the repressed educational opportunities during the Japanese colonial period. In addition, socioeconomic factors play a role. The obsession with education is attributed in large part to the importance of credentials in the current Korean society. Diplomas are frequently regarded as the most important criterion for employment, marriage, and interpersonal relationships. Educational achievements are considered a way to upward social mobility in Korea, and this has pressed the government to offer more educational opportunities to the public.

In this sociocultural background, the public policies for educational development have largely been successful, given the scarce public funding for education.

Education Policy—Response to the Needs of a Knowledge-Based Economy

Limitations of Previous Development

Government policies for teacher education and recruitment, such as high salaries and other benefits that upheld the quality of teaching, seemed to be effective despite limited resources for improving schooling conditions. By exempting from taxes the acquisition and sale of properties and by providing subsidies and loans to cover the shortage of remuneration and operating costs, policy incentives to mobilize the private sector provided more educational opportunities with the limited public resources. And contributions from households, which were motivated by socioeconomic and cultural factors, were important for successful implementation of national education development policies.

Under these conditions, Korea's education system has responded well to the basic educational needs of the population and was successful in delivering the human resources required for Korea's industrialization efforts. However, the rule-driven and teacher-centered education policies caused a sheer quantitative expansion of the education system without increasing quality, diversity, and relevance. In that policy context, educational institutions could not provide educational services to flexibly meet the changing socioeconomic demand in a KBE, which led to skill mismatches between labor demand and supply.

Also, in spite of the successful quantitative expansion, quality improvement did not follow suit. The government's investment in education increased steadily but not enough to finance the necessary quality enhancements. The public investment is much below that of the average in OECD countries; the investment gap is mostly supplemented by private sources (figure 6.10).

In addition to the increased investment in education, Korea's education system needs to cultivate creativity. The education reforms since the late 1990s have succinctly stated the challenges faced by Korea (Presidential Commission on Education 1995): "Korean education, having registered a marked growth in quantitative terms in the era of industrialization, will no longer be appropriate in the era of information technology and globalization. It will not be able to produce persons who possess high levels of creativity and moral sensitivity, which are required to sharpen the nation's competitive edge in the coming era." In that context, the Korean government began education reform to increase educational autonomy and accountability to meet the challenges of a KBE.

Figure 6.10 Public Spending on Education (percent of GDP), OECD Countries, 2003

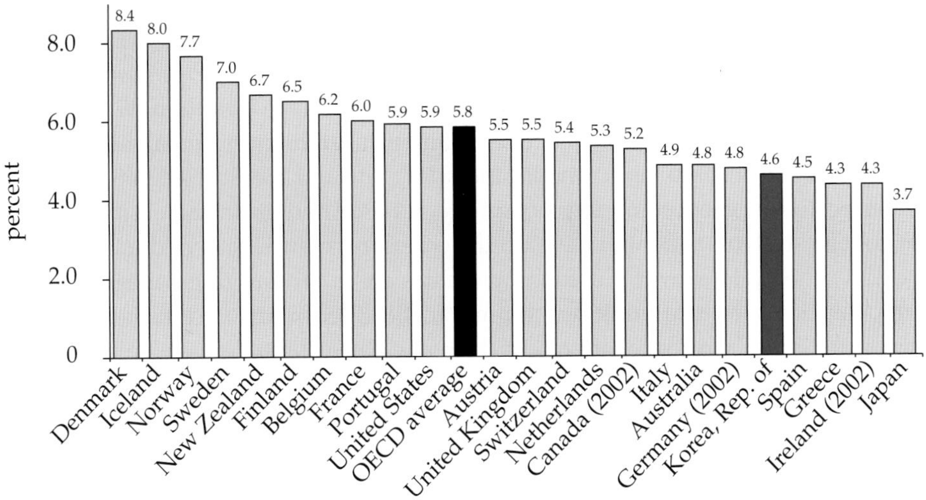

Source: World Bank SIMA database.

Current Issues in Education

Since Korea started economic development plans in the 1960s, it has been able to achieve high economic growth by increasing the input of labor and capital, which required the government to play an active role. In this government-led strategy, which is based on the growth of large-scale industry, the government has been highly centralized and interventionist. The approach has been reflected in Korea's educational development process. Rigid government control over the education system included the curriculum, examination system, tuition fees, number of students, and so forth for both public and private schools. The result of these top-down education policies has been the loss of autonomy and lack of accountability by individual institutions.

As a result, strategic partnerships and connections, along with the institutional and organizational structures that govern such partnerships, among knowledge-producing institutions such as corporations, universities, and research institutions are weak. Such systemic weakness is also found in the international exchange of people and knowledge, such as the debilitated establishment of foreign universities and research institutions in Korea and inadequate participation in joint international research projects. In addition, the brain drain from Korea has accelerated with the increased international competition for highly skilled workers.

Universities have focused on the traditional mission of training scholars and the leaders of society. They have remained passive in the practical application of knowledge and failed to respond effectively to job market realities. The universities have not succeeded in specializing in a manner that reflects the uniqueness of local industry and culture—consequently, their role as a center for creating and disseminating knowledge in the local community has remained weak. Therefore, the training of high-quality human resources and the acquisition of advanced technology have relied on such alternative means as overseas education.

Owing to the expansion of compulsory education and the universalization of higher education, the quantitative basis for supplying human resources is relatively strong in Korea. In contrast, the educational environment has not improved, with the quality of university education and the capabilities of university research remaining poor.

Korea has a large pool of highly educated workers. More than 80 percent of high-school graduates go to college, but there is a problem of imbalance between academic fields. Professional schools, including law and medical schools, are much preferred to the science and engineering faculties. There is an increasing demand for college students who will develop the core competencies needed in the KBE of the 21st century. However, Korean universities are not improving college students' competencies in critical thinking, communication, self-motivated learning, leadership, problem solving, or cooperation (Kim and Rhee 2003).

The financial crisis of 1997 and the corporate restructuring that followed sharply raised the unemployment rate, to 6.8 percent in 1998 and 8.4 percent in the first quarter of 1999. The unemployment rate decreased afterward, but new entrants into the labor market increasingly face difficulties in finding jobs, and switching occupations and seeking reemployment is increasing among the adult population. Jobs for young members of the workforce tend to be less available, so many young people lose the opportunity to experience work and start improving their professional skills.

Meanwhile, although the proportion of women who are economically active has been increasing it was still less than 55 percent. In particular, participation of highly educated women is very low compared to that in advanced industrial countries (figures 6.11 and 6.12). Both development and use of women are low in the engineering and S&T fields. Job creation remains low in the high-value-added areas in which women have relative advantages.

Separation between the education and training system and the labor market made the use of human resources ineffective. The basic information infrastructure for creating links between the education and training system and the labor market, such as forecasting the supply of and demand for labor, information on employment, the certification system, and so forth, needs further development. The mis-

Figure 6.11 Korea–Labor Force Participation Rates by Sex, 1980–2005

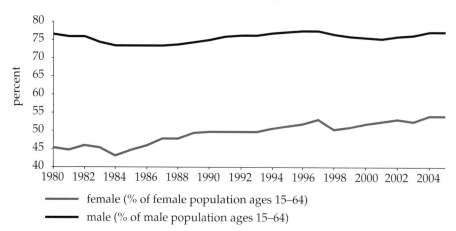

Source: World Bank SIMA database.

Figure 6.12 Female Labor Force Participation Rates, OECD Countries, 2005

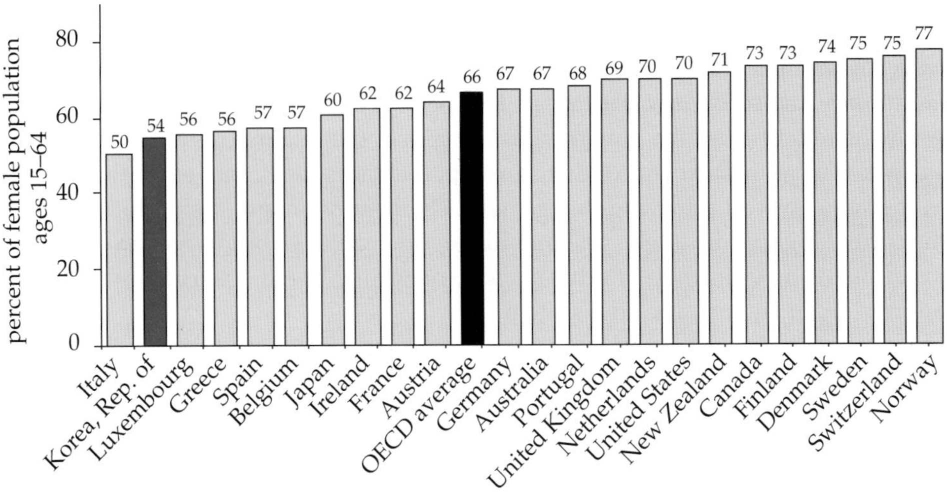

Source: World Bank SIMA database.

match between employment and academic training is serious; there is also a mismatch of skills between supply and demand in the workforce, so that highly educated people are employed in low-level jobs.

> Because of weak university-industry linkages, Korean university graduates are not appropriately trained for Korea's current industrial needs.

Responding to these issues, primary and secondary education now focus more on excellence and creativity than on generality, and tertiary education provides competitive, high-quality education and research. In that context, Korea's education policy and system have been moving forward from the past industrial model toward a knowledge-based model since the mid-1990s, as shown in table 6.5.

Table 6.5 Comparison of Educational Models in Industrial Economies and KBEs

Classification	Industrial model	Knowledge-based model
Government role	Provider of education and training	Facilitator
Human resources input	Labor force	Knowledge and skills
Governance and management	Bureaucratic and centralized	Deregulated and decentralized
Leading sector	Central government and education institution	Education institution, industry, and local government
Policy priority	General education and equity in educational access	Higher education, lifelong learning, excellence, and competitiveness
Policy strategy	Linear expansion	Diversification, innovation, and performance-based funding

Source: Author's compilation.

Higher Education Reform

Higher education draws more attention and importance in government education policies as the economy is transformed toward a KBE. A clear shift has occurred, with government increasing its spending on the higher education sector more than on primary and secondary education. This policy change is caused by two factors. On one hand, because the government recognizes the quality of human resources as the key factor in further economic growth, it regards the higher education sector as the key player in achieving that growth. On the other hand, the performance of the current higher education system in Korea is perceived to be lower than expected in terms of the efficiency of educational spending. These observations call for reforms in the higher education system.

Regulatory Reform

Higher education institutions have insisted that they must have a high degree of freedom from external intervention and of control to perform effectively. The government has steadily carried out such regulatory reforms in higher education since the mid-1990s. As existing laws and regulations on higher education have been revised to give more power to higher education institutions, the Ministry of Education and Human Resources Development (MOE & HRD) is expected to do more planning, coordination, financing, and evaluation.

The main thrust of recent regulatory reforms in higher education is to make the institutions more entrepreneurial and responsive by granting a greater level of autonomy in setting the number of students to be admitted, hiring teaching staff, and managing academic affairs. For example, until 1998, the number of students admitted to colleges and universities was determined by the government based on educational conditions, such as student-faculty ratio, and human resources requirements at the national level. Beginning in 1999, private universities, with the exception of medical schools, teachers' colleges, and universities located in and around the Seoul metropolitan area, were allowed to determine the number of administrative personnel or professors by submitting a proposal stating their standards and plans. Regulatory reforms in the late 1990s also resulted in allowing foreigners to become professors at national public universities, opening the doors to high-quality human resources from overseas. Since 2002, colleges and universities have been permitted to set the amount of tuition fees, depending on each university's specific financial situation.

> Higher education reform focuses on encouraging tertiary institutions to be more entrepreneurial and responsive to industrial needs by granting a greater level of autonomy in both academic and administrative affairs with regard to students and staff.

Despite government efforts, higher education laws, policies, and practices still have regulatory elements regarding many areas in which institutions of higher education are generally considered to have autonomy (Rhee 2003). For instance, institutional activities such as the establishment of universities, organization, curricula, student selection, and staffing are regulated by the Higher Education Act and the related enforcement decree.[1]

Academic Restructuring

Korea has achieved a stage of mass higher education, but it is not easy to see any differences among colleges and universities. Because most institutions of higher learning are interested in quantitative expansion, they underestimate the important missions given to them, such as quality assurance and specialization in unique characteristics. Now, similar departments, colleges, and graduate programs can be easily found in almost all universities. To make the higher education system more diverse, the government pushes colleges and universities to identify their unique strengths and then revise their curriculums, strategic focus, and missions accordingly. During 1998–2002, approximately W 730 billion were granted to support universities' restructuring activities.

Furthermore, the government recently announced a University Restructuring Plan (2004). The key objectives of the plan are to (a) lay the foundation for improving the quality of higher education beyond the growth in quantity, (b) improve the efficiency of tertiary education investment, (c) develop human resources that meet the needs of society, and (d) support development of Korean universities to become world-class institutions (MOE & HRD/KEDI 2004b, 2004c). To achieve these goals, the government provided W 80 billion to 23 institutions of higher education in 2005 and will continue to support them until 2008 if they maintain their qualifications for the project.[2] In addition to the financial incentives, colleges and universities undergoing restructuring or downsizing will be given favorable credits on applications for government-funded higher education projects, such as BK21 and NURI (see boxes 6.1 and 6.2).

Although it is too early to tell whether the government's university-restructuring initiatives will succeed, a fair number of colleges and universities are in the process of restructuring and downsizing. In 2005, 8 national colleges and universities in local provinces were consolidated into 4 universities, and 38 institutions of higher education announced their intention to downsize their enrollments by about 10 percent over the next three years. Nevertheless, it remains to be seen whether the isomorphic institutions of higher education will be able to become distinctive.

Upgrading Research Capability

Until recent years, most applied research has been left to the government research institutes and private sectors. The institutions of higher education in general were not really interested or willing to build up competencies in engineering and science. To strengthen the research capacity of universities, the MOE & HRD set up a plan suggesting two large projects: the second phase of BK21 (2006–12; see box 6.1) and the Five-Year Plan for the Development of Basic Sciences (2005–09). Korea's

---

1. In Korea, the basic rules regarding operation, financing, and status of teaching staff for education systems, including schools and lifelong education, must be stipulated by law according to article 31, paragraph t of the Constitution of the Republic of Korea.

2. Two main conditions to be eligible for the restructuring project are downsizing as planned and putting more internal resources into the fields with competitive advantage.

aim for the two projects is to have about 15 universities with world-class reputations by 2010. The post–BK21 will be more specialized for S&T, whereas the five-year plan is for the humanities and social sciences. The former project is being planned in close cooperation with the ministries dealing with high-tech or national strategic industries, with consideration of the industries' intersectoral character (Jang 2004).

However, at the beginning, BK21 was under strong criticism that it favors a small number of large-scale, research-oriented universities. One critic even argued that it is designed to support Seoul National University (Park 2000). Nevertheless, it is evident that BK21 has greatly improved research capacity of universities. Lee (2002) showed that the amount of research funds that went into BK21 project teams had a positive relationship with research productivity measured by research papers per faculty member. It is also known that the number of research papers written by the faculty members involved in BK21 and published in the Science Citation Index (SCI) journals, such as x increased from 3,765 in 1998 to 7,477 in 2003, or about 42 percent of the SCI journal articles of the nation (MOE & HRD/KEDI 2005).

Strengthening the Link between Universities and Industry

In a historical sense, there has been poor interaction between universities and business at the technical level. One reason is that most large firms have built up their own training and education facilities. As Korea enters the knowledge-based society, the product cycle of knowledge grows shorter and the creation of knowledge determines the future of the entire nation. In this setting, the establishment of a national innovation system that can create, share, and spread new knowledge is welcomed as a novel national strategy and must be based on active exchange and cooperation

---

Box 6.1 Brain Korea 21

BK21 is a national human resource development project that aims to fulfill the demand for high-quality human resources, which Korea will need to thrive in the fierce competition of the knowledge-based society of the 21st century. The ultimate objective of the project is to meet the needs of the times for creative and high-quality R&D human resources.

The seven-year project, which started in 1999 has contributed greatly to improving the research capability of universities and developing excellent human resources. For the past six years, universities involved in BK21 have changed their administrative systems and improved student selection methods to move toward becoming research-oriented institutions. For example, they enhanced research capability by introducing pay for performance based on professors' research achievements, thus creating a favorable environment for research.

The second phase of the BK21 project began in February 2006, and is scheduled to continue until 2012. Based on the research infrastructure built during the first phase of the project and the "selection and concentration" strategy, the second phase will focus on the S&T sector that will have more direct impacts on nation's economic development. Support will be provided for the development of high-caliber researchers (in particular, students in their master's degree and doctoral programs), international exchange and cooperation, and innovative curriculum development.

among human resources of universities, government research agencies, and private industry.

In an effort to foster proactive collaboration and create a channel for communi-

> It is imperative the Korea develop a national innovation system whereby knowledge is generated and shared, and R&D is coordinated and collaborated on by universities, government research agencies, and the private sector.

cating the demands and needs of industry to the education community, the government is formulating a new industry-academia collaboration system, which is based on the Act on the Promotion of Industrial Education & Industry/Academia Collaboration. Taking into consideration the diverse regional characteristics and unique circumstances of universities and industries, the MOE & HRD has classified cases of industry-academia collaboration into three groups (see table 6.6). Policy implementation and financial support will be closely tied to the collaborative system to eventually create a university system that fully incorporates the industry-academia collaboration framework.

In addition to financial support, the government introduced two new features into the higher education system. One is a contract-based education system that enables close ties between industry and academia. This system has been established to allow the needs of the industrial sector to be directly reflected in the operation of the university curriculum. For example, new majors as well as departments may be established under contract between universities and private enterprises. The contract may stipulate matters related to the student quota, student selection process, curriculum, teaching and learning processes, and so forth. Upon graduation, students enrolled in the program will receive favorable employment opportu-

Table 6.6 Types of Collaboration between Industry and Academia

Type 1	*Human resources endowed with world-class research and development capabilities*
	• Project to upgrade universities that conduct research in their graduate schools, turning them into research centers (BK21, 1999–2005): W 1.5 trillion • Project to support academic research environment (2002–04): W 660 billion
Type 2	*Human resources for high-tech development*
	• Innovation project (NURI) to reinforce the capabilities of universities outside the Seoul metropolitan area and vicinity (2004): W 220 billion • Project for the specialization of universities in the Seoul metropolitan area (2004): W 60 billion
Type 3	*Human resources for industrial technology*
	• Selection of universities to be industry-academia collaboration universities by each region (2004): W 30 billion • Project to identify unique characteristics of junior colleges (2004): W 175 billion

Source: Yoon 2003.

nities from the companies. The other feature is a school-enterprise system that enables the practical application of the research conducted through the industry-academia collaboration (Jang 2004).

It is fair to say that the link between universities and industry is expected to get stronger because a new regional governance system, the Regional Innovation Committee (consisting of key stakeholders in each major city and each province) has been set in place to facilitate communication among the key stakeholders. Financial support from both central and local governments is available; however, the collaboration among them is not as active as expected.

Provision of Lifelong Learning for Human Resource Development (HRD)

Human resource development was a relatively new term in Korea in the early 1990s, but its origin can be traced to early vocational education programs under the first economic development plan (1962–66). Now human resource development is widely perceived by both employers and employees to be one of the key factors for long-term corporate success and individual growth.

Government initiatives in the early years included supports for establishing training institutions such as the Korea Productivity Center (KPC), Korea Management Association (KMA), and Korea Standards Association (KSA). During the 1980s, these institutions began to develop systematic training programs tailored to Korean firms. The first national training conference was held in 1980 to discuss visions for and strategies of training in Korea. Since then, many companies have established their own training departments and training centers with instructors trained by the KPC, KMA, and KSA. To help establish systematic training programs, magazines on personnel management and vocational training were published in 1989 and 1990 to provide basic theories, methods, and information to human resource development practitioners.

In the early 1990s, the human resource development profession also became involved in developing a professional certification process and established undergraduate, graduate, and continuing education programs for its practitioners. Training and development programs expanded to include training in skills and technical expertise, management, organizational development, global business, customer

---

Box 6.2 New University for Regional Innovation

NURI is a government-funded project for local universities that is aimed at diversification and specialization, higher employment rates for local university graduates, and creating a greater role for local universities as centers of regional innovation by strengthening ties within a region with local governments, companies, and research institutions.

The government will invest W 1,360 billion in the NURI project, and the fund will be allocated to 13 cities and provinces based on population and number of students and universities. The project, which started in 2004, has not yet been assessed for its achievement. In 2004, 112 project groups were selected for their outstanding achievements. The MOE & HRD plans to conduct annual assessments and an interim assessment (in the third year of the project), which will include an assessment of budget execution and performance versus targets and make recommendations.

satisfaction, quality control, cultural issues, and multimedia use. This period brought about significant changes that affected the growth of the human resource development field until the economic crisis in 1997.

The economic crisis in 1997 forced Korean firms to restructure, with the side effect of reducing resources and opportunities for employee training. According to a survey on corporate training in the top 200 companies (MOE & HRD/KEDI 1998), more than 70 percent of the companies reported decreases in training expenses. Employers in Korean firms had a dilemma in that the only way to overcome the economic crisis was to have companies invest in human resource development to provide core competencies of a globally competitive level; however, they were reluctant to invest their limited resources in human resource development. What was worse, many firms had eliminated their human resource development staff, and as a result, their expertise was to some extent lost from those firms' business functions.

The government's policy foci and tasks have changed in accordance with changes in the human resource development environment (see table 6.7). In recent years, the development and use of competent and adaptable human resources have grown in importance. Individuals invest financial and other resources in their lifelong learning as a strategic imperative to survive and enhance employability in the era of ongoing downsizing. Business enterprises now find themselves competing to attract, develop, and retain employees to build knowledge-based organizations. Many firms participate in the lifelong learning movement in Korea. The Korean government has made great efforts to transform the nation into a knowledge-based society by developing regional learning societies in cooperation with local governments.

Table 6.7 Shifts in the Human Resource Development Paradigm in Korea

	1960–80	*1980s*	*1990s*	*2000–05*
Environment changes	• National economic development plans • Rapid economic growth	• Continuous high growth	• Globalization • Knowledge-based society • Economic crisis	• Networked learning society
Human resource development	• Vocational and technical education	• Outreach programs	• Strategic human resource development	• Individuals' right to lifelong learning
Focus of government policies	• Investment in vocational high schools and colleges	• Investment for the disadvantaged	• High performers and experts	• Investment in learning for all
Major policy tasks	• Financial supports for vocational and technical education	• Training for the unemployed • Training supports for SMEs	• Cost-saving policies (e-learning) • Encouragement of private sector investment	• Creation of ubiquitous learning environments • Learning accounts • Learning partnerships

Source: Prepared by Korea Research Institute for Vocational Education and Training.

Conclusion

Some key policy lessons can be drawn from the Korean experience in developing skills and human resources for the KBE: (a) education and training are critical, (b) education and training need to be relevant to the particular needs of industries and various sectors of the economy, and (c) education and training need to develop over time to keep pace with the changing needs of the economy.

The Korean economy has made enormous progress over the past four decades, and education has played a pivotal role. The primary lessons of those experiences are straightforward: investment in human resource development pays off in the long run and is even more crucial in the KBE. It is clear that the early governments were fully aware of the importance of human resources in rebuilding the economy that was demolished during the Korean War, because they strategically invested in human resource development.

What Korea has implemented as part of its human resource development may have some implications for developing or underdeveloped countries that are in the process of restructuring their educational systems to narrow the economic gap between themselves and countries that are economic leaders. Progressive quantitative expansion from compulsory elementary to higher education should be first, followed by qualitative improvements in each educational level. However, it doesn't necessarily mean that this model should work for developing or underdeveloped countries, because they may have different problems in a world that has changed substantially. In Korea's process, the government's policy of intervention turned out to be critical. For example, during the developmental stages in the 1960s and 1970s, when the key industries, such as manufacturing, needed a skilled workforce, the government responded by creating vocational high schools and vocational colleges. Although expanding the educational system usually comes up first as a handy policy option to revitalize the national economy, budget constraints are always considered to be a limiting factor. Korea's governments dealt with this issue by using private resources. By having secondary and tertiary education be partially funded by the private sector, they reduced financial burdens and didn't harm equity when the education sector experienced its dramatic expansion.

Although Korea's experiences worked out well, the Korean government faces new challenges in maintaining cost-effective human resource development in national strategic areas and lifelong learning. Reforming the higher education sector and establishing a lifelong learning system to upgrade human resource capability are national tasks for all countries. Most governments, including Korea's, are under pressure to reduce the growth of public spending on education and find other sources of funding for the expected expansion of their education system. Thus, finance-driven reform measures have been introduced, and policies give priority to cost-effectiveness (Kim 2002). Following the policy framework, new reform measures to increase educational quality and accountability, such as performance-based funding for higher education, have been introduced in Korea.

As a result of Korea's previous success in establishing an education system infrastructure and expanding higher education opportunities, the country is taking a new approach to educational reform that focuses more on qualitative performance of the system in terms of both the quality of human resources' skills and research productivity. To achieve those purposes, the role of the government is changing, from that of regulator to facilitator, and competition between educational institutions is being enforced to make education and training systems more cost-effective and productive. The active government intervention that once made educational development possible is now counted as the main cause of the educational system's inefficiency. Similarly, current reforms emphasize the relevance of university education and the responsiveness of higher education institutions to social and economic needs. Thus, the new challenge for the Korean government in the current education reform process will be to maintain consistent policies of deregulation and decentralization. Finally, because the development of a KBE requires the creation of sustainable learning opportunities and learning societies, the public and private sectors now have a mutual responsibility to develop learning partnerships. To fulfill this purpose, private firms are becoming important partners in the learning society as they provide ever more opportunities for continuous learning to their employees and their regions. The government's role in this process will be to establish a learning infrastructure to foster learning and eliminate barriers to the creation of a learning society. In short, knowledgeable workers, lifelong learning organizations, and a networked learning society have become, and will remain, key success factors for individuals, organizations, and nations.

7

Harnessing the Potential of Science and Technology

Sungchul Chung and Joonghae Suh

Considering the relationship between industrialization and S&T, the Republic of Korea's innovation system (KIS) has evolved in line with the stages of industrial development in the country. When Korea launched its industrialization drive in the early 1960s, it suffered from many of the problems that were common among poor economies in those days. Korea, a resource-poor country, had neither the capital nor the technology required for industrialization. It was then a barren land as far as S&T were concerned. Korea thus had to opt for an outward-looking development strategy—a development strategy reliant on foreign resources, capital, markets, and technologies.

The 1960s were a period of technological learning for the development of light industries. During the 1970s, Korea focused on the development of heavy machinery and chemical industries, and it was during this period that the government created the Government Research Institutes (GRIs) in the fields of heavy machinery and chemicals to compensate domestic industries for their technological weaknesses. At this stage, Korea relied on foreign sources rather than domestic R&D for the technologies required for industrialization; therefore, its S&T policy was geared to facilitating learning from foreign technologies while developing a domestic S&T infrastructure.

It was only in the early 1980s, stimulated by changes in economic environments, that Korea embarked on serious efforts to develop indigenous R&D. Industrial development had reached such a stage that Korean industries could no longer rely on imported technologies and cheap domestic labor to compete in international markets. However, as Korean industries grew to be potential competitors in the international market, foreign companies became increasingly reluctant to transfer technologies to Korea, making it inevitable for Korea to develop an indigenous base for research and innovation.

To meet the challenge, Korea required a supply of highly trained scientists and engineers, as well as financial resources, to support R&D activities that are by nature uncertain and risky. Korea was fortunate in this respect, because, thanks to Koreans' aspiration for education, the country had a large pool of scientists and engineers and also because the large Korean conglomerates were financially able to venture into new technologies. By the early 1990s, Korea's R&D investment exceeded 2 percent of GDP, of which private industries accounted for more than 80 percent. This was a period when Korea's R&D grew rapidly, and the country's efforts to attain technological competence became successful. By the end of the decade, Korean industries had emerged as new leaders in memory chips, cellular phones, LCDs, and other technologies, and they established themselves in world markets in such areas as shipbuilding, automobiles, home appliances, and telecommunications.

The Asian financial crisis of 1997 struck a serious blow to innovation in Korea. Private businesses responded to the crisis by severely cutting R&D investments. To counteract the economic effects of declining R&D investments in the private sector, the government increased R&D spending to 5 percent of its budget, focusing on the development of IT and related industries. During this period, IT sectors played key roles in innovation in Korea, leading the country's recovery from the economic crisis as well as its move toward a KBE.

This chapter provides an overview of the research and development, and innovation system of Korea. It also identifies the strengths and weakness of the system and attempts to draw policy lessons for developing countries..

Industrialization and Technology Development

Initial Conditions

When Korea first launched its industrialization drive, it was an underdeveloped country with a poor resource and production base, a small domestic market, and a large population, and it depended on foreign powers for national security. The economic situation in the early 1960s in Korea was more than bleak: Korea's GNP in 1961 was only US$2.3 billion (in 1980 prices)—US$87 per capita. At the time, the main source of income was the primary sectors, with the manufacturing sector accounting for only 15 percent of GNP. International economic interactions were also very limited. In 1961, Korea's export volume was only US$55 million and imports were US$390 million. All these indicate that Korea was then one of the poorest countries in the world, suffering from all the socioeconomic problems that poor countries faced in those days.

The S&T situation was even bleaker. There were only two public institutions for scientific research and technological development: the National Defense Research and Development Institute, which was created right after the end of the Korean War, and the Korea Atomic Energy Research Institute, which was founded in 1959. On this base, the Korean government invested US$9.5 million on R&D in 1963, employing less than 5,000 research scientists and engineers.[1] As far as S&T were concerned, Korea was a barren land.

---

1. There are no statistics on R&D human resources for the early 1960s in Korea. The number here is an estimate based on the figure for 1969, which was 5,337 (MOST 1984).

Technology Acquisition for Industrialization

> When the S&T capability was at the earliest stage in the early 1960s, Korea focused on promoting the inward transfer of foreign technologies and developing domestic capacity to digest, assimilate, and improve upon the transferred technologies and adapt them for domestic production.

In 1962, Korea launched the first five-year economic development plan This and subsequent plans created huge demand for new technologies that were in no way available from domestic sources. Lacking in technological capability, Korea had to rely almost exclusively on imported foreign technologies. At the early stage, Korea pursued two objectives in this respect: promoting the inward transfer of foreign technologies and developing domestic absorptive capacity to digest, assimilate, and improve upon the transferred technologies. Of the various alternative channels for technology acquisition, such as FDI, foreign licensing, and importation of turnkey plants, FDI is often advocated as an effective means for developing countries to acquire new production skills and management expertise, such as in the case of Singapore. Unlike in other developing countries, however, FDI played a less important role in Korea as a source of capital and technology in the early years of industrialization.[2] In contrast to the relatively minor contribution of FDI to Korea's acquisition of foreign technologies, combinations of arm's length methods such as reverse engineering, original equipment manufacturing (OEM), and foreign licensing have been critical to transferring technologies and supplementing local efforts (table 7.1).

> In the early years of industrialization, Korea relied on reverse engineering, OEM, and foreign licensing as means of tapping and assimilating foreign technologies.

Korea resorted to long-term foreign loans to finance industrial investments. The Korean government brought in large-scale foreign loans and allocated them to investments in selected industries, which led to massive importation of foreign capital goods and turnkey plants. To acquire the necessary technologies, industries later reverse engineered imported capital goods.

---

2. FDI played a less important role because of government policy that restricted it in various ways, such as ownership restrictions, repatriation restrictions, technology transfer requirements, and export requirements. Such a restrictive policy was used partly because multinationals were then viewed by many Koreans as perpetuating economic and technological dependence, thus reinforcing the asymmetrical relationship between the industrialized and the developing countries (Koo 1986; Vernon 1977; Stewart 1978). Also, foreign investors did not view Korea as an attractive place for investment. Even though Korea had a very open and liberal policy on FDI in the 1960s, few investments were made, primarily because of questions about Korea's political stability and economic outlook.

Table 7.1 Channels of Foreign Technology Transfer to Korea, 1962–2005
(US$ millions)

	FDI	Sum of foreign licensing and capital goods imports	Foreign licensing	Capital good imports
1962–66	45.4	316.8	0.8	316
1967–71	218.6	2,557.3	16.3	2,541
1972–76	879.4	8,937.6	96.6	8,841
1977–81	720.6	28,429.4	451.4	27,978
1982–86	1,767.7	52,162.9	1,184.9	50,978
1987–91	5,635.9	125,311.4	4,359.4	120,952
1992–96	8,405.2	228,160.8	7,317.8	220,843
1997–2001	57,850.8	265,228.0	13,192.4	252,034
2002–05	39,918.4	318,608.2	14,630.6	303,977

Source: National Statistical Office.

Private companies' responses to such restrictive policies varied across industries. In the case of light industries such as shoes, clothing, textiles, and some intermediate goods for import substitution as well as export, the major sources of technological learning were OEM arrangements and technical training as part of the importation of turnkey plants. Korean firms benefited most from the OEM arrangements because they offered opportunities to work with foreign buyers who provided everything from product designs and materials to quality control at the end of production. This was especially so in the case of the garment and electronics industries (Hobday 1995).

During the 1970s, Korea made massive investments in the machinery and chemical industries. For the development of chemical industries, Korea relied largely on importing turnkey plants, which included technical training programs as part of the packages. In the case of heavy machinery, foreign licensing was an important channel for technology acquisition (Chung and Branscomb 1996). To compensate for the technological weakness of domestic industries, the government created GRIs in the fields of heavy machinery and chemicals, such as the Korea Institute of Machinery and Metals, the Electronics and Telecommunications Research Institute, the Korea Research Institute of Chemical Technology, the Korea Research Institute of Standards and Science, the Korea Institute for Energy Research, and the Korea Ocean Research and Development Institute. These institutes worked with private industries to build the technological foundation for industrial development.

To compensate for the technological weakness of domestic industries in the 1970s, the Korean government created GRIs to work with private industries to developed the necessary technological foundation for industrialization.

In short, Korean industries were dependent more upon informal channels for technology acquisition than on formal channels. The Korean approach to technology acquisition resulted in both positive and negative effects. On the positive side, this policy enabled Korea to acquire technologies at lower costs and precluded the constraints often imposed by multinationals on local firms' efforts to develop their own capability. The approach was effective in maintaining independence from the dominance of multinationals. The negative effect was that Korea had to give up an important access to new technologies that might have been available through direct equity links with foreign firms. By restricting FDI, Korea failed to set global standards in domestic business operation. Much worse, large-scale foreign loans that had been used to finance the massive importation of capital goods, plants, and foreign licensing contributed to the financial crisis in 1997. The most important lesson here is that had Korea not had its well-educated workforce, the country would not have succeeded in acquiring and using technologies through informal modes of technology transfer.

Domestic Technological Activities

As industrial development continued into the 1980s, the technological requirements of Korean industries became more complex and sophisticated. At the same time, advanced countries began to view Korea as a potential competitor in the international market. As a result, foreign companies became increasingly reluctant to transfer new technologies to their Korean counterparts. To facilitate international technological interaction of private industries, the government loosened its regulation of FDI and liberalized foreign licensing during the 1980s. However, the deregulation and liberalization did not lead to significant increases in FDI inflow and foreign licensing.

> With increased technological capability, Korea became a potential competitor in the global market, and, consequently, opportunities to assimilate imported technology became less readily available. This necessitated the development of indigenous capability for research and innovation.

The government viewed this as a signal that to sustain the development, it would have to build indigenous R&D capability. The government launched the National R&D Program in 1982 and took various policy measures to promote and facilitate private R&D activities (see box 2.3 in chapter 2 on the policy initiatives of the early 1980s). Private industries responded to the policy by investing heavily in R&D. Thus, the relationship between technology imports and R&D changed. The ratio of technology imports to business R&D declined sharply, from about 40 percent in 1981 to 20 percent in the mid-1980s, to 10 percent in the early 1990s, and staying around 20 percent after 2000 (see figure 2.8 in chapter 2). This implies that Korean industries turned to indigenous R&D for technology acquisition. R&D investment has since undergone a quantum leap. Korea's R&D investment, which stood at only W 368.8 billion (US$526 million, 0.81 percent GDP) in 1981, rose to W 24,155 billion (US$23.6 billion, 3 percent of GDP) in 2005 (figure 7.1). Over a period of 25 years, investment in R&D increased almost 19 times in real terms, with an average annual growth rate of almost 12 percent. It can be seen from figure 7.2 that Korea ranks sixth among the OECD countries in terms of GERD as a share of GDP.

Figure 7.1 Gross Expenditure on Research and Development in Korea, 1964-2005

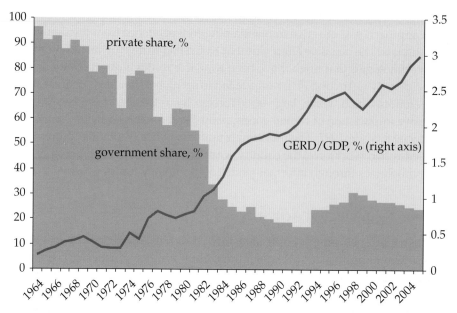

Source: Ministry of Science and Technology.

Figure 7.2 GERD (Share of GDP), Average for 2002–05

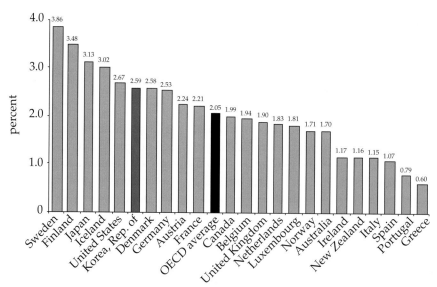

Source: World Bank SIMA database.

Consistent increases in R&D investment by the private sector over the past 40 years have contributed significantly to the rapid increase in Korea's GERD.

The rapid increases in total R&D expenditure were made possible by active expansion of investment by the private sector. During the earlier years of industrialization, private sector R&D spending was negligible. In 2004, the private sector accounted for 75 percent of the nation's total R&D investment. Because private industries lead R&D investment, R&D activities in Korea are very much focused on applied research and technology development, reflecting the interest of private industries. In the 1980s, about 83 percent of R&D funds were used for applied research and technology development, and the share increased to 87 percent in the 1990s. Korea spends far less on basic research than advanced countries such as the United States, Japan, France, and Germany. The general tendency is that the richer a country is, the more it invests in basic scientific research; however, Korea's investment in basic scientific research has declined over time despite economic growth, which is against conventional expectations.

Many factors may have contributed to the rapid increase in private sector R&D investments, but such an increase basically has been possible because Korean firms have been put under market pressure for technology development. The government contributed to such development in two indirect ways. First, the outward-looking development strategy (export-driven) of the government drove domestic industries to international markets, exposing them to fierce competition. To survive the competition, they have had to keep up with technological changes by investing heavily in R&D.

> Korea's export-driven development strategy compelled domestic firms to invest heavily in R&D to remain globally competitive, resulting in increases in productivity and efficiency.

Second, the government's industrial policy that favored large firms gave birth to a unique business organization in Korea called the chaebol, a conglomerate that is similar to the *zaibatsu* of Japan before World War II. Chaebols enjoy greater financial affluence as a result of the economies of both scale and scope of their business operation. Chaebols, which are usually big international operators, have deeper pockets and are able to engage in risky and expensive R&D projects that are unthinkable for small and medium firms. This is explained by the fact that the top 20 firms receive about 57 percent of the total industrial R&D investments in Korea (KITA 2004).

Most important, Korea has been able to increase R&D investments at such a rate because it has an abundant, highly educated labor force that could meet the increasing demand for R&D services in both the private and public sectors. Considering that R&D investment by both developed and developing countries is more constrained by the lack of human resources than financial limitation, Korea clearly had prepared itself well for development by investing heavily in education and human resource development.[3]

---

3. OECD (2003d) emphasizes the importance of the supply of skilled scientists and engineers as one of the framework conditions for achieving R&D spending targets.

> Korea has been able to increase R&D investments at a rapid rate because of the availability of educated human resources to meet the growing demand for R&D services. Indeed, it is often the case that the countries are constrained by the lack of adequately trained human resources rather financial resources when it comes to investing in R&D.

R&D in Korea had been growing rapidly and continuously until Korea was hit by the financial crisis in 1997. R&D was one of the most damaged victims of the crisis. In a survey undertaken in early 1998, many companies responded that they would cut R&D investments and R&D personnel by almost 20 percent in response to the crisis. Actually, industrial R&D expenditures decreased by 10 percent in nominal terms, from W 884.4 billion in 1997 to W 797.2 billion in 1998, and R&D personnel dropped by 15 percent, from 102,000 in 1997 to 87,000 in the next year. This was a serious blow to the KIS. If the crisis had continued for several more years, the KIS would have collapsed. Fortunately, however, Korea recovered from the crisis in a relatively short time. It took only two years for the industrial R&D to recover and rise above the level achieved before the financial crisis (see table 7.2).

Two factors account for the rebound of R&D investment. One is the government's efforts to make up for the decrease in industrial R&D expenditures by increasing government R&D expenditures. The government's share of GERD increased from less than 20 percent of total expenditures before the crisis to 27 percent after the crisis. Government R&D funds flew into private industrial sectors—in particular, small technology-based firms—and helped them maintain and expand innovation activities. The other factor is the promotion of IT and IT-related ventures that led to an IT boom in the early 2000s. The government's commitment to IT development is well reflected in the fact that the share of IT in government R&D expenditures rose to 33.5 percent in 2002 from 13 percent in 1997. Such a pro-IT policy fueled innovation in that sector, which then affected innovation activities in other sectors. This policy not only helped the KIS recover vitality but also promoted Korea's transition toward an information society.

Government and Public Sector R&D

Since the early 1960s, the government has played a key role in Korea's development. The government first initiated S&T development as part of the national economic development plan, and it has led the development, not just as a rule setter but also as a target setter as well as a financier. As discussed in the preceding section, S&T policy in Korea has been closely linked to industrial development, and thus policy priorities have been adjusted in response to the changes in industrial development targets. In the 1960s and 1970s, the government set specific policy goals and led the private industries in pursuing the goals. However, as industrial development proceeds, it has become increasingly difficult for the government to intervene in economic and R&D activities because of the increased scale and complexity of industrial activities. Therefore, the pattern of government intervention in S&T has also changed from direct involvement as a target setter and commander-in-chief type of leader to indirect involvement as a facilitator and promoter. This is

Table 7.2 Basic Statistics on Korea's R&D, 1965–2005

	1965	1970	1975	1980	1985	1990	1995	2000	2005
R&D expenditure									
(in billion won)	2.1	10.5	42.7	282.5	1,237.1	3,349.9	9,440.6	13,848.5	24,155.4
Government	1.9	9.2	30.3	180.0	306.8	651.0	1,780.9	3,451.8	5,877.2
Private sector	0.2	1.3	12.3	102.5	930.3	1,698.9	7,659.7	10,387.2	18,106.8
Government versus private sector	61:39	97:03	71:29	64:36	25:75	19:81	19:81	25:75	25:75
University R&D	NA	0.4	2.2	25.9	118.8	244.3	770.9	1,561.9	2,398.3
GRI R&D	NA	8.9	28.1	104.5	367.2	731.0	1,766.7	2,032.0	3,192.9
Corporate R&D	0.2	1.3	12.3	81.4	751.0	2,374.5	6,903.0	10,254.7	18,564.2
R&D as percentage of GNP	0.3	0.4	0.4	0.8	1.6	2.0	2.5	2.4	3.0
Manufacturing sector R&D									
expenditure (in billion won)	NA	NA	16.7	76.0	688.6	2,134.7	5,809.9	8,584.9	16,463.7
Percent of sales	NA	NA	0.4	0.5	1.5	2.0	2.7	2.2	2.7
Number of researchers	2,135	5,628	10,275	18,434	41,473	70,503	128,315	159,973	234,702
GRI	1,671	2,458	3,086	4,598	7,542	10,434	15,007	13,913	15,501
Universities	352	2,011	4,534	8,695	14,935	21,332	44,683	51,727	64,895
Private sector	112	1,159	2,655	5,141	18,996	38,737	68,625	94,333	154,306
R&D expenditure per researcher									
(in thousand won)	967	1,874	4,152	15,325	27,853	47,514	73,574	86,568	102,920
Researchers per 10,000 population	0.7	1.7	2.9	4.8	10.1	16.4	28.6	34.0	48.6
Number of corporate R&D centers	0	1	12	54	183	966	2,270	7,110	11,810

Source: Ministry of Science and Technology.
Note: GRI = government research institute.
NA = not available.

a natural course of change in view of the growth of private industries in R&D and of changes in management and information capabilities.

> S&T and innovation polices in Korea have been closely linked to industrial development, and thus policy priorities have been adjusted in response to the changes in industrial development targets over the decades.

Evolution of Public Sector R&D

When the government first launched the National R&D Program in 1982, its R&D expenditures were only W 263 billion, but the expenditures exceeded W 5 trillion in 2004, which implies 13.6 percent average annual growth rates (see table 7.2). Together with the increases in investment, the nature of the National R&D Program has also changed over time (see table 7.3). In the formative stage (roughly during the first four years, 1982–85), the main objective of the program was to facilitate the absorption of foreign technologies. In other words, the program's focus was on the development of technologies required for the local production of major products, parts, components, and materials that were considered essential to industrial development in those days. During this period, the National R&D Program relied totally on a bottom-up approach for project selection, and priority was given to those proposals involving private enterprises.

The next five years, 1986–90, can be dubbed a takeoff stage, because the objective of the program was gradually switched from the simple internalization of foreign industrial technologies to the development of core technologies that private industries were not able to tackle because of the technical and financial risks. The program also aimed at building up a technological base for high-technology industries. Accordingly, project selections were partly linked to long-term technology development plans.

At about the end of the takeoff stage (around the end of the 1980s and the early 1990s), other ministries began to establish their own R&D programs to solve the

Table 7.3 *Changes in the National R&D Program by Stages*

	Formation stage (1982–85)	*Takeoff stage (1986–90)*	*Maturing stage (1991–)*
National R&D Program objective	Internalization of foreign technologies	Development of core technologies	Creative research, future-oriented research
Planning	No planning: bottom-up	Based on a loose long-term plan	R&D planning, technology foresight
Main actors	GRIs	Main: GRIs Minor: Universities and industries	Main: GRIs, with increased role of universities and industries

Source: MOST 1997b.

problems in the areas of their purview. The Ministry of Commerce, Industry, and Energy launched the Industrial Base Technology Development Program in 1987 and the Alternative Energy Development Program in 1988. The MIC created the Information and Communications Technology Development Program in 1989, and several other ministries followed these actions in the subsequent years (see table 7.4). Until 1987, the National R&D Program of MOST was the only government-sponsored R&D program, and MOST was the sole player in public sector research. But with the emergence of other ministries on the scene, the role of MOST has been reduced gradually. In 2003, the share of MOST in government R&D expenditures stood at only 20.5 percent.

The rapid growth of government R&D investment is the result of increased political pressure for economic and social contributions to the investment. The

Table 7.4 Government Ministries' R&D Programs

Ministry	Year initiated	Major program	Management agencies
MOST	1982	Specific R&D Program	Korea Institute of Science and Technology Evaluation & Planning Korea Science and Engineering Foundation
Ministry of Commerce, Industry, and Energy	1987, 1988	Industrial Base Technology Development Program Alternative Energy Development Program	Korea Institute of Industrial Technology Evaluation and Planning
MIC	1989	ICT Development Program	Institute of Information Technology Assessment
Ministry of Environment	1992, 1996	Environmental Engineering Technology Development Program Environmental Basic Technology Development Program	National Institute of Environmental Research
Ministry of Construction and Transportation	1994	Construction Technology Development Program	Korea Institute of Construction Technology
Ministry of Agriculture and Forestry	1994	Agricultural Technology Development Program	Agricultural R&D Promotion Center
Ministry of Health and Welfare	1995	Health and Medical Technology Development Program	Korea Health Industry Development Institute
MOE & HRD	1983	Basic Scientific Research Support Program	Korea Research Foundation

Source: MOST 1997b; National Science and Technology Council (NSTC) 2004.

question has been, What good do the government R&D programs do for the future of the nation? At the same time, the private industrial sector, as a major financial contributor, became increasingly skeptical about the economic value of the results of government R&D investments. However, as individual ministries created their own R&D programs, the problem of interministerial resource allocation emerged as an important policy issue. In other words, the diversification of government R&D programs brought up a new set of issues, such as duplication of research efforts, delineation of R&D areas among different ministries, interministerial R&D priority setting, and efficient allocation of the R&D budget.

All of these issues boil down to the question of how to allocate the limited resources and to which areas. The question is not only technological but also economic and political, in that government R&D programs are justified only by the taxpayers' consent to the investment. To deal with the issues, in the mid-1980s, the government adopted the concept of technology planning and evaluation in implementing the government R&D programs. In other words, in setting priorities for technology development, the government used a strategic approach based on long-term planning. Industries and academia participated in the process so that the interests of private industries and academia could be reflected in the planning of the government R&D programs. During this period, collaborative research among industry, academia, and the GRIs was first undertaken as part of the government R&D programs. The International Cooperative Research Program was also launched during this period.

Yet it was not until 1992 that a Korean system of public sector R&D management took shape. In that year, the government launched the Highly Advanced National (HAN) Project, a 10-year, interministerial R&D program to develop core technologies for industrial development into the 21st century.[4] The HAN Project was the first government R&D program developed through a full cycle of planning, including technology foresight, ex ante planning, and interministerial consultation. Through these stages, the government R&D expenditures grew very rapidly, from W 263 billion in 1982 to W 4,664 billion in 2003. As a result of this growth, MOST, as a funder of R&D, has been reduced from being the sole player in public sector R&D to just one of the major players.

Because of the cross-sectoral nature of innovation, the Korean government developed the HAN Project, a 10-year, interministerial R&D program to develop core technologies for Korean industrial development in the 21st century.

Government Research Institutes

GRIs are the major players in government R&D.[5] They operate with the financial assistance of the government but are independent, nongovernmental organizations operating under the provisions of the civil laws and the Law for the Creation and

---

4. OECD (1996, pp. 72–74) contains detailed explanations on the HAN project.
5. This section draws upon NSTC (2004), and the statistics cited are for 2002, unless otherwise indicated.

Promotion of the Government Research Institutes (1999). Therefore, GRI researchers are not government employees.

Korea has 28 GRIs for S&T fields, and they conduct 42 percent of the government R&D programs in terms of expenditure. GRIs employ about 8,600 scientists and engineers, of whom about 40 percent hold doctorates and 50 percent hold master's degrees. Of the total R&D expenditures by GRIs in 2003, 45.5 percent was devoted to technology development, 35.4 percent went to applied research, and the remaining 19.1 percent went to basic research. More than 93 percent of research funds came from the government, and the inflow of funds from industries was less than 7 percent, signifying that despite the overwhelming industrial research orientation of GRIs, industry-GRI research interactions are not that pronounced.

> Even though the original objective for establishing the GRIs was to develop industrial technologies together with the private sector, industrial-GRI research collaborations are currently minimal.

KIST, the first GRI, was established as an integrated technical center to assist industrialization by finding solutions to simple technical and practical problems and helping to internalize imported technologies. With the development of the HCIs in the 1970s, the demand for technical support, such as that KIST provided in the 1960s, increased in various industries. To meet the demand, in the 1970s, the government spun off from KIST a number of specialized institutes in the priority industrial areas: electronics, telecommunications, energy, machinery, chemicals, shipbuilding, and marine resources. These institutes operated under the patronage of the ministries that were responsible for the development of the respective industries. To accommodate these institutes as well as private R&D labs, the government started the development of the Daeduck Science Town in the 1970s.

In the early 1980s, the environments surrounding GRIs changed rapidly. Private industries began to establish in-house R&D systems to build up technological capability to cope with increasing market competition. Universities, which had been heavily oriented toward reaching, also launched various efforts to develop research capability. These two developments squeezed the position of GRIs, and the ground for GRIs was much eroded.

Debates on the Role of Government Research Institutes

Except in the early years, when business enterprises and universities were weak in R&D, GRIs have been continuously criticized about their appropriate roles in the KIS. Critics say that GRIs have not contributed as much as they have spent, and that they have overexpanded their range of activities to claim more resources, causing duplication among GRIs and leading to severe waste of resources. Another line of criticism is that the demand for GRI services has changed and therefore the roles of GRIs should be redefined. In response, the government downsized GRIs and merged some of them to reduce overlaps. They then put GRIs under the jurisdiction of MOST, in the hope of promoting interinstitutional flows of research personnel and resources.[6] Along with this, they launched the National R&D Program and enacted the Law for the Promotion of Government Research Institutes (1982), which provided the legal base for GRIs. GRIs were transformed from industrial and technical research centers into institutions for government R&D.

After almost 20 years of operation, the criticisms of GRIs had not subsided, and in the late 1990s, GRIs had to undergo another round of major reform and reorganization. Reasons for the reorganization were that resources were being wasted because of barriers to interinstitutional mobility that existed between and among GRIs. Also, GRIs tended to work for the interests of their patrons (the ministries) rather than those of the nation. This suggests that the reform of GRIs in the early 1980s failed to accomplish its goals. The government again not only downsized GRIs, in terms of both budget and personnel, but also redefined their functions and classified them into three different groups that were put under three newly created research councils. The research councils report directly to the prime minister's office.[7]

In accordance with the amendment to the Framework Law for Scientific and Technological Innovation, in 2004, the three research councils and their member institutes were moved from the prime minister's control and put under the NSTC for better coordination. The GRIs' R&D activities are now geared more to the development of future-oriented technologies and technologies in the public domain, but still the debates on the roles of GRIs have not come to an end.

Universities

Universities are a rich pool of high-quality scientists and engineers. They have about 60,000 highly qualified researchers, 38,000 of whom hold doctorates and 20,000 who have master's degrees. Universities harbor more than 30 percent of the total research force of Korea; however, doctoral level research scientists and engineers are extremely concentrated in universities (72.3 percent; see table 7.2).

Even though universities command the largest pool of qualified scientists and engineers, they account for only 10.1 percent of the gross national R&D expenditures, which is smaller than the combined share of GRIs and national labs (12.6 percent). This reflects the situation of Korean universities and particularly that of research environments. First, in many universities, professors cannot afford to engage in serious research because of excessive teaching obligations. Amazingly, the student-professor ratio at Korean universities exceeds 34 to 1. Even at national universities, which are in much better situations, the ratio stands at 29 to 1 (MOE & KEDI 1998).

Second, many universities place more emphasis on teaching at the undergraduate level, so graduate programs have not been well developed. Universities also are very poor in research facilities, and university education is not linked to research. Kim Young-Gul, an engineering professor, describes the situation: "Only a few academic institutions in Korea provide anywhere near sufficient research support. In most uni-

---

6. There were exceptions to this reform, and some GRIs were allowed to remain under the patronage of individual ministries.

7. Some GRIs were allowed to stay under MOST or other ministries if this was deemed necessary for efficient operation. For example, the Korea Atomic Energy Research Institute is under MOST, even after the reorganization.

versities, a newly recruited professor must start with an empty laboratory space and very meager university support for expendable supplies and equipment" (1996).

Third, university professors are not put under pressure for research. Once employed, they are almost automatically tenured. Even though they must meet some requirements in order to stay at the teaching job, those could be met without serious research efforts. Therefore, university research is very much concentrated in a few top universities.

University R&D activities are more directed toward basic research than others sectors' (see table 7.5). Of the total R&D expenditures in universities in 2005, 35 percent were devoted to basic research, 34 percent went to applied research, and 31 percent went to development. Naturally, universities rely more on the government for research funds—85 percent of the university research funds are from the government. In 2005, about half of the funds were spent on engineering research, whereas scientific research received only 19 percent. Other major areas are medical science (16 percent) and agriculture (6 percent).

Overall, universities in Korea have not been as important in R&D as their foreign counterparts are. Various factors may be behind this, but the fundamental reason is the extreme orientation of Korean universities toward teaching. To reorient Korean universities toward becoming more research-oriented institutions, the government has taken various measures, including the BK21 program, which supports selected universities in their transformation into research-oriented and graduate education–oriented institutions. The MOE & HRD has been pouring W 90 billion into the program every year since 1999. Universities also have been making efforts to reform the education and research systems. BK21 and other government efforts to upgrade university research and education have started to bear fruit in various ways. Most significant is the growth of scientific publications, of which universities are the major producers. Korea now ranks 15th in the world in terms of the number of scientific publications, but what is more impressive is the fact that Korea recorded the highest growth rate in science publication over the past decade.

Table 7.5 R&D Structure at Universities

		1998	2000	2003	2005
R&D expenditure (billion won)		12,650 (11.2% of GERD)	15,619 (11.3%)	19,327 (10.1%)	2,398 (9.9%)
Source of fund (%)	Government	52.1	60.4	75.1	84.6
	Industries	47.7	39.4	24.5	15.2
	Foreign	0.2	0.2	0.4	0.2
Type (%)	Basic research	40.1	42.4	36.0	34.8
	Applied research	33.8	30.5	32.8	34.4
	Development	26.1	27.2	31.2	30.8
Areas (%)	Sciences	18.5	20.0	18.9	18.9
	Engineering	49.1	50.3	50.2	49.6
	Agriculture	7.0	6.5	5.9	5.9
	Medicine	17.6	11.4	16.3	16.0

Source: MOST.

Outcomes of R&D Activities

Evaluations of the results of the R&D efforts in Korea are mixed. Some critics say that Korea's R&D inputs, such as human resources and financial inputs, exceed other countries' but that its outputs lag way behind. Others say that R&D results have not been effectively linked to industrial uses. All in all, the major criticism is that Korea's R&D investments have not been efficient enough to be economically justified. Most of the criticisms are targeted at public research. However, those criticisms are based on anecdotal evidence rather than formal analyses.[8]

Despite such criticisms, one cannot deny the positive contributions that the R&D efforts have made. Rapid growth in R&D investment has led to a remarkable increase in patent registration, both in Korea and abroad. The number of patents granted by the Korea Industrial Property Office increased from 1,808 in 1981 to 49,068 in 2004, with an average annual growth rate of about 15 percent. What is more encouraging is the growth of patents granted to Koreans. Only 12.8 percent of the total patents registered in 1981 (232) were granted to Koreans, but the figure rose to 72.6 percent in 2005, recording an average annual growth rate of more than 22 percent (see table 7.6).

Patents granted by the USPTO are sometimes used as an indicator of a nation's international technological competitiveness. Only five U.S. patents were granted to Koreans in 1969, but that grew to 586 in 1992 and to 4,591 in 2005, which is equivalent to 2.9 percent of all USPTO patents or 6.1 percent of USPTO patents granted to non-U.S. entities for 2005 (figure 7.3). According to a patent analysis by the U.S. Department of Commerce, Korea has established world prominence in technology areas such as ICTs, pharmaceuticals, advanced materials, and automotive (Albert 1998). These advances indicate that Korea has been rapidly gaining in technological competitiveness.

Another important development is the remarkable increase in the number of scientific and technical articles published by Koreans in internationally recognized academic journals. Articles published by Koreans increased from only 27 in 1973 to 13,746 in 2003, which is relatively large compared to the other East Asian newly industrial-

---

8. Two studies on the economic effects of R&D investments in Korea are Chung and Jang (1993) and Nadiri (1993). The results in general support R&D investments, but the studies do not provide any direct justification of R&D investments, such as costs and benefits of R&D.

Table 7.6 Korean Patent Office: Patent Applications and Granted Patents

		1981	*1985*	*1990*	*1995*	*2000*	*2005*
Applications	National	1,319	2,703	9,082	59,236	72,831	122,188
	Foreign	3,984	7,884	16,738	19,263	29,179	38,733
	Total	5,303	10,587	25,820	78,499	102,010	160,921
Granted	National	232	349	2,554	6,575	22,943	53,419
	Foreign	1,576	1,919	5,208	5,937	12,013	20,093
	Total	1,808	2,268	7,762	12,512	34,956	73,512

Source: Korea Patent Office.

Figure 7.3 USPTO Patents Granted to East Asian Newly Industrialized Economies Inventors, 1980–2005

Source: World Bank SIMA database.

ized economies (NIEs): 3,122 scientific and technical journal articles were published by Singaporean authors, and the Taiwanese had 9,270 articles. However, note that when the size of the population is taken into account, the Korean journal publication performance becomes weaker when compared with the other NIEs (figure 7.4).

Figure 7.5 displays the KAM spidergram for innovation indicators using data for Korea and the averages for the G7 and high-income countries for the most recent year. As expected, Korea's performance is at par with and even exceeds the high-income country average for many of the indicators. Korea is particularly strong in sci-

Figure 7.4 Scientific and Technical Journal Articles Published by East Asian Newly Industrialized Economies Authors, 1981–2003

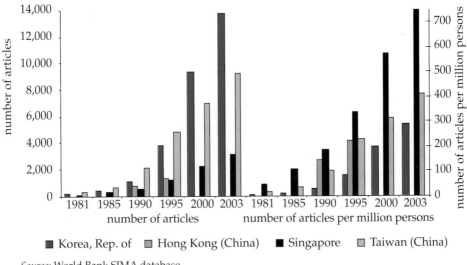

Source: World Bank SIMA database.

Figure 7.5 Innovation Indicators: Republic of Korea, G7, and High-Income Countries

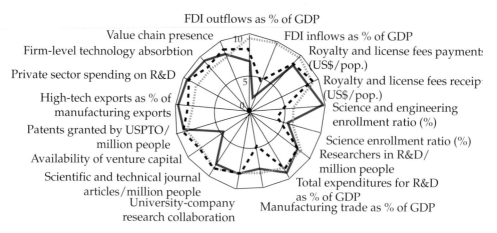

	Korea, Rep. of		G-7		High income	
Variable	Actual	Normalized	Actual	Normalized	Actual	Normalized
FDI outflows as % of GDP, 2000–04	0.71	6.58	2.98	8.29	14.90	9.78
FDI inflows as % of GDP, 2000–04	1.04	1.89	2.23	3.90	14.46	9.58
Royalty and license fees payments (US$/pop.), 2004	92.52	8.56	95.28	8.62	291.95	9.76
Royalty and license fees receipts (US$/pop.), 2004	37.22	8.41	107.69	9.28	83.00	9.02
Science and engineering enrollment ratio (%), 2004	41.09	9.88	21.59	4.24	23.79	5.76
Science enrollment ratio (%), 2004	10.25	5.35	8.80	3.81	10.76	5.99
Researchers in R&D/million people, 2004	3,187.00	8.09	3,411.71	8.48	3,367.55	8.44
Total expenditure for R&D as % of GDP, 2004	2.64	9.25	2.21	8.66	1.97	8.57
Manufacturing trade as % of GDP, 2004	55.37	7.58	31.45	4.23	60.82	8.02
University-company research collaboration, 2006[a]	4.60	8.28	4.64	8.49	4.30	8.02
Scientific and technical journal articles/milion people, 2003	287.57	7.94	612.98	8.80	535.89	8.66
Availability of venture capital, 2006[a]	3.10	4.14	4.54	8.10	4.50	7.93
Patents granted by USPTO/million people, avg. 2001–05	88.44	8.86	146.45	9.43	86.64	8.84
High-tech exports as % of manufacturing exports, 2004	32.80	9.34	19.67	8.16	17.69	7.87
Private sector spending on R&D, 2006[a]	5.10	9.22	4.91	9.14	4.43	8.06
Firm-level technology absorption, 2006[a]	5.90	8.97	5.51	8.06	5.48	7.87
Value chain presence, 2006[a]	5.50	8.25	5.83	8.82	5.15	8.07

Source: KAM, December 2006 (www.worldbank.org/wbi/kam).

a. Ratings are from 1 (worst) to 7 (best).

ence and engineering enrollment, R&D expenditure, high-tech exports, and private sector R&D spending, with these variables scoring above the 90th percentile. However, Korea shows some weak performance in three of the indicators: FDI inflows as a share of GDP, science enrollment ratio, and the availability of venture capital.

R&D efforts also have contributed to the development of high-tech industries in Korea. Because of their in-house R&D, Korean industries recently emerged as world leaders in semiconductor memory chips, cellular phones, and LCDs and also established themselves in the world market in the numerous areas such as shipbuilding, home appliances, automobiles, and telecommunications, to name a few.

Supportive Measures for Industrial Technology Development

Overview

Korea has implemented various kinds of policy measures that aim to promote industry's technological activities. These measures can be broadly classified by their characteristics into four schemes: NRDPs, infrastructural programs, institutional support systems, and incentive systems (see table 7.7). The government's industrial technology policy has focused mostly on technology programs, and other policy measures played a minor role. For example, as of 2000, the government as a whole spent W 3 trillion on NRDPs, which accounted for 82 percent of the government's total R&D budget. To complement mission-oriented NRDPs, the government has other policy measures intended to enhance technology diffusion and fill the institutional gap between innovation actors. The list of policy tools for these objectives includes educating and training research personnel, compiling and diffusing technical information, encouraging establishment of cooperative R&D facilities, and promoting spin-off activities from public research. The direct funding from the government budget for GRIs is classified as institutional support. The budget for GRIs is in general composed of two sources: on average, one-third of the GRIs budget is funded directly by the government, and the rest is filled with revenues from contract research projects that are mostly implemented under the name of national R&D programs.[9] Incentive measures are intended to induce and assist private enterprises' technology development activities. The measures include tax exemption for firms' R&D spending, financial support with preferential loans, and subsidizing of technology development.

Evolution of Korea's Incentive Schemes for Industrial Technology Development

The first incentive measure, in which corporate tax was reduced or exempted for FDI firms that satisfied a technology requirement, was applied in the early 1960s (see table 7.8). Several incentive measures also were introduced during the 1970s. A majority of supportive measures implemented during the latter period, however, aimed to promote or facilitate technology transfer rather than internal R&D. The list of incentives was considerably expanded or modified again during the 1980s.

---

9. Institutional support funding enables GRIs to undertake more long-term, basic research; contract research from NRDP are more mission-oriented.

Table 7.7 The Scheme of Korea's Industrial Technology Policy

	NRDPs	Infrastructure and diffusion	Institutional support	Incentives
Objectives	Develop core industrial technologies	Enhance intermediary functions and fill the gaps among innovation actors	Nurture GRIs and strengthen GRIs' research capabilities	Induce or assist private enterprises' technology development activities
Tools	Ministries' R&D programs	Research personnel, technical information, cooperative R&D facilities, regional R&D centers, spin-offs, and so on	Funding for GRIs' operational expenses and basic research	Tax exemptions, financial support, subsidy for technology development
Effects on industry	Expand knowledge and the technology pool for industrial use	Facilitate diffusion and make better industry use of technologies	Bring up helper or partner for industry's technology development	Strengthen industry's own technological capabilities

Source: Author's compilation.

The upsurge of incentive measures during this period was not accidental; rather, it reflected the changes in private enterprises' technological activities, which had activated in-house R&D at a much larger scale during the same period. Responding to that trend, the government shifted its industrial policy to promoting in-house R&D rather than importing technology. The change was formalized by the enactment of the Industrial Development Law, which marked a turning point of industrial policy from sectoral support to functional support. Since that time, the direction of incentive policy has been moving toward more indirect incentives, such as emphasizing construction of S&T infrastructure and human resources development. Furthermore, in accordance with the WTO's subsidy rule, industrial policy emphasizes R&D support while reducing conventional measures.

Changes after the Financial Crisis

Quick Recovery of Industrial R&D

The financial crisis in 1997 and the restructuring efforts afterward have had an unexpected effect on Korean businesses. Profitability has become more important than market expansion, and firms' technological development spending is no exception. Companies, particularly large firms, have endeavored to downsize and streamline R&D laboratories in line with business restructuring. Large firms' downsizing has forced many R&D personnel to leave, and many of them have established small-scale, specialized R&D laboratories or technology-based small firms. As shown in

Table 7.8 Chronology of Major Technology Policies

	Before the 1970s	1970s						1980s				1990s	
		1973	1974	1976	1977	1978	1979	1981	1982	1984	1986	1991	1992
R&D investment promotion		Technology development reserve funds system	Tax credit or special depreciation for investment in equipment to develop technology and human resources		Duty abatement or exemption on goods for academic research			Tax credit for technology and human resources development expenses	Tax exemption for real estate of private enterprises' affiliated research centers	Tax exemption for research devices and samples		Duty abatement or exemption on goods for research	
Technology transfer promotion	Deduction and exemption of the corporate tax for the foreign investment accompanied by the technology requisite							Reduction and exemption of tax amount on technology transfer income / Income tax exemption for foreign technologists					
Technology commercialization promotion									Provisional special consumption tax rate for technology commodities		Reduction and exemption of tax for start-up venture SMEs		

Source: MOST 1997c.

155

Box 7.1 The Efficacy of Government Policies

Despite the wide array of policy measures for industrial technology development, very few studies have been done on policy effectiveness. Exceptionally, the late professor Linsu Kim made persuasive judgments on three aspects of these: policies to create market needs for technology development, policies to increase S&T capabilities, and policies to provide the link between demand and supply (Kim, L. 2003).

Demand-side policies can cover three areas: export promotion, competition policy, and government procurement. Export promotion, by pushing firms into highly competitive international markets, has been more influential than other policies in forcing firms to expedite technological learning. Exporters also created capacity in excess of local market needs to achieve economies of scale. This led to crises and forced them to accelerate technological learning to maximize capacity use.

Competition policies also increased the need for technological effort. The government enacted the Fair Trade Act in 1980 to prohibit unfair practices in the market and to restrict the growth of the chaebols. At the same time, the government began to liberalize the local market, bringing down tariff and nontariff barriers, thus forcing Korean firms to compete against multinational firms not only in the export market but also in the domestic market. In 1986, the government introduced legislation to protect intellectual property rights, preempting the reverse engineering of foreign products. These policies forced Korean firms to further intensify technological effort.

Government procurement is often mentioned in the literature as an important tool in creating local demand for technological effort. However, except for significant government procurement of personal computers at the formative stage of that industry in the early 1980s, this policy did not play a significant role in Korea in creating demand for technological effort.

Major supply-side policies cover human resource development, technology transfer, and domestic R&D. The formation of human resources enabled Korean industry to master mature production technologies through reverse engineering in the early years. However, the Korean government made a critical mistake in neglecting to invest in research-oriented tertiary education in preparation for knowledge-intensive industries, creating a major bottleneck in innovative technological learning in the 1990s. Korea restricted reliance on FDI, enabling local firms to retain managerial independence and allowing them to set the direction of technological learning. The government gradually relaxed restrictions on licensing in the 1970s as Korean industries progressed into more complex technologies. The government's role in R&D was relatively small relative to other countries, accounting for only about 20–25 percent of total R&D in the 1990s. The government's R&D was largely directed at keeping increasingly weaker GRIs afloat and running mission-oriented national projects. Some national projects had significant results, such as the development of electronic switching systems and Code Division Multiple Access (CDMA) mobile telephone systems. In general, however, R&D policy neglected diffusion-oriented projects such as upgrading the quality of tertiary education and university research.

Preferential financing and tax incentives are the major instruments that lubricate the links between demand and supply. The impact of the preferential financing on furthering R&D activities, however, is dubious. Its interest rates, ranging from 6.5 to 15 percent, were far higher than similar loans in other countries. Tax incentives were another indirect mechanism to make funds available for corporate R&D. Preferential financing and tax incentives definitely provided funds for corporate R&D activities and lowered their costs, but they were peripheral in promoting R&D in Korea.

figure 7.6, the number of corporate R&D centers increased rapidly after the financial crisis, and most newly established corporate R&D centers are small.[10]

The increasing number of small-scale, specialized R&D centers or technology-based small firms is changing the industry's landscape. First, a direct effect is the increases in SMEs' R&D expenditure and intensity. Second, the existence of technologically agile small firms will make changes in business relationships, particularly between large firms and small firms. Table 7.9 compares SMEs' and large enterprises' changes in R&D expenditures and in number of researchers. SMEs' total R&D expenditures doubled between 1997 and 2000, whereas large enterprises' increased by only 5 percent. The increases in total R&D expenditures reflect the fact that the number of SMEs that spend on R&D activities is also sharply increasing, as manifested by the sharp increases in the number of SME R&D centers.

R&D intensity of SMEs, defined by the ratio of R&D expenditures to sales, also increased from 2.8 percent in 1997 to 3.9 percent in 2005. In contrast, R&D intensity of large enterprises increased only marginally from 2.07 percent in 1997 to 2.13 percent in 2000. Therefore, not only are more SMEs spending on R&D, but also SMEs are spending on more intense R&D activities than before the financial crisis. The same observation and conclusion can also be applied to the case of researchers. During the period from 1997 and 2000, SMEs strengthened their R&D activities by doubling the number of researchers (more than tripling the number with doctorates), whereas the number of researchers used by large enterprises remained almost the same as before the crisis.

---

10. In addition to the restructuring by large firms, other factors contribute to the increases in small corporate R&D centers. Among these are the government's drive to create venture companies and changed capital market conditions for start-up companies.

Figure 7.6 The Growth of Corporate R&D Centers, 1996–2005

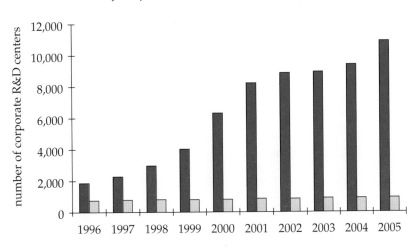

Source: Korea Industrial Technology Association 2006.

Table 7.9 Changes in R&D Activities

	R&D expenditure, in billion won (and as percentage of sales)				Researchers (doctoral level)			
	1997	2000	2003	2005	1997	2000	2003	2005
SMEs	1,090.2	2,106.4	3,425.4	3,921.4	17,703	36,494	52,332	62,792
	(2.82)	(3.14)	(3.57)	(3.00)	(474)	(1,543)	(2,291)	N.A.
Large enterprises	7,755.1	8,148.2	11,084.2	14,642.9	56,990	57,839	71,698	91,514
	(2.07)	(1.81)	(2.05)	(2.13)	(3,613)	(3,878)	(5,562)	N.A.

Source: MOST, *Survey of R&D Activities,* various years.
N.A. not available.

The Role of Foreign-Owned Companies

Before the financial crisis, foreign-owned companies played a minor role in the Korean economy. As shown in table 7.1, inward FDI had been quite low for many years; before the financial crisis, foreign-owned companies played a minor role in the Korean economy. This is more evident in technology and innovation issues. For example, technology transfer in the private sector mostly went through licensing contracts rather than FDI (OECD 1996). Also, technological activities of foreign-owned companies are mostly centered on product modification to meet local demand conditions.

The situation changed drastically after the financial crisis of 1997 (figure 7.7). FDI inflows into Korea increased sharply thereafter because of the favorable investment environment, depreciation in the local currency and asset values, the Korean government's promotion of investment through deregulation, the increased number of company offerings as a result of corporate restructuring, and privatization of government-owned companies (KPMG Consulting 2001). The effects of the FDI

Figure 7.7 Comparison of Inward FDI Stock as a Percentage of GDP

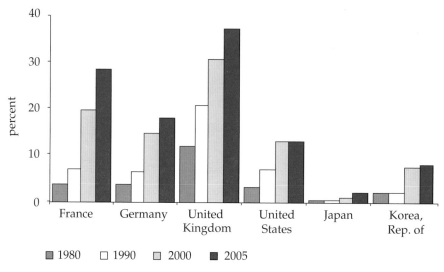

Source: United Nations, *World Investment Report 2006.*

increases on Korean industry's technological activities are not easy to determine because no comprehensive study has been done on the technology-related activities of foreign-owned companies. Instead, the effects can be inferred from changes in the Korean economy.

Table 7.10 shows the number of foreign-owned companies that spend on R&D, classified by the share of foreign ownership. From 1997 to 2000, the number increased from 329 to 462, a 40 percent increase in three years. In 2000, of the 462 companies, 333 were minority-owned foreign companies and the remaining 129 were majority-owned foreign companies. The total number of both foreign and domestic companies spending on R&D also increased, showing a 30 percent increase between 1997 and 2000. Therefore, the number of foreign-owned companies spending on R&D outpaced the number of domestic companies spending on R&D.

Clusters and the Regional Innovation System

As part of its industrialization, Korea has built many industrial complexes across the country. The building of industrial complexes started from scratch at the beginning of the industrialization process, because Korea is poorly endowed with natural resources and differences between localities' industrial qualifications were negligible. Population density might be a criterion: Seoul and its vicinity, as well as other urban areas, have been favored as the industrial complexes, but otherwise, great discrepancies exist across regions. According to the Korea Industrial Complex Corporation (KICC 2005), as of 2004, Korea had 550 industrial complexes, which host 34,083 companies and employ 1.2 million workers. The location of industrial complexes is concentrated in two regions. The capital region (Seoul and its vicinity, Inch'ŏn metropolitan area, and Kyŏnggi province) has 41 percent of companies and 33 percent of workers, and the southeast region (cities of Pusan and Ulsan in south Kyŏngsang province, and Taegu in nouth Kyŏngsang province) has 31 percent of companies and 43 percent of employees. These two regions contain three-quarters of Korea's industrial complexes.

The building of industrial complexes was intended to have synergistic effects by gathering individual firms and related supporting institutions in one place. Naturally, industrial clusters mirror the regional distribution of industrial complexes; however, the questions are whether the industrial clusters act as a mechanism for

Table 7.10 Foreign-Owned Companies that Spend on R&D

	Share of foreign ownership			
	Minority-owned (less than 50 percent)	*Majority-owned (50–100 percent)*	*100 percent*	*Total*
1995	236	23	15	274 (2,150)
1997	256	40	33	329 (2,522)
1999	287	97	61	445 (2,601)
2000	333	74	55	462 (3,269)

Source: MOST, *Survey of R&D Activities,* various years.
Note: Numbers in parentheses are the total number of companies, both foreign and domestic, that spend on R&D.

interaction and learning, and what is expected from clusters. If well-connected, industrial complexes are valuable assets for the development of innovation networks and clusters. But most of Korea's industrial complexes do not act as a mechanism for interfirm networks and learning. Although various supporting institutions aim to help resident firms, the frequency of use and the degree of satisfaction with the services offered are less than expected. Also, only a small portion of resident firms are doing collaborative R&D with other firms or innovators, such as universities and GRIs.[11]

After their role as the drivers of industrialization over the past decades, industrial complexes or industrial clusters in Korea now face a new challenge—to become knowledge-based, technology-intensive centers of industrial activities. The existence of an industrial base in a region greatly influences the nature of the economic activities in that region. Together with other innovators and supporting institutions, industrial complexes can be the cornerstone of the regional innovation systems. The question is whether the industrial base of a region can act as a learning mechanism for the region.

Because the industrial activities and complexes differ, there are also differences in the regions' research capabilities. The capital region—Seoul, Inch'ŏn, and Kyŏnggi province—takes the lion's share of Korea's R&D resources, with the exception of Taejŏn, where Daeduck Science Town is located (see figure 7.8). Recently the Korean government started to develop innovation clusters and construct effective regional innovation systems across the country. Of the government's initiatives, the most comprehensive one is the Regional Balanced Growth Plan. The basic concept of the plan, which started in 2004, is to make regional economic development self-sustaining and self-reliant for each region or province by combining research activities of university and public research institutions with industrial activities. Despite some success stories (see box 7.2), there are many difficulties to overcome in achieving the goal of establishing self-sustaining regional innovation systems. The most important of those tasks is the strengthening of research and innovation capabilities in which local and regional universities are expected to play a key role.

Conclusion and Policy Lessons

Strengths and Weaknesses of the Korean Innovation System

Korea has achieved enormous development in S&T over the past four decades. By making continuous and massive investments in human resource development and R&D, Korea succeeded in building up a unique innovation system in a technologically barren land. Some of the factors that have influenced the KIS most are (a) an outward-looking development strategy, (b) an industry-targeting development

---

11. Kim and Suh (2003) have detailed their analysis of Korea's major industrial clusters: the Daeduck valley in Taejŏn; the Gumi electronics cluster, a biotechnology cluster in Kyŏnggi province; the Taegu textile industry, and the Chang-won machinery industry. All these regional clusters have been assessed to determine whether they are acting as innovation clusters. Most of Korea's industrial custers receive negative assessments.

Figure 7.8 Regional Distribution of R&D Resources in Korea

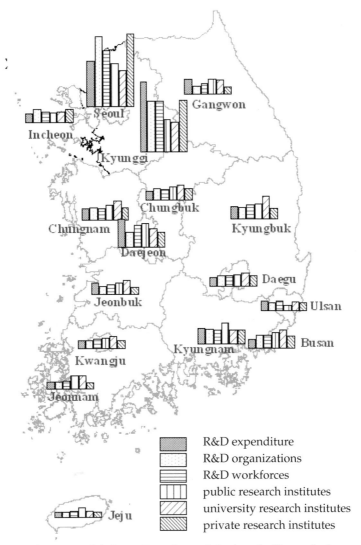

Source: Courtesy of Dr. Young-Sub Kwon, Korea Research Institute for Human Settlement (KRIHS), based on data from MOST (2004).

policy, (c) a large-firm-oriented industrial policy, (d) human resource development, and (e) government-led S&T infrastructure building. These are also the sources of the KIS's strengths and weaknesses.

> Some of the key determinants of Korea's S&T and innovative capability are (a) an outward-looking development strategy, (b) an industry-targeting development policy, (c) a large-firm-oriented industrial policy, (d) human resource development, and (e) government-led S&T infrastructure building.

The strength of the KIS is its dynamism, which is fueled by the government's strong commitment to technology-based national development and private enter-

---

Box 7.2 The Case of Wŏnju Medical Equipment Cluster

Kangwŏn province has been the most underdeveloped region in Korea. The industrial activities of this province, with its mountains and high hills, are mostly centered on coal mining and cement production, with some agricultural products in high mountain areas. However, since 2002, the top export product of the province has changed from cement to medical equipment because of the development of Wŏnju Medical Equipment Cluster (WMEC). The medical school of Yonsei University at the Wŏnju campus in Kangwŏn initiated the concept of the WMEC: to combine university research and industrial development. The Yonsei medical school has a medical engineering department that has produced quality research and a large number of graduates for many years. The concept began to materialize in 1996, when the Wŏnju city government built a 10,000-square-meter medical equipment production complex and tried to attract domestic companies to the complex. The choice of location for the medical equipment complex was not accidental. Medison Company, one of Korea's leading companies in medical equipment production, already operated a plant near Wŏnju with a small number of parts suppliers.

The development of the WMEC has been undertaken in three ways: technology development, business incubation, and production for the market. The Yonsei medical school plays a key role in technology development. Yonsei University created a medical equipment research center at its Wŏnju campus and has actively participated in the Wŏnju Medical Equipment Technopark project, in which regional universities, including the Yonsei medical school, Wŏnju Chamber of Commerce, and Wŏnju city government work together as partners. The business incubation center, where new businesses and new products are developed, is also a partnership project of these institutions, including the Wŏnju city government and local universities. The industrial complex established by the city government hosts those already established companies that are producing consumable products.

The WMEC is a rare success story in Korea—creating new business by combining university research and industrial development. Three things contribute the success of the WMEC: the existence of quality research in the region, the financial support of the local government, and active participation of the industry.

---

prises' efforts to gain technological competence. Despite the short history of R&D in Korea, the country already has rich yields from the endeavor in the forms of patents, scientific papers, and exports of various technology-intensive products such as semiconductors, cellular phones, LCDs, and automobiles.

Yet there are problems, too. R&D activities in Korea have grown very rapidly, led by private industries under the active promotion policy of the government. Even though Korea spends a larger share of GDP on R&D than other countries, it still lags far behind advanced industrial countries in terms of the absolute size of R&D expenditures.

Second, the discussions so far show that Korea has nearly reached the level of an advanced country in terms of scientific and technological inputs, but it still has a long way to go to reach the level of advanced countries in terms of R&D productivity. The most important source of inefficiency is the lack of interactions and exchanges among the major actors of innovation, such as universities, research institutes, and industries. Intersector mobility of scientists and engineers is extremely low in Korea.

Third, the weakness in basic sciences poses a fundamental problem for the KIS, because scientific capability determines the technological potential of a nation. Because Korean R&D efforts have been overly devoted to industrial technology development, basic scientific research has been neglected to a substantial extent. The lack of a strong scientific base already limits technological progress in Korea. In fact, the weakness in science results not just from the funding policy that favors technology development but also from weak university research capability. Therefore, strengthening the university research base poses a major policy challenge.

Fourth, excessive reliance on private industries for R&D investments has made the innovation system very vulnerable in two ways. On one hand, the system has placed so much emphasis on applied R&D that it failed to build up the strong foundation required for the long-term development of S&T. On the other hand, the R&D system has responded too sensitively to changes in economic and business environments. For instance, large Korean enterprises responded to the financial crisis of 1997 by cutting their R&D spending by about 14 percent, destabilizing the R&D system. If the crisis had continued for several more years, the whole system would have collapsed.

Fifth, despite Korean industries' remarkable performance in technological development, those industries harbor fundamental structural problems that have to be redressed to sustain the technological dynamism. First, the extremely high concentration of R&D activities poses a serious problem. High concentration means that only a few large firms are actively involved in R&D. If this persists for long, it will dichotomize Korean industries into technologically advanced and retarded firms and sectors. This situation will result in reduced interfirm and interindustry interactions, which are the key elements of innovation. The second problem is the weakness of SMEs in R&D. This is important because even chaebols would not be able to sustain competitiveness without technologically strong domestic SMEs. The third problem is the insufficient interactions among industries, universities, and GRIs. The lack of active interactions between R&D performers increases the gap between public R&D and industrial needs.

Sixth, the industrial structure shows the weakness of upstream sectors, particularly in the capital goods industry. This weakness is closely related to the predominance the chaebols, and the government's industrial policy. In accordance with the aggressive export-promotion policy that complements the limited domestic market, the imported technologies are both mature in life cycle and of a kind that can render economies of scale in production. Also, the production structure has centered on end products. Strengthening upstream industrial links is one of the most urgent tasks for the Korean economy, but the speed of adjustment upstream into capital goods needs to be balanced against (a) the competencies and strategies of the chaebol, (b) opportunities for joint ventures with foreign suppliers, and (c) the integration with foreign capital goods suppliers through international production networks. Particularly in the era of rapid technological changes, when production processes are fragmented and therefore much easier to expand using global production networks (GPN), upgrading local suppliers' technical and managerial skills is very important (Ernst and Kim 2002).

By using the USPTO count of patents granted as an indicator of R&D productivity, figure 7.9 shows that Korea indeed has been slowly losing ground and being overtaken by other economies with stronger innovation systems.

Figure 7.9 USPTO Patent Count, Selected Countries, 1984–2005

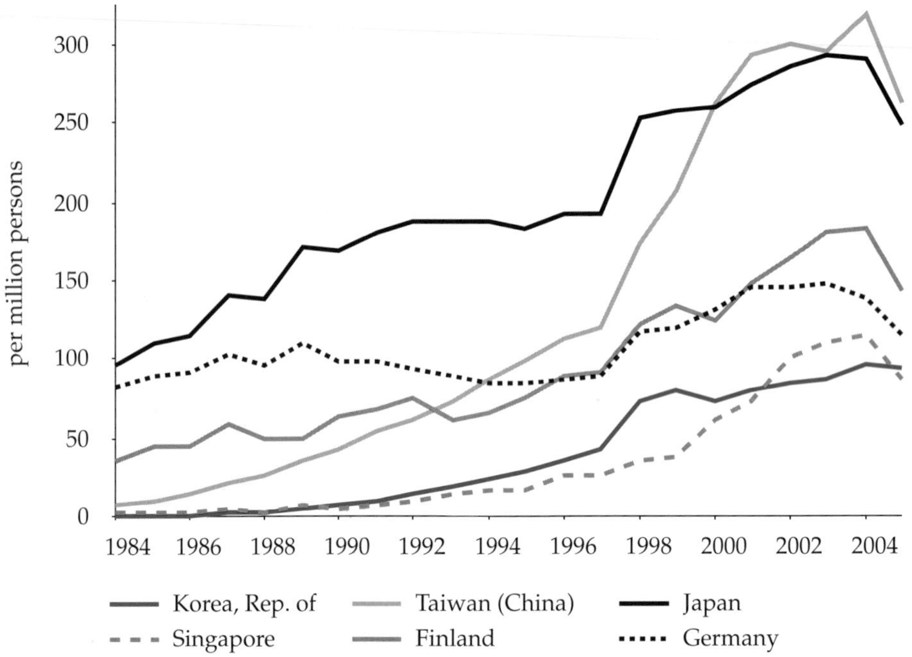

Source: Constructed by World Bank staff based on data from the USPTO Web site (http://www.uspto
.gov/web/offices/ac/ido/oeip/taf/reports.htm#by_geog) and World Bank SIMA database.

Lessons for Developing Countries

Korean experiences offer some lessons for policy makers responsible for education, trade, and technology development in developing countries. There is no doubt that education builds a nation's ability to absorb new knowledge and technology. Education gives rise to individuals' initial tacit knowledge, which is an essential building block in technological learning. Therefore, the government should assume full responsibility for taking measures necessary to promote human resource development. For example, investing in education in advance, as Korea did in the 1960s and 1970s, is essential in laying a foundation for industrial development.

To help workers cope with changes in technology, the government should provide vocational and technical training or take steps to promote such training at workplaces. As an economy becomes more advanced, technological competence becomes a critical factor. To build up that competence, the economic decision makers must nurture high-caliber scientists and engineers who are capable of dealing with the developments on the frontiers of S&T. In other words, advanced education in S&T should come first in preparing for entrance into a developed world. In the case of Korea, education and industrialization helped each other in sustaining and accelerating mutual development. Education made technological learning and therefore industrialization possible, and industrialization enhanced the rate of return on investment in education, further promoting demand for education.

Korea's industrialization evolved from imitation to innovation. In the initial stage, Korean industries attained technological capability through informal channels for technology transfer, such as production arrangements for OEM, reverse engineering of imported machines, technical training as part of turnkey plant importation, and so on. Contrary to the experiences of other developing countries, FDI played a modest role in technological learning in the course of development in Korea. To lay the initial technological foundation, many Korean industries resorted to nonmarket processes, relying on the technological absorptive capacity of their workers for technology acquisition. This approach enabled them to acquire technology at lower cost and maintain independence in business operations. But Korea paid a great price for this: it had to abandon many of the technological opportunities that foreign direct investors might have offered.

By adopting an outward-looking development strategy, the government drove Korean industries out into the competitive international market, putting them under great pressure to pursue technological learning or development. Korean industries responded to such pressures by investing heavily in technology development. By developing technological competence, they have been able to survive international competition and establish world prominence in such high-technology areas as telecommunications, semiconductor memory chips, LCDs, automobiles, and shipbuilding. A protectionist policy may be effective in creating the initial market opportunities for domestic industries, but if such a policy is prolonged, industries will develop immunity against market pressure for innovation. It may be for this reason that export-oriented firms and economies achieved technological learning more rapidly than import-substituting firms and economies (Kim 1997).

In sum, Korea owes very much to its human resources and the outward-looking development strategy for its achievements in technological development and industrialization. Two major lessons form the Korean experiences: First, human resources are the key to S&T development and thus to economic growth, and second, nothing can better motivate private businesses to invest in technology development than market competition. However, for Korea to sustain its past development into the future, it has to further strengthen basic scientific research capability and improve framework conditions for innovation, the core of which is competitive markets.

8

Assessment and Lessons

Jean-Eric Aubert and Joonghae Suh

Lessons Learned

Korea is an example for developing countries in many ways. Admittedly, there are unique aspects of the country that limit the direct applicability of lessons to be derived:[1] ethnic and cultural homogeneity, a strong Confucian tradition that places high value on education, achievement and loyalty to the nation, a security threat, and political leadership. In addition, some features of the country are typical of the Asian model of development and growth, which cannot be easily replicated in other cultures—among them, a strong state involvement in the orientation and management of the economy, very high saving and investment rates, and an industrial organization well-fitted to mass production. Nevertheless, there are a number of key features of the Korean experience that illustrate how a country can gradually build a KBE with approaches to follow and pitfalls to avoid.

Synchronizing the KE Pillars with Economic Development

Korea has been exemplary in developing each of the pillars of the knowledge economy at the level, type, and pace that complement the other KE pillars, and together the KE pillars complemented the various stages of the economy's development. For example, in the 1960s, when the economy was starting out with subsistence agriculture and light manufacturing, the main focus of education was on providing universal primary and secondary education. At the same time, the universal pri-

---

1. Contrasting Korea-specific contexts and characteristics with other countries or country classifications will be useful for delineating the applicability of the Korean experiences. Readers can refer to some earlier works. For example, using six factors of classifying countries, Ernst and O'Connor (1989) distinguish five developing country groups, among which Korea belongs to first-tier Asian newly industrializing economies. Focusing on the role that FDI played in building technological capabilities of various nations, Lall (2003) contrasts the capability-building strategy of Korea and Taiwan (China) with the FDI-dependence strategy of other countries, including China and Malaysia.

mary and secondary education of the labor force was also critical to the technology assimilation efforts of the manufacturing industries. Similarly, in the 1990s and beyond, when Korea was deploying world-class industries in communications, IT, and advanced electronics, there was the necessary expansion of the higher education system to ensure an ample supply of workers with tertiary education for the intensive R&D programs. At the same time, the modern and high-technology information infrastructure was being established to facilitate the timely and prompt dissemination of information and knowledge from abroad and around the country.

To reiterate, Korea developed the KE pillars by adopting a gradual, step-by-step approach that emphasized coordination and complementarities among the various KE pillars, and also with the country's stage of economic development and industrialization. In the early years, these complementarities took place even without an explicit KE agenda. The KE approach is thus important in minimizing mismatches in terms of quantity and type in any of the KE pillars and hence reducing misallocations and wastage of the extremely scarce resources of any developing country.

> The KE approach emphasizes a gradual, step-by-step coordinated and complementary development of the various KE pillars synchronized with the country's stage of economic development.

Education, Human Resource Development, and Lifelong Learning

Education builds a nation's ability to absorb new knowledge and technology, because it gives rise to individuals' basic competence, which is an essential building block in technological learning. Therefore, the government should assume full responsibility for taking the measures necessary to promote human resource development. For example, investing in primary and secondary education in advance, as Korea did in the 1960s and 1970s, is essential in laying a foundation for industrial development. In addition, to help workers cope with changes in technology, the government should also provide vocational and technical training and constant retraining, or take steps to promote such training at workplaces.

> Education is an essential building block in technological learning. Therefore, governments should invest in all levels of education, with priorities and sequencing to depend on the stage of economic development and industrial strategy.

As an economy becomes more advanced, technological competence becomes a critical factor. Building that competence requires high-caliber scientists and engineers who are familiar with the developments on the frontiers of S&T. More specifically, advanced education in S&T should come first in preparing for entrance into a developed world. In the case of Korea, education and industrialization were mutually complementary in sustaining and accelerating mutual development. Education made technological learning, and therefore industrialization, possible, and industrialization enhanced the rate of return on investment in education, further promoting demand for education.

Advanced education in S&T should come first in preparing for entrance into a developed world.

Technological Adoption and Innovation

Korea's industrialization evolved from imitation to innovation. At the initial stage, Korean industries attained technological capability through informal channels for technology transfer, such as production arrangements for OEM, reverse engineering of imported machines, and technical training as part of turnkey plant importation. These practices were necessarily coupled with strong reliance on the technological absorptive capacity of the workers. Thus, contrary to the experiences of other developing countries, FDI played a modest role in technological learning in the course of development in Korea. These channels of informal technology transfer enabled Koreans to acquire technology at lower cost and maintain independence in business operations. However, this independence probably came at a significant price because Korea had to abandon many of the technological opportunities that foreign direct investors would have offered.

Korea opted for a technology assimilation strategy through informal channels to maintain independence, but by doing so, it is likely to have forgone technological opportunities that foreign direct investors would have offered.

Today Korea continues to import a significant amount of technology and know-how from abroad, but it has developed a strong indigenous R&D platform and spends almost 3 percent of its GDP on R&D. These approaches for education and technology illustrate both the pragmatism and the discipline that should inspire developing countries in their knowledge efforts. As a whole, it is estimated that for Korea, TFP growth, including knowledge-related contributions, accounted for more than two-thirds of the growth of GDP per capita over the period 1960–2005 (see figure 1.3). This demonstrates the need for accumulating not only physical capital but also intellectual capital for successful takeoff and growth.

Market-Oriented Role of the State

One of the most important lessons from Korea's economic development process is the necessity of a market-oriented approach for the transformation to a knowledge economy. Korea's economic success was not based on policies that substituted for the market. Instead, the success of Korea's development policies up to 1997 was the result of policies that complemented and facilitated the functioning of the market. However, a contributing factor in the 1997 financial crisis was the continued discretionary resource allocation on the part of the government in the early 1990s. This had resulted in a very weak financial sector that was saddled with large debts from the bankrupt chaebols. The financial crisis thus showed the limitations of the government's market intervention and underscored the importance of a market-based approach for sustained economic development. A market-based approach requires the existence of competitive forces and, as such, policies that in one way or another foster competition. Transparency of financial markets, accountability of the government, a level playing field for all market participants, liberalized trade, and foreign investment regimes are all crucial characteristics of a market-based knowledge economy.

> A market-based development strategy liberates competitive forces that are crucial for mechanics of the knowledge economy.

Export-Led Industrialization

By adopting an outward-looking development strategy, the government exposed Korean industries to competition in the global market, which compelled them to invest heavily in technological assimilation and innovation to remain competitive. This was true in the 1970s and 1980s, when Korea developed its heavy industries. This outward-looking development strategy was complemented by intensive development of government R&D programs and strong fiscal incentives for the firms in the early 1980s. More recently, stimulated by the same strategy, the resulting increases in competitiveness have enabled Korean firms to gain significant shares in global markets in high-technology areas such as telecommunications, semiconductor memory chips, and LCDs. Protectionist policies may be effective in creating initial market opportunities for domestic industries, but they eventually lead to complacency in terms of innovation because of the lack of exposure to competitive forces.

The Pivotal Role of the Government

The Korean government has played a very significant role throughout the entire development process. Since the beginning of the industrialization process, Korea's visionary government provided effective leadership that ensured a stable and conducive macroeconomic environment, providing mass education and training of the population, encouraging the assimilation of foreign technologies and developing a domestic R&D initiative, and establishing an accessible and modern information infrastructure. As the economy developed and became larger and more complex, it was best to leave economic activities to market forces, and the government consequently adopted a less-direct interventionist approach and changed its role to that of an architect and regulator.

> An effective, visionary government is critical to the implementation of a KE approach to long-term economic development.

One characteristic of the Korean government that deserves special recognition is its long-term fiscal prudence, which allowed the government to implement a series of post-1997 economic reforms even though it had incurred astronomical costs. Initiatives such as removing NPLs and recapitalizing financial institutions, establishing social programs such as unemployment insurance, and providing financial support for low-income families required public funds and contributed to enormous fiscal pressures. However, because of its long history of fiscal prudence and financial credibility, the Korean government was not saddled with public debt and was able to issue new bonds to finance the necessary reforms.

Top-Down and Bottom-Up Approaches to Build a National Consensus

Because the KE approach is broad, in that it permeates many areas of the economy and involves many actors, it is important to use both top-down and bottom-up approaches to build a national consensus and achieve a set of coherent strategies across the different of parts of the government, the private sector, and civil society. Top-down and bottom-up approaches are both key for successful reform processes. In the case of Korea, the sensitization of the society as a whole, including opinion leaders and politicians, to the notion of the knowledge economy had begun before the 1997 crisis as a bottom-up initiative of the *Maeil Business Newspaper,* the principal business newspaper in Korea. Before the crisis, the paper's management had organized policy forums that introduced the concept of the knowledge economy and highlighted its benefits, and the public was informed of the basics of the KE approach. The 1997 crisis may have actually energized existing KE awareness campaigns, which led to the government finally initiating its top-down approach—the government sought policy evaluations and advice from international organizations on the KE approach. Thus, in 2000, a report was jointly prepared by the World Bank and the OECD: *Korea and the Knowledge-Based Economy: Making the Transition.* The report inspired subsequent government plans. In a typical Korean manner, all concerned government departments were mobilized to elaborate new policy measures with quantified objectives and budget estimates for implementing those measures. Meanwhile, to maintain and enlarge the KBE mobilization, the *Maeil Business Newspaper* has pursued its awareness actions toward varied target groups: business, civil servants, households, children, and even prisoners.

> Because the KE approach permeates many areas of the economy and involves many actors, it is important to use both top-down and bottom-up approaches to build a national consensus and achieve a set of coherent strategies across the different of parts of the government, the private sector, and civil society.

Indeed, without the resulting national consensus, efforts to reform and restructure the Korean economy would likely have been unsuccessful, because institutional reforms inevitably invoke resistance from vested interests, which frequently retards the reform process. For example, the legalizing of layoffs was made possible only through dialogues among the government, the private sector, and the labor unions, all of whom shouldered a portion of the costs associated with labor reform. No doubt there are specific features of Korean society that have facilitated its rapid adhesion to the KE concept. However, the general concept of a simultaneous top-down, bottom-up approach is one that warrants the consideration of policy makers implementing economy-wide strategies.

> The general concept of a simultaneous top- down, bottom-up approach is one that warrants the consideration of policy makers implementing economy-wide strategies.

Recovery from the 1997 Crisis

The 1997–98 Asian financial crisis was particularly strong in the Republic of Korea because of the vicious circle of the insolvent financial system and its significant amount of NPLs to the chaebols, and the consequent capital flight. The situation was created by the traditional opacity that characterizes the Korean financial system—as well as other Asian systems—and by the nature of the relationships that linked big industry (chaebols) to the government and the banking system. Measures to improve the transparency of financial markets, ameliorate corporate governance, and introduce more competition into the economy contributed to the recovery process. Meanwhile, the government adopted a less-direct interventionist approach and changed its role to become more an architect and a regulator.

> Every country needs to have sound economic fundamentals if it wants to succeed as a KBE.

However, Korea did not respond by using only traditional financial and economic policies. It also put into place a vigorous KE approach to boost the economy after the crisis to recover a high-growth path. In fact, since the early 1990s, there had been increasing signs of the gradual loss of industrial competitiveness and the need to adapt the economy to the rapid globalization process. An exhaustive plan inspired by the goal of a KBE was elaborated. Actions orchestrated by MOFE and financially supported by the Ministry of Budget and Planning were launched in several directions: ICTs, education, and innovation with clear targets to be reached. Most of the objectives, but not all, were reached as planned. This two-pronged approach—financial- and knowledge-based—has been effective. Although the rate of unemployment rose to more than 10 percent in 1998, it came down to less than 5 percent four years later.

> The combination of financial, economic, and knowledge-based reforms contributed to the rapid recovery of the Korean economy after the 1997 crisis.

Successful Reforms and Initiatives

After several years of reforms, the government can clearly claim success in two policy areas of the four-pillar framework. First, the overall financial system has been put in order and NPLs have been cleaned up. Of course, it was very costly for taxpayers, but the situation was rapidly and significantly improved, and trust came back quickly for both domestic and foreign investors. Undertaking reforms was vital to regain the economy's global competitiveness and recover a growth path, which explains why the measures were quickly implemented and generally met relatively little resistance. Some aspects of the reforms that were not so vital, such as those concerning corporate governance or the control of industrial power, were less successful or less actively pursued.

> A well-functioning and credible financial system is vital to the global competitiveness of the economy. Korea has successfully implemented reforms and restored public confidence in the financial system.

Another very impressive achievement is the development of the telecommunications infrastructure and the IT industry. In fact, Korea, like other Asian countries, enjoys a natural easiness with the hard dimension of technology and invests massively in telecom lines, Internet equipment, multimedia, and so forth. Investment in IT infrastructure and its use in non-IT sectors has positively contributed to the productivity growth in Korea (see table 5.6). The Korean policy was articulated on three key areas: a very active informatization policy (setting up e-government, bridging the digital divide, and building an advance infrastructure), an industrial policy (oriented toward R&D, human resources, and venture capital), and a clearly enforced regulatory and competition policy (privatization and market liberalization). Integrating the three policy areas in a complementary manner has been the key for the success of the overall IT strategy, and it is a lesson that could inspire policy makers worldwide, in both developing and developed countries. Korean society today enjoys highly well-developed information infrastructures,[2] which have become the basis of the exceptional development of related industries.

> The success of Korea's IT strategy hinged on the implementation of a well-integrated approach involving an active informatization policy, an industrial policy, and a clearly enforced regulatory and competition policy.

Challenges

Korea has made substantial progress in numerous dimensions related to the knowledge economy. However, there are some areas still that require further reform before Korea can continue its transformation into an advanced knowledge economy.

---

2. Until recently, Korea has recorded sizable deficits in TBOP (technology balance of payments): US$2.4 billion in 2003. Korea's TBOP payments in 2003 were US$3.2 billion, which amounts to 20.2 percent of GERD (OECD 2005c).

Modernizing the Education System for the Knowledge Economy

Korea's education and human resources development system has been a driver of productivity growth over the high-growth years, but it now faces a challenge to substantially upgrade its quality and build a more-open system. For example, Korea's share of professional and technical workers within the labor force is far lower than the average of G-7 countries,[3] which implies that there is further potential for productivity improvement when the government makes an effort to upgrade the employment structure. Public spending on education needs be increased to a level comparable to that in other OECD countries, and the quality and availability of management education also need further improvement.

Education and training in Korea are still being largely provided in a routine way, which poses significant challenges as Korea now enters the information and knowledge era. Teacher-centered, one-way teaching; rote memorization, the lack of diversity in educational programs; and preoccupation with preparing for entrance exams have left little leeway to nurture creativity and initiative, which are necessary qualities of a workforce in a vibrant knowledge economy. Measures were announced in the 2000 KE master plan to reform the education system, but progress so far remains modest.

The low profile of public education creates problems in human resources supply. According to an opinion survey of executives on the usefulness of university education, Korea ranked 50th among 61 countries, showing that Korean universities failed to sufficiently meet the needs of the economy (IMD 2006). As a partial consequence of noncreative Korean graduates, strategic partnerships among universities, private corporations, and research institutions are weak, with little participation in joint research projects and a significant loss of opportunity for indigenous research and development.

> The dated Korean education system has yet to evolve to be able to deliver workers with initiative and creative talents and capable of meeting the new skill and knowledge requirements of the knowledge economy.

Meanwhile the competitive nature of the education system has been reinforced, and as a consequence, private schools have flourished, funded by families excessively engaged in getting their children into elite establishments from an early age. This trend contributes to increased inequality in Korean society. In fact, an important group in the resistance to change was the teachers themselves, including those at the primary and secondary levels. The reforms would work better if teachers were asked to participate in the process not as the victims of the reform but as the beneficiaries in the long run. In many countries, the education systems prove to be the most difficult part of society to reform. Korea has not been an exception to this rule.

---

3. See the appendix in chapter 1 and figure 6.5.

Experience around that world has shown that it is always very challenging to implement reforms of education systems. However, reforms have a higher probability of succeeding if teachers are asked to participate in the reform process, not as the victims of the reform but as the beneficiaries in the long run.

Efforts to enhance the quality of human resources without reforming the education system have inevitable limits. To nurture creativity and independent thinking, the government intends to completely abandon the current rigid and bureaucratic school system and work to create a whole new educational environment that can meet the diverse demands and views of parents and students (Government of the Republic of Korea 2004). The new system would allow greater autonomy of individual schools and local administrations as well as enable students to have diverse choices regarding their education. The new system will put an end to rigid government control over higher education's curricula, examination system, tuition fees, and number of students in each discipline. In particular, this change would allow higher education institutions to become more entrepreneurial, accountable, and responsive to industrial needs. The education reform agenda also includes improving the quality of faculty, curricula, and teaching techniques while strengthening support for the underperforming students and the economically disadvantaged group.

In addition to the changes associated with the new education system, further reforms are needed if the Korean education system is to fully meet the needs of the knowledge economy. More specifically, three-party collaboration among government, universities, and industry is needed to encourage universities to proactively respond to the new demands of the economy.[4] For example, universities should use their specialty areas to develop innovative programs that cater to industrial needs. Another area that needs a concerted effort from the government and industry is the establishment of a more efficient system of job training. For workers to stay in touch with rapid technological advances, formal links are needed between higher education institutions and other forms of education and training, such as adult education, job training, and employer-based training. In particular, lifelong education should be strengthened. Currently only 19 percent of Korean adults participate in lifelong education, which is low compared with the 35 percent average for the OECD countries (OECD 2005c).

Diversification and Coordination within the Innovation System

The innovation and S&T system is another area in which progress has been difficult. Although Korea has experienced dramatic increases in R&D efforts, the innovation system still has significant issues to resolve. For example, a disproportionately large amount of R&D is conducted by the private sector, particularly by the chaebols. This has made the innovation system in Korea vulnerable in

---

4. The New Industry-Academia Collaboration System that is currently being designed is a step in the correct direction.

two ways. First, applied R&D have been overemphasized and insufficient resources have been devoted to R&D in basic sciences, which is a necessary investment for the long-term development of S&T.

A second disadvantage is the small number of chaebols dominating industrial innovation activities, which is the problem associated with the domestic diffusion of innovation. The internal diffusion of technological innovation is not very active in Korea. The lack of technological diffusion among domestic firms is well demonstrated by the fact that repetitive importation of foreign technologies is common. Furthermore, the diffusion from research institutions to private firms is not as effective as expected. More organic cooperation between domestic firms, particularly between large firms and SMEs, and more active collaboration between research institutions and private firms are imperative for the technological advancement of the Korean knowledge economy. In this regard, positive signs of change have been seen since the financial crisis, such as the emergence of innovation networks between conglomerates and SMEs (Suh 2003). Korea needs to sustain this trend.

> A disproportionately large amount of Korean research and development is being conducted by the private sector, resulting in insufficient R&D investment in basic sciences and weak domestic diffusion.

Related to this situation, efforts to improve the relevance and importance of the other institutions in the innovation system have been largely deemed unsuccessful. GRIs, although sources of important technological progress in certain sectors such as telecoms, have not adequately evolved despite repeated attempts to make them more collaborative with industries. Korean universities have not been able to sufficiently respond to the industries, in terms of providing both appropriate human resources and relevant and collaborative industrial research. University research remains at a low level of activity and performance, with few resources (10 percent of national R&D expenditures), even though it employs the bulk of doctorate holders (70 percent of the national total). Interactions between the different innovation actors are still poorly developed, so it is in this sense excessive to speak of an innovation system. On top of that, mediocre coordination persists at the top level. MOST, which is responsible for ensuring coordination among the different institutions, has difficulty involving other key partners, such as the Ministries of Industry and Labor and MOE & HRD, in a coherent strategy. These difficulties persist even though the S&T minister's status was raised to deputy prime minister and the National S&T Council was convened to gather all key ministers concerned.

> Efforts to improve the relevance and importance of GRIs and universities in the innovation system have not been successful. In addition, interactions between the different innovation actors are still poorly developed, despite the efforts of MOST and the convening of the National S&T council.

For a national innovation system to be effective, it must tap into global knowledge, and foreign investment could have played an important role. However, Korea kept foreign investments at arm's length to maintain independence. This stand-alone strategy will not be effective in the current globalized knowledge economy. Therefore, technological cooperation between domestic firms and foreign firms needs to be aggressively promoted. In the past, the Korean economy has benefited from the inflow of advanced foreign technologies via informal channels. Now, new modes of cooperation, such as cross-licensing and strategic alliances, need to be used more. Facing rapid changes in technological opportunities and the expansion of globalization, private enterprises need to strengthen the development of human resources and international R&D networks.

> For a national innovation system to be more effective, it must tap into global knowledge. A stand-alone strategy in the current globalized economy is doomed to be ineffective. Therefore, technological cooperation between domestic firms and foreign firms needs to be aggressively promoted, so that Korean firms can participate in and benefit from international R&D networks.

These challenges in the education and innovation pillars of the Korean economy have persisted for some time. For example, the problems with the innovation system were pointed out in an OECD S&T policy review in 1995 (OECD 1996), and they have yet to be resolved, despite the drastic economic crisis experienced by the country and subsequent economy-wide reforms. Korea may encounter further difficulties in maintaining its current rate of economic growth if appropriate, concrete steps are not taken to promptly and properly resolve these issues.

Polarization of Korean Society

Another challenge facing the Korean economy is that the economic development has not been balanced across the different sectors of the economy, and the benefits of economic growth have not been trickling down to all household groups. Thus, economic inequality among different household groups has increased since the 1990s. This polarization has been amplified by the 1997 recession and takes place in several dimensions. For example, workers in the manufacturing sector are earning significantly more than workers in the service sectors, and workers in large enterprises (300 or more employees) are economically better off than those in SMEs. Similar disparities are observed between workers in the HCIs and those in the light manufacturing industries, between those in and those not in the IT sector (as discussed in chapter 5), and between permanent and contractual workers.

> Economic development in Korea has not been balanced across the different sectors of the economy, and the economic benefits have not been trickling down to all household groups, resulting in increased income inequality.

Two initiatives are being implemented by the government in an effort to achieve more balanced economic development across the different parts of the economy: first, the promotion of the SME sector, and second, the economic regionalization process. Korea is showing encouraging signs on both. For example, the SMEs sector has shown a significant increase in R&D. This is concomitant with the development of venture capital businesses, boosted in the early 2000s. Moreover, a significant number of industrial clusters are being formed around the country that present promising opportunities for diversification and decentralization of activities away from the national capital.

The negative effects of high levels of income inequality on economic growth and political stability have been well documented in the literature; therefore, efforts to address this social issue need to be continued and expanded before income inequality becomes a hindrance to long-term economic growth.

Conclusion

Korea's design and implementation of knowledge-based development strategies and the resulting rapid and sustained knowledge-led economic growth over the past four decades provide a wealth of valuable policy lessons for other developing economies. First, and particularly important, are the coordinated and complementary expansion of the four pillars of the KE framework—economic incentive and institutional regimes, educated and skilled workers, an effective innovation system, and modern and accessible information infrastructure—that evolved in tandem with the economy's various stages of development. These pillars provided the economy with the necessary means to effectively acquire and use knowledge to improve productivity and enhance long-term economic growth. Second, the strong and effective leadership provided by the government, which led to the coordinated development of the education, innovation, and ICTs pillars, was particularly important during the earlier stages of industrialization, when appropriate institutions to coordinate an economy-wide development agenda were not yet sufficiently established. The role of Korean government has appropriately mellowed in recent times to allow the market to further spur economic activity. Third, the economy-wide reforms and the array of policy measures that were implemented after the 1997 crisis serve as good examples of making the best use of opportunities to improve economic conditions. The government initiated the formalization of the action plan, which was orchestrated by MOFE, but also sought support from the civil society and some media groups. One outcome of those measures was the successful wiring of the Korean economy and the public, resulting in a first-class information infrastructure.[5] And fourth were the exemplary ways in which the educational basis has been built and gradually expanded and the way technology has been gradually mastered and upgraded throughout the stages of industrialization.

Although Korea has made these advances, it needs to continue and increase efforts in reforming its higher education and innovation systems. These pillars have not sufficiently evolved in recent years to meet the demands of the current global economy, in part as a result of several pockets of resistance inherent in the Korean society and culture. In addition, a more proactive policy response is required to

---

5. For example, in 2004, 86 percent of Korean households had a broadband connection via a computer or mobile phone, the highest record among OECD countries (OECD 2005d).

achieve more-balanced economic development across the different sectors and niches of the economy. Concrete steps to resolve these issues will eventually become critical to Korea's continued transition to the knowledge economy and further sustained economic growth. To sum up these four decades of change, it has been easier to invest in hard infrastructure than to change mentalities, traditions, and institutional behaviors rooted in culture and history. This is not a new insight; most, if not all, societies must endure this painful experience. Only by seeking a better understanding of a country's unique features and inner functioning can its cultures truly progress.

References

Albert, M. B. 1998. *The New Innovators: Global Patenting Trends in Five Sectors.* Washington, DC: U.S. Department of Commerce.

Amsden, A. 1989. *Asia's Next Giant: South Korea and Late Industrialization.* Oxford: Oxford University Press.

Aoki, Masahiko, Kim Hyung-Ki, and Masahiro Okuno-Fujiwara, eds. 1997. *The Role of Government in East Asian Economic Development: Comparative Institutional Analysis.* Oxford and New York: Oxford University Press.

Bank of Korea. 2000. *Input-Ouput Tables 2000.* Seoul: Bank of Korea.

———. 2006. "Real Gross Domestic Product: The 1st Quarter of 2006." Economic Statistics Department. Press release, April 25.

Bresnahan, T. F., E. Brynjolfsson, and L. M. Hitt. 2002. "Information Technology, Workplace Organization and the Demand for Skilled Labor: Firm- level Evidence." *Quarterly Journal of Economics* 117(1), 339 376.

Bureau of Statistics. Various years. *Economically Active Population Survey.*

Cha, Dong-Se, Kwang Suk Kim, and Dwight H. Perkins. 1997. *The Korean Economy 1945–1995: Performance and Vision for the 21st Century.* Seoul: Korea Development Institute.

Chen, Derek H. C., and Carl J. Dahlman. 2004. "The Knowledge Assessment Methodology: Linking the Knowledge Economy with World Bank Country Operations." Mimeo. Washington, DC: World Bank Institute.

Cho, Lee-Jay, and Yoon Hyung Kim, eds. 1991. *Economic Development in the Republic of Korea.* Honolulu: University of Hawaii Press.

Cho, Yoon Je, and Joon Kyung Kim. 1997. "Credit Policies and the Industrialization of Korea." KDI Research Monograph 9701. Seoul: Korea Development Institute.

Chung, S. C., and L. M. Branscomb. 1996. "Technology Transfer and International Cooperation." In *Korea at the Turning Point*, eds. L. M. Branscomb and S. C. Choi. Westport, CT: Praeger.

Chung, S. C., and J. Jang. 1993. "The Economic Effects of R&D." Policy Research Series 93-04. Seoul: Science and Technology Policy Institute. (In Korean)

Chung, Un-Chan. 2004. "The Korean Economy before and after the Crisis." In *The Korean Economy Beyond the Crisis*, eds. Duck-Koo Chung and Barry Eichengreen. Cheltenham, UK: Edward Elgar.

Dedrick, Jason, and Kenneth L. Kraemer. 1997. *Asia's Computer Challenge: Threat or Opportunity for the U.S.?* University of California, Irvine: Center for Research on Information Technology and Organizations.

Duclos, Jean-Yyves, Joan Esteban, and Debraj Ray. 2004. "Polarization: Concepts, Measurement, Estimation." *Econometrica* 72 (6).

Ernst, Dieter, and David O'Connor. 1989. *Technology and Global Competition: The Challenge for Newly Industrialising Economies.* Paris: OECD.

Ernst, Dieter, and Linsu Kim. 2002. "Global Production Networks, Knowledge Diffusion, and Local Capability Formation." *Research Policy* 31: 1417-1429.

Fukagawa, Yukiko. 1997. Kankoku: Senshinkoku Keisai-ron Tokyo: Nihonkeisaishinbun. [Translated by Chan-Uck Park. 1998. *The Korean Economy at Great Transformation Period.* Seoul: Nanam Publishing.]

Gonzales, Patrick, Juan Carlos Guzman, Lisette Partelow, Erin Pahlke, Leslie Jocelyn, David Kastberg and Trevor William (2004). *Highlights From the Trends in Internal Mathematics and Science Study (TIMSS) 2003* (NCES 2005-005). U.S. Department of Education, National Center for Education Statistics. Washington DC: U.S. Government Printing Office.

Government of the Republic of Korea. 1962. *The First Five-Year Economic Development Plan 1962–1966.* Seoul: Government of the Republic of Korea.

———. 1982. *The Fifth Five-Year Economic Development Plan 1982–1986.* Seoul: Government of the Republic of Korea.

———. 1992. *The Seventh Five-Year Economic and Social Development Plan 1992–1996.* Seoul: Government of the Republic of Korea.

———. 1999. *DJnomics: A New Foundation for the Korean Economy.* Published for the Ministry of Finance and Economy. Seoul: Korea Development Institute.

———. 2004. *Dynamic Korea: A Nation on the Move.* Kwachon, Republic of Korea: Ministry of Finance and Economy.

Hobday, M. 1995. *Innovation in East Asia: The Challenge to Japan.* Aldershot: Edward Elgar.

Hong, Dong-pyo, and others. 2003a. *Analysis of Korea's IT Industry Growth and Productivity,* KISDI , Issue Report, 03-05. (In Korean)

Hong, Dong-pyo, and Seoghoon Kang. 2003b. "An Analysis of the Sources of Growth and Productivity of the Korean IT Industry." *KyongJeHakYonGu* 51 (4). (In Korean)

———. 2003c. *Structural Changes by Sector and Responses in the Digital Economy (I),* Korea Information Strategy Development Institute. (In Korean)

———. 2004. *Structural Changes by Sector and Responses in the Digital Economy (II),* Korea Information Strategy Development Institute. (In Korean)

Hong, Wontack. 1994. *Trade and Growth: A Korean Perspective.* Seoul: Kudara International.

IITA (Institute of Information Technology Assessment). 2002. *Report on R&D Statistics in Information and Communication Technology.* Seoul: IITA. (In Korean)

IMD (Institute for Management Development). 2006. *IMD World Competitiveness Yearbook 2006.* Lausanne, Switzerland: IMD.

———. 2005. *IMD World Competitiveness Yearbook 2005.* Lausanne, Switzerland: IMD.

ITU. (International Telecommunication Union.) 2003. Broadband Korea: Internet Case Study. Geneva: ITU.

———. 2003. "Case Study: Korea, Promoting Broadband Workshop, April 2003." http://www.itu.int/ITU-D/ict/cs/korea/material/CS_KOR.pdf.

Jang, Ha-Joon. 2003. *Globalisation, Economic Development and the Role of the State.* London: Zed Books Ltd.

Jang, Kiwon. 2004. "Roles of Local Higher Education Institutions in the Republic of Korea." Paper presented at the OECD experts meeting, Paris, France.

KAIT (Korea Association of Information and Telecommunication). 2004. *Statistical Reports on IT Industry.* Seoul: KAIT.

Kang, Dong Soo. 2004. "Financial Restructuring and Reforms." In *Economic Development and Economic Crisis Management in Korea,* eds. Chin-Seung Chung and Kwang Choi. Seoul: KDI School of Public Policy and Management.

KDI (Korea Development Institute). 2002. *Open Society, Flexible Economy: Korea's Vision and Missions toward the Years 2011.* Seoul: Korea Development Institute.

KEDI/MOE&HRD (Korea Educational Development Institute and the Ministry of Education and Human Resources Development). 2005. Educational Statistics System. Seoul: MOE&HRD.

KICC (Korea Industrial Complex Corporation). 2005. *Statistics on Industrial Complexes.* Seoul: KICC.

Kim, Anna. 2002. "The Korean Student Loan Scheme: Its Financial Efficiency and Equity Issues." *The Journal of Korean Education* 29 (2): 455–75.

———. 2003. "The Meaning and Significance of Social Class in Educational Research." *The Journal of Korean Education* 29 (2): 5–30.

Kim, Anna and Byung-Shik Rhee (2003). "An Analytic Study of Identifying Personal and Institutional Influences on the Perceived Development of Core Competencies of College Students," *The Journal of Korean Educatio,* 30(1), pp. 367-392.

Kim, Dong-Ju, and Joonghae Suh, eds. 2003. *Innovative Clusters and Regional Economic Development: International Perspective.* Seoul: Korea Development Institute.

Kim, Hyun-chang. 2004. "Competitiveness of Korea's Component/Material Industry and Policy Issues." (In Korean)

Kim, Kyeong-won. 2003. "Post-crisis Transformation of the Korean Economy: A Review from 1998 to 2002." Seoul: Samsung Economic Research Institute.

Kim, Linsu. 1997. *Imitation to Innovation: The Dynamics of Korea's Technological Learning.* Cambridge, MA: Harvard Business School Press.

———. 2003. "The Dynamics of Technology Development: Lessons from the Korean Experience," In *Competitiveness, FDI and Technological Activity in East Asia,* eds. Sanjaya Lall and Shujiro Urata. Cheltenham, UK: Edward Elgar.

Kim, Young-Gul. 1996. "Innovation and the Role of Korea's Universities." In *Korea at the Turning Point,* eds. L. Branscomb and Y. Choi. West Port: Praeger.

KISDI (Korea Information Strategy Development Institute). 2004. *Korea's Digital Economy.* KISDI Issue Report, 04-24. KISDI, Seoul. (In Korean)

———. 2005. "IT Component/Material Industry Promotion Plan." Mimeo. Seoul: KISDI. (In Korean)

KITA (Korea Industrial Technology Association). 1997, 2004. *Major Indicators of Industrial Technology.* Seoul: KITA.

Ko, Sangwon, and others. 2005. *IT Industry Outlook of Korea 2006.* Seoul: Korea Information Strategy Development Institute.

Koh, Sangwon. 1998. *Human Resource Management Profile of Korea.* Policy Monograph 98-08. Science and Technology Policy Institute, Seoul.

Koo, Bohn-Young (1986). "Role of Government in Korea's Industrial Development." In K. Lee, ed., *Industrial Development Policies and Issues.* Seoul: Korea Development Institute.

KPMG Consulting. 2001. *Foreign Direct Investment in Korea,* Seoul: Korea Investment Service Center.

Lall, Sanjaya. 2003. "Foreign Direct Investment, Technology Development and Competitiveness: Issues and Evidences." In *Competitiveness, FDI and Technological Activity in East Asia,* eds. Sanjaya Lall and Shujiro Urata. Cheltenham, UK: Edward Elgar.

Landes, David S. 1998. "Homo Faber, Homo Sapiens: Knowledge, Technology, Growth, and Development." In *The Knowledge Economy,* ed. Dale Neef. Boston: Butterworth-Heinemann.

Lee, Suk-Chae. 1991. "The Heavy and Chemical Industries Promotion Plan (1973–1979)." In *Economic Development in the Republic of Korea: A Policy Perspective,* eds. Lee-Jay Cho and Yoon Hyung Kim. Honolulu: University of Hawaii Press.

Lee, Young Ki. 2002. *Analysis of Government Funds to Higher Education Institutions and Efficiency Measures.* Seoul: KDI.

McMahon, Walter W. 1995. "Endogenous Growth in East Asia: The Contribution of Secondary Education to Growth and Development in Japan, South Korea, Malaysia, Thailand and Indonesia." Paper presented at World Bank-KEDI Secondary Education Study Tour, Seoul, Korea, June 25–30.

MIC (Ministry of Information and Communication). Various years. *White Paper on Informatization.* MIC, Seoul. (In Korean)

———. 2002. *e-Korea Vision 2006: The Third Master Plan for Informatization Promotion (2002–2006).* Seoul: MIC. (In Korean)

———. 2003a. *e-Korea Vision 2007: Broadband IT Korea 2007.* Seoul: MIC. (In Korean)

———. 2003b. *Informatization Strategy in Korea.* Seoul: MIC.

———. 2004. *Basic Implementation Plan for Broadband Convergence Network.* (In Korean)

Min, Hee-chul. 2005. "Polarization of IT and Non - IT and Countermeasures", Joint Workshop Report 7 of NRCEHS and Research Institutes 2005, *A Plan to Reduce Industry Polarization,* 3rd Theme, The National Research Council for Economics, Humanities, and Social Sciences (NRCEHS) (in Korean).

Ministry of Labor. Various years. *Report on the Labor Demand Survey.* Seoul: Ministry of Labor.

MOE & KEDI (Ministry of Education and Human Resources Development). *Statistical Yearbook of Education.* Seoul: MOE&HRD. (various years)

———. 2000. *Statistical Yearbook of Education.* Seoul: MOE & KEDI.

———. 2004a. "Key Policies of the Ministry of Education and Human Resources Development in 2003." Internal document. Seoul: MOE&HRD.

———. 2004b. "New University for Regional Development Project." Internal document. Seoul: MOE&HRD.

———. 2004c. *Securing Independence of College Education and Strengthening the National Competitive Edge.* Seoul: MOE&HRD.

———. 2005. *A Comprehensive Analysis and Evaluation of the First-stage Brain Korea 21.* Seoul: MOE&HRD.

MOFE (Ministry of Finance and Economy). 1999. *Korea: An Economy Transformed.* Kwachon, Republic of Korea: MOFE.

———. 2000. *Korea's Three-Year KBE Action Plan.* Kwachon, Republic of Korea: MOFE.

———. 2004. *Economic Surveys: Korea.* Kwachon, Republic of Korea: MOFE.

MOST (Ministry of Science and Technology). 1984. "Survey of R&D Activities." Seoul: MOST. (In Korean)

———. 1997a. "1996 Report on the Survey of R&D in Science and Technology." Kwachon, Republic of Korea: MOST.

———. 1997b. "Fifteen Years of the National R&D Program." Kwachon, Republic of Korea: MOST. (In Korean)

———. 1997c. "Thirty Year History of Science and Technology." Kwachon, Republic of Korea: MOST. (In Korean)

———. 1998a. "97 Nyun Gukka Yungu Gaebal Saub Chosa, Bunsuk, Pyungga Gyulgwa" [Analysis of the 1997 National R&D Programs]. Kwachon, Republic of Korea: MOST. (In Korean)

———. 1998b. "1997 Report on the Survey of R&D in Science and Technology." Kwachon, Republic of Korea: MOST.

———. 1999. "The Basic Direction of Policy and Strategies." Document submitted to the National Science and Technology Council, March 1999. (In Korean)

———. 2004. "Supportive Programs to Promote Innovation." Kwachon, Republic of Korea: MOST. (In Korean)

Nadiri, I. M. 1993. "Output and Labor Productivity, R&D Expenditure and Catch-up Scenarios: A Comparison of the US, Japanese, and Korean Manufacturing Sectors." Mimeo. Department of Economics, New York University, NY.

Nam, Duck-Woo. 1997. *Korea's Economic Growth in a Changing World.* Seoul: Samsung Economic Research Institute.

Nam, Il Chong. 2004. "Corporate Restructuring and Reforms." In *Economic Development and Economic Crisis Management in Korea,* eds. Chin-Seung Chung and Kwang Choi. Seoul: KDI School of Public Policy and Management. Nam, Il Chong, and Yeongjae Kang. 1998. "The Plan for Privatizing Public Enterprises." Seoul: Korea Development Institute.

National Statistical Office. 2003. "2002 Informatization Research." Seoul: National Statistical Office. (In Korean)

———. 2003. "White Paper on Internet Korea." Seoul: National Statistical Office.

———. 2004. *Mining and Manufacturing Industries Statistics Report,* Seoul: National Statistical Office.

———. 2006. *Mining and Manufacturing Industries Statistics Report,* Seoul: National Statistical Office.

NSTC (National Science and Technology Council). 2004. *National R&D Priority Setting for the Year 2005.* Seoul: NSTC. (In Korean)

OECD (Organisation for Economic Co-operation and Development). 1996. *Reviews of National Science and Technology Policy: Republic of Korea.* Paris: OECD.

———. 1998. *Basic Science and Technology Statistics.* Paris: OECD.

———. 1998. *Education at a Glance.* Paris: OECD.

———. 2003a. *Education at a Glance.* Paris: OECD.

———. 2003b. *Seizing the Benefits of ICT in a Digital Economy.* Paris: OECD.

———. 2003c. "Meeting R&D Funding Targets: Policy Implications." Paris: Directorate for Science, Technology and Industry, OECD.

———. 2003d. *Meeting R&D Funding Targets: Policy Implications.* DSTI/STP(2003)2. Paris: OECD.

———. 2004a. *ICT Diffusion to Business: Peer Review Country Report: Korea.* Paris: OECD.

———. 2004b. *Understanding Economic Growth: A Macro-level, Industry-level, and Firm-level Perspective.* Paris: OECD.

———. 2004c. *Learning for Tomorrow's World: First Result from the PISA 2003.* Paris: OECD.

————. 2005a. *Economic Survey of Korea.* Paris: OECD.

————. 2005b. *Education at a Glance.* Paris: OECD.

————. 2005c. *Main Science and Technology Indicators.* Paris: OECD.

————. 2005d *Science, Technology and Industry Scoreboard.* Paris: OECD.

————. 2005e. *Promoting Adult Learning.* Paris: OECD.

————. PISA 2003 Database.

Paik, Sung-Joon. 1999. "Educational Policy and Economic Development." In *Economic Development and Educational Policies in Korea.* Proceedings of a study on the Republic of Korea, organized by KEDI, World Bank, and KOICA, May 24–June 17. Seoul: KEDI.

Park, Bu-Kwon. 2000. "Failure Foreseen: Reforming SNU through Brain Korea 21." *Journal of Korean Education Research* 6 (1): 19–55.

Park, Hun Joo. 2004. "Political Economy of Economic Development." In *Economic Development and Economic Crisis Management in Korea,* eds. Chin-Seung Chung and Kwang Choi. Seoul: KDI School of Public Policy and Management.

Park, Jeong-gyu and Jong-rim Ha. 2005. "Analysis of the Effects of IT Use on the Enhancement of Total Factor Productivity." *Monthly Statistics Report,* Bank of Korea, 23–54. (In Korean)

Park, Yung Chul, Wonho Song, and Yunjong Wang. 2004. "Finance and Economic Development in Korea." Working Paper 04-06. Institute for International Economic Policy, Seoul, Korea. Pilat, Dirk, and Anders Hoffman. 2004. "Competitiveness Challenge for OECD Economies: Lessons from the OECD Growth Project." Paper presented at the Korea Development Institute 33rd Anniversary Conference, Seoul, April 22–23.

Political Risk Service Group. 2004. International Country Risk Guide Dataset.

Presidential Commission on Education. 1995. *The New Education System towards Globalization and Information Society.* Seoul: Ministry of Education.

Presidential Commission on Education Reform. 1997. *Education Reform for the 21st Century.* Seoul: Presidential Commission on Education Reform, Republic of Korea.

Public Fund Oversight Committee. 2004. "White Paper on Public Funds." Ministry of Finance and Economy, Seoul.

Rhee, Byung-Shik. 2003. "Differences in Perceptions between Policy-makers and University Faculty Regarding Educational Regulations in Korean Higher Education." *Korean Journal of Higher Education* 14 (1): 121–43.

Rodrik, Dani. 2004. "Industrial Policy for the Twenty-First Century." CEPR discussion paper. Centre for Economic Policy Research. http://ksghome.harvard.edu/~drodrik/.

Shin, Gwan- ho, Young-su Lee, and Jong-hwa Lee. 2004. "Analysis of Korea's IT Investments by Industry on Productivity." *International Economy Research* 10 (2): 127–55. (In Korean)

Stewart, F. 1978. *Technology and Underdevelopment.* London: Macmillan.

Suh, Joonghae. 2003. "The Emergence of Innovation Networks and Clusters, and Their Policy Implications." In *Innovative Clusters and Regional Economic Development: International Perspective,* ed. Dong-Ju Kim and Joonghae Suh. Seoul: Korea Development Institute.

Tae, Wan-son. 1973. *The Economic Development of Korea: Past, Present and Future.* Seoul: Samhwa Publishing.

U.S. Department of Commerce. 1997. *Korea's Strategy for Leadership in Research and Development.* Washington, DC: U.S. DOC, Office of Technology Policy.

————. 2003. *Digital Economy 2003.* Washington DC: Economics and Statistics Administration, U.S. Department of Commerce.

United Nations. 2005. *World Investment Report 2005.* UNCTAD.

Vernon, R. 1977. *Storm over Multinationals.* Cambridge, MA: Harvard University Press.

Wade, L. L., and B. S. Kim. 1978. *Economic Development of South Korea: The Political Economy of Success.* New York and London: Praeger.

Woo, Cheonsik. 2004. "The Knowledge-Based Economy and Korea in the Post-crisis Era." In *Economic Development and Economic Crisis Management in Korea,* eds. Chin-Seung Chung and Kwang Choi. Seoul: KDI School of Public Policy and Management.

World Bank. 1993. *The East Asian Miracle: Economic Growth and Public Policy.* New York: Oxford University Press, for the World Bank.

———. 2006. Knowledge Assessment Methodology (updated March 2006). http://www.worldbank.org/kam.

World Bank and OECD. 2000. *Korea and the Knowledge-based Economy: Making the Transition.* Paris: Organisation for Economic Co-operation and Development, and Washington, DC: World Bank.

Yoo, Gyeong Joon. 2004. "Structural Reform of the Labor Sector." In *Economic Development and Economic Crisis Management in Korea,* eds. Chin-Seung Chung and Kwang Choi. Seoul: KDI School of Public Policy and Management.

Yoon, Deok-Hong (2003). "Industry-Academia Collaboration." A paper presented by the Deputy Prime Minister at Education Reform Special Committee Meeting at the Federation of Korean Industries. October 15, 2003. p. 5.